CASE STUDIES FOR TEACHING SPECIAL NEEDS AND AT-RISK STUDENTS

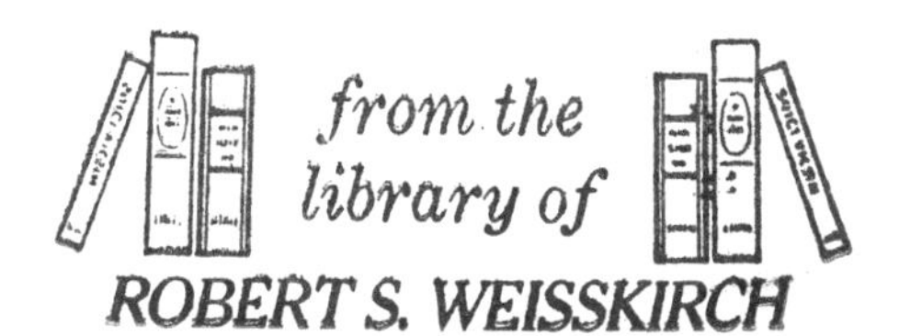

CASE STUDIES FOR TEACHING SPECIAL NEEDS AND AT-RISK STUDENTS

Judith B. Buzzell
Southern Connecticut State University

and

Robert Piazza
Southern Connecticut State University

Delmar Publishers Inc.™
I(T)P™

NOTICE TO THE READER

Cover design by: design m design w

Delmar Staff

Executive Editor: Lucille Sutton
Associate Editor: Erin J. O'Connor
Project Editor: Carol Micheli
Production Coordinator: Sandra Woods
Art/Design Coordinator: Karen Kunz Kemp

For information, address
Delmar Publishers, Inc.
3 Columbia Circle, Box 15-015
Albany, New York 12212

Delmar Publishers' Online Services

To access Delmar on the World Wide Web, point your browser to:
http://www.delmar.com/delmar.html
To access through Gopher: gopher://gopher.delmar.com
(Delmar Online is part of "thomson.com", an Internet site with information on more than 30 publishers of the International Thomson Publishing organization.)
For information on our products and services:
email: info@delmar.com
or call 800-347-7707

2 3 4 5 6 7 8 9 10 XXX 00 99 98 97 96 95

Printed in the United States of America
Published simultaneously in Canada
by Nelson Canada,
a division of The Thomson Corporation

Library of Congress Cataloging-in-Publication Data

Buzzell, Judith & Piazza, Robert.
Case studies for teaching special needs and at-risk students / Judith Buzzell, Robert Piazza.
p. cm.
Includes bibliographical references and matrix.
ISBN 0-8273-5298-0
1. Special education—United States—Case studies. 2. Classroom management—United States—Case studies. 3. Problem solving—Case studies. 4. Teaching—Case studies. I. Buzzell, Judith. II. Title.
LC3981.P53 1994
371.9'0973—dc20 93-17633
CIP

This book
is dedicated to
our spouses and children

Lloyd and *Joshua*
Janice, *Kristen*, and *Kimberly*

About the Authors

Judith B. Buzzell, Assistant Professor in the Education Department of Southern Connecticut State University, taught for many years at both the early childhood and secondary levels. A graduate of Teacher's College, Columbia University, she began her teaching career in a New York City public high school. Subsequently, she worked on a Piagetian-based elementary school curriculum project at Yale University, and was a teacher and Assistant Director at the Gesell Institute Nursery School. Presently, she uses the case method in her teaching of early childhood education and secondary school methods courses.

Robert Piazza, Professor in the Special Education Department of Southern Connecticut State University, taught at both the elementary and junior high school levels. He received his B.S. and M.S. degrees from Southern Connecticut State University and is a graduate of the doctoral program at Teacher's College, Columbia University. He presently coordinates the learning disabilities area within his department and teaches graduate level diagnostic and seminar courses.

Contents

Contributing Writers

Joseph Amato, B.S., M.S., is a special education teacher who has been teaching for 7 years.

Susan Dimond Block, B.S., M.S., 6th Year Diploma, is a health and science teacher. She has taught for 20 years in both public and private schools and universities.

Sally Francia, B.S., M.S., is a teacher of the hearing impaired. She has been in elementary education for 20 years.

Barbara Heinisch, B.S., M.A., 6th Year Diploma, is an Associate Professor of Special Education and Director of the Adaptive Technology Lab at Southern Connecticut State University. She has taught at various levels for 21 years.

Deirdre Peterson, B.S., M.S., is a special education teacher and consultant. She has been in the field of elementary education for 10 years.

Linda Pica, B.S., M.S., 6th Year Diploma, is a special education coordinator who has worked in this area for 5 years.

Linda Maynard Powell, B.S., M.S., is a history and social studies teacher. She has taught 9th-12th graders for 22 years.

Denise LaPrade Rini, B.S., M.A., is adjunct faculty for the Department of Communication Disorders at Southern Connecticut State University. She has worked at various levels for 21 years in the area of speech-language pathology.

Loretta L. Rubin, B.A., M.S., is a staff developer and facilitator. She has taught elementary education for 21 years.

Tracie-Lynn Zakas, B.S., M.S., is a special education teacher who has been teaching for 7 years.

Matrix of Cases

Case Title	I Don't Believe This is Happening	A Case of Prejudice?	Lofty Aims	Two Steps Forward, One Step Back	A Matter of Perspective	The New Child in my Class	A Different Kind of Student	How Much Can you Expect?	At Risk
Case Number	1	2	3	4	5	6	7	8	9
Pre-School	✓	✓	✓						
Elementary				✓	✓	✓	✓	✓	✓
Middle and Secondary									
Urban		✓	✓			✓	✓		✓
Non-urban	✓			✓	✓			✓	
Language Arts					✓		✓	✓	
Other Content Areas									
Collaboration and consultation	✓		✓	✓	✓	✓		✓	
Parent Communication	✓	✓	✓		✓	✓	✓	✓	
Instructional Strategies			✓	✓	✓		✓	✓	✓
Case Study Meetings				✓	✓	✓	✓		
Behavioral Strategies	✓	✓	✓		✓	✓			✓
Assessment-labeling and categorization	✓					✓	✓	✓	
Multicultural Issues		✓							✓
Peer Relationships	✓	✓	✓	✓	✓	✓			
Motivation						✓			✓
Retention				✓	✓		✓		
Learning Disabilities							✓		
Social and Emotional Problems	✓	✓			✓	✓			✓
Mental Retardation									
Physical Handicaps			✓			✓			
Visual Impairment				✓				✓	
Hearing Impairment								✓	
Communication Disorder					✓				
Gifted									
Autistic/pervasive developmental disorder					✓				
Other At-Risk Issues	✓	✓							✓

Who's in Charge? 10	A Question of Ownership 11	Case of Inclusion 12	A Child's Disability—A Teacher's Handicap? 13	The First Mistake 14	Chen Yang 15	True Assessment 16	The Performance 17	Pandora's Box 18	The Reluctant Freshman 19	The Letter 20	The Case of Competition 21	Acceptance or Achievement 22
✓	✓	✓	✓	✓	✓	✓						
							✓	✓	✓	✓	✓	✓
		✓			✓	✓	✓	✓		✓	✓	✓
✓	✓		✓	✓					✓			
✓	✓		✓		✓				✓			
✓	✓	✓		✓		✓			✓	✓	✓	✓
✓	✓	✓		✓	✓	✓	✓		✓	✓		
✓	✓	✓	✓	✓	✓	✓	✓		✓	✓		
✓	✓	✓	✓	✓	✓		✓		✓		✓	✓
✓	✓	✓	✓	✓		✓			✓			
			✓					✓		✓	✓	
✓		✓		✓		✓		✓	✓			✓
					✓	✓		✓			✓	✓
		✓			✓		✓	✓				✓
		✓									✓	✓
✓		✓						✓				
✓				✓		✓			✓			
					✓		✓			✓	✓	✓
		✓										
			✓									
	✓											
✓							✓		✓			
												✓
					✓	✓		✓		✓	✓	✓

Preface

Case Studies on Teaching Special Needs and At-Risk Students brings to teacher education lively and instructive stories of teachers' real life experiences. Each case portrays a challenging situation and dilemmas that teachers have faced in regular education and special education classrooms. Many focus on the collaboration between regular and special educators in mainstreamed settings. The cases describe teachers working with the atypical learner, such as a gifted child or a child with a visual impairment or a physical or learning disability. There are also cases on teaching children who are at risk for educational failure resulting from a variety of factors, such as teenage pregnancy, recent immigration, prenatal drug exposure, or sexual abuse.

The case method is a relatively new and exciting approach in teacher education. These cases are based on the Harvard Business School case-based approach to instruction in which students' decision-making skills are developed through the analysis of practicing professionals' problems portrayed in case studies. Generally, the cases are open-ended, and there is no one, "right" way to solve the problems—just as real teachers must regularly evaluate and handle complicated situations for which there is no one, surefire solution.

Cases familiarize learners with the real world of teaching and help them to develop the skills and felt understanding that a more traditional textbook approach may not. They help learners to develop analytical skills necessary for teasing out the essential factors in a flesh-and-blood problem. They promote problem-solving skills needed for developing strategies to contend with hands-on problems. They encourage learners to apply educational theory to true-to-life teaching circumstances. The cases are not simply compelling stories: they have been carefully crafted to meet complex pedagogical objectives.

Our book is designed for use in special education courses covering a range of exceptionalities in children and in courses on educating children in the least restrictive environment. Increasingly, such courses are required of students in regular education as well as special education.

The book could be a course's primary text, with additional background provided through lectures, readings available in the library and/or instructor's handouts. It could also serve as a supplementary text to a traditional textbook on exceptional children or mainstreaming. Regardless of the context in which the book is used, these cases should produce spirited discussion and debate of engaging stories that raise some of the most important issues facing teachers in America today.

Our cases have been developed from observations of and interviews with practicing teachers, primarily, but also parents, students, and administrators in Connecticut. In order to ensure confidentiality, the names of the students, teachers, administrators, schools, and locations have been changed. We have attempted to provide balance and variety in the book. The settings include urban, suburban, and rural schools. The cases involve early childhood, elementary, middle school, and secondary classrooms. Most of the traditional special needs categories are represented by students at-risk for a range of reasons. The matrix on pages xii and xiii will assist the instructor and learner in quickly identifying the topics, subject area, grade level, setting, at-risk factors, and special need addressed in each case.

The term *Planning and Placement Team (PPT)* is used throughout the book. This team alternatively may be called a *child study team, a committee for the disabled*, or other terms in various parts of the country. It is often composed of special services professionals (such as a school psychologist, special educator, social worker, guidance counselor, and speech and language clinician), school administrators, school nurses, regular education teachers, and parents. The main function of the team is to assess and plan individualized education programs for students in need of special education.

We realize that the success of the case method as a teaching technique relies both on the quality of the cases themselves and on how familiar and comfortable the instructor is with this approach. Therefore, a separate *Instructor's Guide* accompanies this book. It offers suggestions for teaching the cases by providing the following for each case: a synopsis, an analysis of the major issues, sample questions, possible lines of discussion, and follow-up activities. The *Instructor's Guide* is the result of field-testing the cases in teacher education classrooms prior to publication.

Acknowledgments

We are indebted to many colleagues, friends, and family members who have taught, advised, encouraged, and supported us during the writing of this book.

For sparking our interest in the use of the case method in teacher education, we thank Traci Bliss, now Associate Commissioner of Teacher Education for the State of Kentucky. As Executive Director of the Institute for Effective Teaching, Department of Higher Education, State of Connecticut, she energetically sponsored several case method projects. While participating in these, we were stimulated and guided by the insights and thoughtful suggestions of Judith Kleinfeld, University of Alaska, Fairbanks; Judith H. Shulman, Far West Laboratory for Educational Research and Development, San Francisco, CA; Cynthia Ingols, formerly of Harvard Business School and presently Director, Corporate Classrooms Inc., Cambridge, MA; and Marina McCarthy, Harvard University, Cambridge, MA.

We are grateful for the help of grants from the Institute for Effective Teaching, State of Connecticut; the Connecticut State University; and the Consortium for Urban Education (a Rockefeller Foundation–funded initiative that brought together the Yale University Child Study Center, the New Haven Public Schools, and Southern Connecticut State University). From the Consortium, we thank in particular Kathryn Newman, Southern Connecticut State University; Marc Palmieri, New Haven Public Schools; and Joanne Corbin, Yale Child Study Center.

Of the many administrators and faculty at Southern Connecticut State University who recognized the merit of this project and supported our efforts, we would like to express our appreciation particularly to our Dean, Bernice Willis, and the chairpersons of our departments, John McGowan, Jean Flintzer, and Joel Meisel of the Education Department and Irving Newman of the Special Education Department. Also, special thanks to Jean Polka for her careful typing of the manuscript.

We would like to thank our reviewers for their tireless effort in contributing their thoughtful critiques which resulted in a much improved text; Lisa Bloom, Western Carolina University, Cullowhee, NC; Joan M. Goodship, University of Richmond, Richmond, VA; John H. Hoover, University of South Dakota, Vermillion, SD; Ann Knackendoffel, Kansas State University, Manhattan, KS; Dean Richey, Tennessee Technical University, Cookville, TN; Robert Rueda, University of Southern California, Los Angeles, CA; Eugene Scholten, Grand Valley State University, Allendale, MI; Cathleen A. Smith, Douglas College, New Westminster, BC Canada; John Wheeler, University of South Dakota, Vermillion, SD. We are also indebted to our editor, Erin O'Connor, for conscientiously facilitating this effort.

Our families gave unending support and encouragement. Lloyd Buzzell incisively and painstakingly reviewed the cases, and Jan Piazza offered the keen perspectives of a special education resource teacher.

Most of all, we thank the teachers who opened up and so generously shared their stories. We deeply admire their dedication to their own students and gratefully acknowledge their contribution to the students who will reflect on and benefit from their experiences when using the cases in teacher education courses.

Introduction

Why Use Case Studies?

In this book you will be reading a series of case studies. Each case study is a story that presents problems that a real teacher faced in working with children with special needs or with children who are educationally at-risk. The situations addressed by the cases include the following:

1. Including learners with a disability in the regular classroom.
2. Teaching children who are at-risk.
3. Coping with teacher stress and burnout.
4. Selecting appropriate assessment, programming, and teaching options.
5. Developing appropriate strategies for behavioral management.
6. Collaborating and consulting among professionals.
7. Communicating and collaborating with parents.
8. Helping children with the effects of drug abuse.
9. Considering grouping and grading problems.
10. Focusing on multicultural education issues.

Studying cases can prepare you to be a teacher in several ways. The cases encourage you to "think like a teacher" (Kleinfeld, 1992). Schön (1987) points out that they help you to "frame" problems and consider various strategies and their possible consequences. In discussions of the cases, you can share perspectives with others, examine your assumptions, and develop self-awareness. You can use your background knowledge and past experiences as a resource. By taking the position of the teacher, you have an opportunity to vicariously experience problems that teachers typically encounter. Cases can also model the ways a master teacher identifies, reflects upon, and acts upon a teaching problem.

In short, cases help you to see the relationship between educational theory and teaching realities. They link theory to practice. In supporting the case method, Shulman (1992) states:

> Educators have long been critical of academic programs dominated by the twin demons of lecture and textbook, each a method designed to predigest and

> deliver a body of key facts and principles through exposition to a rather passive audience of students. These educators were critical of methods of recitation used by teachers to check whether the students had "mastered" the expounded materials in the lecture or textbook. They argued that students had grown bored, dulled by uninspired pedagogy, mindlessly memorizing and rotely rehearsing. They were surely not learning to connect theory to action, nor were they coming to think analytically.

Although long established in schools of law and business, the use of case studies is not common in schools of education. However, educators increasingly are recognizing the importance of this method for teacher education (Shulman, 1987). The Carnegie report, *A Nation Prepared: Teachers for the 21st Century* (1986), calls for using "cases illustrating a great variety of teaching problems" as a major focus of instruction. John Goodlad (1990), a leading researcher on educational change, states:

> The ability to deal with the complexities of conducting schools would be very much enhanced in teachers who come through preparation programs organized in part around a commonly encountered set of case studies. (p. 294)

The rest of this introduction is a guide to the following: (1) how the cases are organized and structured, (2) what you should look for and do when reading and preparing for case discussions, and (3) how to best discuss cases.

How the Cases Are Structured

The cases in this book follow the Harvard Business School format, adapted for educational purposes. This type of case differs significantly from clinical child studies that have been used in teacher preparation programs. The typical clinical case focuses on the child and provides detailed diagnostic information. In contrast, cases following the business school tradition focus on the teacher and how to resolve a complex educational problem.

Each case presents a narrative of an actual classroom problem that a real teacher faced. In the case, the teacher must grapple with this difficult dilemma and, generally, there is no single correct solution. You, the reader, must analyze the situation, identify the core issues, and suggest appropriate strategies for solving the problem(s).

Most cases have two or three parts. *Part A* typically describes the teacher's dilemma in three sections:

1. *Flash point; or hook*—This part of the case is designed to catch the reader's interest. You may find a teacher encountering a screaming child with a spaghetti-filled face, or a teacher who must deal with a ticklish problem regarding grouping, grading, behavior management, testing, or curriculum.

Although each flash point may not involve you in an immediate crisis, it will present the case's issues in a compelling way.

2. *Background and setting*—This section includes descriptions of the child and his or her family, the school, the community, and the various education professionals involved. The background gives you a basis for developing your analysis of the situation and coming to well-informed decisions. Look upon the information presented as the contextual stage for the upcoming events. At times, you may want to know more about the characters or the setting, just as teachers actually often wish they had more information than is available. Occasionally, you may feel that too much information is given. At these times, your task is to sort out which information is needed and which is extraneous for arriving at a decision.

3. *Return to the Dilemma*—A fuller description of the dilemma is revealed in the final portion of *Part A.* How did that child get covered with spaghetti? Who threw the tray and why? *Part A* ends with the protagonist in the middle of a problem or dilemma. Now you, the reader, must consider how to solve the problem.

***Part B* should *not* be read and discussed until after the class's analysis of *Part A*.** It may portray how the teacher actually solved the problem so readers can critique the strategies and consider the short-term and possible long-term consequences. *Part B* may also provide anothe perspective on the dilemma—perhaps a student's or a parent's or another professional's. Sometimes there is a *Part C* which shows actual long-term consequences or a later view of the problem.

In summary, these detailed cases give you a realistic portrait of the complexity of teaching and decision making. As Merseth (1991) comments:

> Effective cases . . . are sufficiently detailed, complex, and substantive to foster multiple levels of discussion, analysis, and possible courses of action. Short, vignette-like cases (of which there are a growing number) may be helpful in illuminating a single issue, but rarely do classroom issues present themselves in such tidy packages. (p. 25)

Reading a Case and Preparing for Discussion

Getting ready to participate in a class using the case method requires more preparation on your part than does a lecture class. You need to enter the classroom fully prepared to offer insightful comments and analysis, so that you can be actively engaged during the case discussion. To prepare, respond to the Advance Study Questions that accompany each case study using the following steps as guidelines. These should help you to frame the central issues and conflicts. Readings suggested by your instructor are highly recommended as well:

1. First, read the case by skimming *Part A* for a general idea of the characters, the issues, the setting, the background, and the dilemmas faced by the protagonist. *Do not read other parts of the case until you are told to do so by your instructor.* If you "cheat" and read ahead, you and your fellow participants may not develop the desired problem-solving skills. The goals of the case discussion will be undermined, and, in all likelihood, your instructor will know what you've done. **Because the value of the cases depends on each part being read and discussed before the next part is read, we have grouped all of the part As into the first section of the main text, all of the part Bs into the second section, and all of the part Cs into the third section. This will give you a visual reminder to stop reading after you finish a part.**

2. Reread *Part A* carefully and thoroughly. At this point, you should make notes on your analysis in your notebook. Try to tease out the nature of the dilemma. Don't focus solely on the most obvious or apparent problem. What underlying issues are involved in this case that might affect a choice of strategies for solving the problem(s)? Analyzing a complex teaching dilemma can be like unpeeling the many layers of an onion. Consider, too, how this situation developed.

3. Analyze the dilemma from various points of view. What is the protagonist's (probably a teacher's) perspective? What are the points of view of other characters (perhaps the parents, a student, another teacher) in the story? Do they all perceive the problem(s) in the same way? How and why do their perspectives differ? Jot down your thoughts about these differences in your notebook. Consider also the effect of any special education mandates or regulations which must be taken into account.

4. Reflect upon the actions, if any, taken by the various characters to solve the problem so far. Were these actions successful? Why, or why not? Do some actions seem to aggravate the situation? If so, why?

5. Develop an action plan. What if *you* were the teacher? What would you do to remedy the situation? What, if anything, might be done by the other characters to help solve the problem? Don't limit yourself to just one solution; develop alternative ways to address the problem(s). Be prepared to take risks at this stage. Go out on the proverbial limb if the action you are recommending is appropriate. On the other hand, don't play the devil's advocate by developing nonsensical solutions. Anticipate why others in your discussion group may not like your recommended actions, and be prepared to support your arguments in a reasonable and logical manner.

Discussing Cases Within the Classroom

These cases pose complex teaching dilemmas, and the instructor will attempt to get as many people as possible involved in developing problem-solving strategies. Initially, the instructor may promote disagreements among class members. The instructor may try to heighten controversy and help students broaden their thinking by encouraging different points of view on a dilemma. Thus, debate between individuals within a class may be encouraged.

During the case discussion, your responsibilities are threefold. First, as suggested, you must prepare for the discussion by doing the required reading and developing your own insightful analysis of the situation. Second, you must present your analysis of the problems and your plans for action in a convincing well-supported manner. Last, you must listen attentively to the discussion of others in the class and be prepared to accept, modify, or reject the ongoing discourse.

Try not to monopolize the discussion or become upset when others offer persuasive arguments to counter your suggestions. Developing the independent critical-thinking skills of *all* students within the class is an important goal of the instructor, and one person is never going to be aware of the full range of possible answers.

The case discussion will proceed in stages. Once *Part A* has been thoroughly discussed, your instructor will ask you to read *Part B*. *Part C* will be read and discussed after *Part B*. Slowly, the story will be unveiled.

Again, while analyzing each part of the case, don't assume that the response of the teacher in the case was necessarily right or wrong. In fact, you may find at the end of some cases that the initial dilemma persists—or that new problems have surfaced. Although this may be unsettling, many complex problems teachers face are not neatly resolved. It is precisely because teaching so often involves "messy problematic situations" (Schön, 1991) that cases help to prepare you for the real world of teaching.

REFERENCES

Carnegie Commission. (1986). *A nation prepared: Teachers for the 21st century*. New York: Carnegie Forum in Education and the Economy.

Goodlad, J. (1990). *Teachers of our nation's schools*. San Francisco: Jossey-Bass.

Kleinfeld, J. (1992). Learning to think like a teacher: The study of cases. In J. H. Shulman (Ed.). *Case methods in teacher education* (pp. 33–49). New York: Teachers College Press.

Merseth, K. K. (1991). *The case for cases in teacher education*. Washington, DC: AACTE Publications.

Schön, D. (1987). *Educating the reflective practitioner*. San Francisco: Jossey-Bass.

Schön, D. (1991). *The reflective turn: Case studies in and on educational practice.* New York: Teachers College Press.

Shulman, L. S. (1992). Toward a pedagogy of cases. In J. H. Shulman (Ed.), *Case methods in teacher education* (pp. 1–30). New York: Teachers College Press.

SECTION A

This section contains Part A of each of the following cases:

CASE 1

I Don't Believe This Is Happening

Robert Piazza

CHARACTERS

Student:	Joey
Joey's parents:	Mr. and Mrs. Cummings
Preschool teachers:	Harriet Cooper
	Amanda Carbo
Other students:	Jessica
	Justin
Joey's sister:	Kimberly
Neighbor of Mr. and Mrs. Cummings:	Martha Mongillo
Social worker:	Mr. Donald
Consultant from school system:	Mrs. Murphy

Part A

What Can This Be?

Joey ran across the room to the play circle in a frenzy. He approached Justin who was playing with the red fire truck. Suddenly, out of nowhere, he pushed Justin to the shiny tile floor and began to punch him over and over again. "I want that!" screamed Joey. "Gimme that truck!" Justin was hysterical, as were most of the children in the room. They had all seen what had happened and were wondering what was going to occur next. Two of the children ran to an adjacent room shouting for Miss Harriet, their teacher, who was talking with her co-teacher. Miss Harriet quickly returned to the room, observed the mayhem, and firmly ordered Joey to his cubby. Joey obeyed in silence.

This wasn't the first time Joey had been physically aggressive toward his peers. In the short three weeks since school had begun, Joey had had several outbursts. One time he yelled obscenities to the other children when they were singing "Happy Birthday" to one of their classmates. He then fled to a corner closet to sit alone in the dark. Another time, a red-haired girl named Jessica felt Joey's wrath when he bit her because she reached for one of the crayons that were being shared by the two children at a drawing table. Jessica no longer wanted to sit at the same table as Joey. These episodes had been causing quite a disturbance among the preschoolers in this small midwestern town.

Harriet Cooper had taught several children in the past who displayed emotional difficulties and hyperactive tendencies. None were like Joey. She was afraid that he might cause severe physical harm to another youngster. She thought that she had better not leave the room unattended again, for everyone's sake, including her own.

The School

Busy Beaver Nursery School was located in a small but affluent town called Grandfield in a midwestern state. This school, one of several owned by the same woman within this region, served twenty-two children ranging in ages from three to five. Busy Beaver employed two certified teachers along with two aides. Joey's teacher, Harriet Cooper, had been teaching at the school for two years. She held a B.S. degree in early childhood education, but had yet to begin her graduate studies. She was twenty-four years old.

The preschool program followed the basic nursery format with an "extended day." Children began to enter the classroom at 8:00 A.M., and the day ended between 3:30 and 4:30 P.M. Throughout the day, the youngsters were engaged in whole class, small group, and individualized learning experiences.

When a teacher suspected a child had special needs, appropriate personnel from the Grandfield school system could be called upon for assessment or consultative assistance. In the past, speech and language clinicians, psychologists, social workers, occupational and physical therapists, and others had provided both direct and indirect services to preschoolers at Busy Beaver.

The Family

Joey was adopted by Steve and Linda Cummings, a Caucasian, upper-middle-class couple, who both worked in the banking industry. Steve and Linda had been married for twelve years and were in their mid-thirties. They had been trying to have children of their own for about six of those years before they decided to adopt. After twenty-two months on an adoption agency waiting list, they formally adopted a three-month-old Caucasian baby boy they named Joey. Steve and Linda were given very little background information about Joey. As far as they knew, he was born to an unmarried teenage mother who could not raise the child on her own.

They would later discover that Joey's mother used a moderate to heavy amount of crack cocaine during the first trimester of her pregnancy. Since she did not continue the use of cocaine throughout the entire pregnancy, Joey's symptoms resulting from this exposure were apparently more subtle than those of an infant exposed to crack for the full term of a pregnancy.

Four months after Joey's adoption, Steve and Linda found themselves expecting a child of their own. Kimberly was born later that year after a full-term and uneventful pregnancy.

Joey

The Cummingses were told that Joey's birth weight was 5.8 pounds and that his Apgar rating was 7. During the first year of life, he was not a good eater. He also flapped his legs in an uncontrollable manner at times. Linda described him as a very colicky baby. She remembered that he had a very high piercing cry and she often had much difficulty calming him down. She said, "He seemed much more at ease if I left him alone. So I did." Linda also indicated that between work and the fatigue associated with her own pregnancy she had not given Joey as much attention as she would have liked.

Joey began walking at fourteen months; however, language development was quite delayed. Early play was very scattered, consisting mostly of picking up and putting down toys, rather than exploring and examining them. Joey was also prone to temper tantrums, especially during transition periods, such as when he finished eating and had to get ready to take a nap.

A full-time nanny lived with the Cummings until Joey was nearly two years old. When Kimberly was born, Linda quit her job to care for both of her children, but since then she felt like she hadn't had a minute to herself. When Joey was $3\frac{1}{2}$, Linda enrolled him at the Busy Beaver Nursery School. She felt a bit guilty doing this, thinking that maybe she was doing it more for her benefit than his. She rationalized that trained professionals would be able to improve Joey's behavior. Everything would be just fine.

At School

As Joey began to interact with his peers at school, his extreme behavior became more obvious to Harriet Cooper. Although she was puzzled, she started to see a pattern to his behavior. At times he would have wild outbursts. During other periods, he would become withdrawn, unable to cope with circle activities and games played by the entire group. Although Joey could usually cope with small group work, his dichotomous behavior in large group settings still continued in the third week of school.

After his most recent outburst, Harriet turned to her co-teacher, Amanda Carbo, and said, "I don't know how to handle Joey; at times he is just out of control. At other times he's like a space cadet—I can't even reach him. He doesn't seem to concentrate on any group activities, especially when physical games are played."

Harriet spoke to Mrs. Cummings about the latest violent incident. Although Linda expressed mild surprise, Harriet sensed that these behaviors were more common than Linda Cummings wanted to admit. Just call it teacher's intuition.

When Linda and Joey left, Martha Mongillo approached Harriet. Martha's daughter was in Joey's class, and she was also a neighbor of the Cummings. She had seen the look of frustration in Linda's face and recognized it very well. Martha had also seen Joey "in action" at some of the neighborhood children's birthday parties. Linda had confided in Martha during those early years, expressing the problems she and her husband were having controlling Joey's behavior at home.

"Maybe I shouldn't be telling you this, but I think I can shed some light on Linda's feelings," Martha said. She told Harriet that the Cummingses went through so much trouble to adopt their son that when they began to experience difficulties with him, they had gone through a period of denial. They couldn't believe that their little boy who looked so perfect would act so unsettled and unhappy. Martha remembered Linda crying in the kitchen after one of her first trips to their pediatrician. The doctor had told Linda that Joey was just a colicky baby and that he'd grow out of his irritability in a few months. Very inconsistent sleeping patterns and intense screaming periods continued for six months. During that time, Linda had complained that Steve had started to play basketball with his buddies two to three nights a week.

Martha continued:

> I think Linda was very depressed, and she felt she had a hyperactive child on her hands. After all, working full-time at the bank and then coming home to almost singlehandedly raise their son was a lot. When Linda got pregnant with Kimberly, Linda told me that Joey's sleeping habits improved. Other problems popped up, however. A year or so later when some of the neighborhood children began to play with each other, Joey had trouble sharing and was very aggressive. Gradually, Joey was excluded from birthday parties and other planned recreational activities the neighbors might be having.

Harriet thanked Mrs. Mongillo for providing this information. Although she was almost ashamed that she had agreed to listen to what Martha had to say, it did confirm what she had been observing.

Now the question paramount in Harriet's mind was how she could improve Joey's cognitive and behavioral development. Or maybe it was how she could prevent the children in her class from getting their heads bashed in by one of Joey's violent outbursts.

From Out of the Blue

It was a clear, brisk, and bright fall morning. Linda Cummings had just dropped Joey off at Busy Beaver Nursery School on her way to the grocery store. When she returned home with Kimberly to get the shopping list she had forgotten, she noticed that there was a message on her answering machine. It was from Mr. Donald, a social worker from the adoption agency that had assisted them in adopting Joey. Linda returned his call immediately. Mr. Donald asked if he could meet with her and Steve that evening. He said he had new information that he needed to share with both of them as soon as possible.

Linda, recognizing a sense of urgency in the social worker's voice, quickly responded that 8:00 P.M. that evening would be a good time. She hoped that both children would be sleeping by then. After hanging up the phone, she called Steve at his office to tell him about the phone call and the meeting she had scheduled. He was a bit agitated that he would have to cancel his Wednesday night out to play basketball, but he felt knowing about Joey's past was more important.

That evening at 8:00 P.M. Mr. Donald promptly arrived at the Cummingses' residence. After shaking hands and exchanging a few polite pleasantries, they sat down at the kitchen table.

Mr. Donald got right to the point:

> What we are doing tonight is not a typical procedure of our agency. We don't usually act as a conduit between a child's biological mother and his adoptive parents . . . but in this case we felt that we should. It seems that your son's mother has recently been reading the newspapers and magazines and watching television shows that have discussed the effect of cocaine abuse by a pregnant mother on the developing fetus. She wanted you to know that she was a fairly regular user of cocaine during the first four months that she was pregnant with your son. She feels horrible about this and wanted you to know so that you could possibly minimize any problems he might have in the future.

Although these words exploded in the heads of both Linda and Steve, in reality they were not completely shocked. They told Mr. Donald that they had talked about whether Joey's mother had been a drug or alcohol abuser. After all, Joey's first years of life had certainly been tumultuous. They recognized that his development and behavior fit that pattern.

The truth both hurt and angered them. Why hadn't Joey's mother been more responsible when she was pregnant? Why hadn't the adoption agency been more diligent in finding out about Joey's fetal history? Why hadn't they waited one more year to try to have their own child?

It took two weeks for Steve and Linda to develop the courage to inform Joey's teacher of his "new" medical history. As with the Cummingses, this revelation was not really a surprise to Harriet Cooper. She had read about "crack babies" in her professional journals and knew that Joey's behavior matched some of the case studies she had read. The main problem was what to do now. How should she structure Joey's day? What could she honestly expect of him if he were a "crack baby?" Should he even be at Busy Beaver? Harriet's head was spinning. She said to herself, "I guess this is one of the reasons you have co-teachers. I need to talk to Amanda."

Advance Study Questions

1. What is the major dilemma facing Harriet Cooper?

2. What underlying problems must the preschool teacher resolve? Has her training prepared her for the problems she is having with Joey?

3. How are the problems viewed by Joey's parents?

4. Does a child like Joey belong in a regular preschool situation?

5. Who should be involved when determining an appropriate program for Joey?

CASE 2

A Case of Prejudice?

Judith B. Buzzell

CHARACTERS

Director of the day care center: Mrs. Phillips
Student: Daniel Rieser
Daniel's mother: Mrs. Rieser
Daniel's friends: Jeffrey
Dwight
Daniel's babysitter: LeShanda
Another student: Stephanie
Teachers: Emily
Sarah
Debbie

Part A

In her cramped but cozy office, with shelves lined with books about young children, Mrs. Phillips, the director of the Early Childhood Center, waited for Mrs. Rieser to arrive for her conference. Mrs. Rieser's son, Daniel, a young four-year-old, had begun day care only a month ago in early September. Mrs. Phillips had sensed a tone of urgency in Mrs. Rieser's voice when she called to make an appointment. Although it was early in the year for a parent-teacher conference, Mrs. Phillips readily agreed to the meeting. Mrs. Rieser had said only that she wanted to discuss an attitude that her son was developing. Mrs. Phillips wondered what it could be.

Mrs. Rieser arrived a few minutes late, having rushed over from work. Her face was drawn and her body tense.

The writer gratefully acknowledges the invaluable assistance of Barbara Fussiner in the preparation of this case.

"Thank you for taking this time with me," she said. Then she blurted out her concern. It seemed that on several occasions recently Daniel had told his parents, "I don't like blacks."

"Can you tell me about a time when he said that?" asked Mrs. Phillips.

Mrs. Rieser paused briefly and then described an incident that had occurred in mid-August. She and Daniel were in the backyard. Daniel was happily sailing boats in his wading pool when Mrs. Boyd, a black neighbor, opened her door and her big dog came bounding out. Daniel, who was very frightened of dogs, shrieked at the sight of the snarling animal and ran into his kitchen. Mrs. Rieser dashed after him to comfort him. That evening, Daniel said, "I don't like blacks." When Mrs. Rieser asked him why he felt that way, he shrugged his shoulders and said, "I don't know." She speculated now that perhaps Daniel identified the threatening dog with its black owners.

A week after the incident, Mrs. Rieser and Daniel were standing in a long check-out line at the supermarket. A black woman was a few places ahead of them. Starting to fidget and pointing at her, Daniel commented, "I don't like black people."

Mrs. Rieser was concerned that Daniel was becoming prejudiced. She wanted to know how to help Daniel overcome this attitude and develop a more tolerant view. She also seemed to have a nagging, barely expressed worry that if Daniel openly stated his feelings in public, they would reflect poorly on her husband and her.

The Family

A well-educated white couple, Mr. and Mrs. Rieser prided themselves on being open-minded and accepting of varied racial, ethnic, and religious groups. They had an interfaith marriage and both worked in social service agencies. They tried to act in accordance with their beliefs and hoped that they were good models for their son. They had purposely chosen to live in a neighborhood that reflected the diverse population of their middle-sized northeastern city, Fairville. In this neighborhood, both black and white children played in the backyards. There were various religious groups as well.

In good weather, Daniel often joined Jeffrey, the boy across the street, and his friend, Dwight, to play with their toy cars, balls, or G.I. Joes. Both Jeffrey and Dwight were black and older than Daniel. Daniel looked up to Jeffrey, admiring his sense of imagination. Jeffrey readily accepted Daniel as a playmate.

This integrated middle-class neighborhood, with single-family, older homes, bordered on a very poor, predominantly black neighborhood. Because of the rapidly rising number of break-ins in the area, the Riesers, like many other families, had installed a burglar alarm. The sirens of police cars and ambulances were heard often in the neighborhood, and the Riesers scrupulously turned on the alarm when going out for even the briefest errands.

When Daniel was almost three, his wagon was stolen from his backyard. The wagon had been a childhood toy of his father's and had been restored painstakingly by his grandfather just for Daniel. During the summer before Daniel began day care, a large, bright-red fire engine, a gift from his maternal grandparents, had been stolen. Daniel loved to ride in the fire engine, pushing its pedals and clanging the bell. When the theft was discovered, his parents tried to help Daniel express his feelings of distress and anger. At the same time, they explained why a poor child may have been tempted to steal such an appealing toy. Daniel seemed to understand and said, "Maybe whoever stole my fire engine is poorer than I am and needs it more than I do. Anyway, I still have my yellow car to ride in."

One Saturday night, Mr. and Mrs. Rieser were going out to dinner. They had asked a new baby-sitter, LeShanda, to stay with Daniel. LeShanda was a black teenager. As with any new baby-sitter, the Riesers waited to leave the house until Daniel and LeShanda got acquainted and became involved in an activity. Daniel chose to draw with crayons, and LeShanda drew alongside of him. As they drew, they chatted in a friendly way. Then, when LeShanda offered Daniel a black crayon, he forcefully responded, "I don't like black." LeShanda didn't seem to notice the remark or take it personally; however, Mrs. Rieser hastily commented, "Why not? Black is a nice, strong, dark color."

Although Mr. Rieser was not particularly worried, Mrs. Rieser's concern heightened. "What do I do?" she wondered. "Are Daniel's comments about blacks a sign of growing prejudice, or is this just a passing stage he's going through?"

The Day Care Center

The day care center was a private, nonprofit program subsidized by a community-minded church group. The educational program for children was based on a play-oriented, developmentally appropriate curriculum. Parents were actively involved in an advisory capacity, as well as with tangible work such as cleaning the school.

There were twenty-five children in the program, coming from predominantly middle-class families. Many parents were professionals or faculty and students from nearby Damon University, an old and prestigious private university. Daniel's group this year included a majority of white children (one of whom was Swiss), a Japanese boy, an adopted Korean boy whose parents were both white, and a girl who was biracial (having a white mother and a black father). All the teachers were white.

Tuition for the day care center was steep in order to finance better salaries for the teachers. It was Mrs. Phillips's firm and often-stated belief that salaries for day care teachers must be improved. She saw this as an ethical stand, as well as a pragmatic way to attract and retain an excellent, well-trained staff. One of her long-term goals was to recruit teachers from diverse ethnic and cultural backgrounds. This was one way the program could help foster in children an appreciation of differences. Another initiative was to recruit more children of diverse backgrounds.

As Mrs. Rieser described her concerns, Mrs. Phillips began to think about how to counsel the mother. She wasn't sure whether the antipathy Daniel expressed toward blacks was a case of prejudice or whether his mother was overreacting. She felt she needed more information.

Advance Study Questions

1. What is the nature of Mrs. Rieser's dilemma?
2. What factors do you think have contributed to this situation?
3. What, if anything, should Mrs. Rieser do? Why?
4. If you were the director of the center, how would you respond to Mrs. Rieser?

CHARACTERS

Director of day care center:	Denise Somers
Student:	Sarah Schultz
Sarah's parents:	Dr. and Mrs. Schultz
Teachers:	Jean
	Lisa

Part A

Initial Visit to the Day Care Center

Denise Somers, director of the Early Learning Center, watched apprehensively as $3\frac{1}{2}$-year-old Sarah tried to maneuver herself, crutches and all, out the heavy front door of the center. "Just let me. I can do it!" Sarah insisted when her father tried to help by pushing the door open wider. At that moment, Jamie, a burly 4-year-old, barreled into Sarah in his dash to get outdoors. Sarah's father deftly grabbed his daughter as she started to fall toward the floor. Denise wondered if there would always be someone there to catch Sarah.

It was a blustery mid-February day, so cold that areas of the blacktop on the playground were coated with a thin sheet of ice. Dr. and Mrs. Schultz and their daughter, Sarah, were just leaving after visiting the Early Learning Center to consider enrolling Sarah in the program.

During the visit, the teachers had introduced Sarah to some of the other children and helped her to get involved in the school's activities. Dr. and Mrs. Schultz observed the class for awhile and then met with Denise to discuss the program and their daughter's interests and needs.

The Schultzes began by stating that Sarah had been born with spina bifida. Dr. Schultz, a dentist, explained that spina bifida is a congenital disease involving an abnormality of the vertebrae of the spine. The spine does not properly close around the nerves it is supposed to protect. As a result, the child experiences, in varying degrees, paralysis, diminished sensation in the legs, and bowel and bladder incontinence. There also may be perceptual difficulties that result in learning problems, as well as motor difficulties in the arms and hands.

Although Sarah's case was not severe, she had had several surgeries to fuse the bones of the spine to protect her spinal cord. As Denise listened, she remembered seeing Mrs. Schultz in the neighborhood with her baby, Sarah, wearing a huge body cast. How difficult that must have been!

Since Dr. and Mrs. Schultz had never been sure how Sarah's development would progress, they had assumed the best. For example, they weren't sure if she could become toilet trained, but she had, only a month ago.

Mrs. Schultz proudly described how her daughter's locomotion skills had developed. Born in mid-September, she had used a walker at twenty months and crutches since she was three. She wore a brace on her left foot. Now, at $3\frac{1}{2}$, she could walk with her crutches for three city blocks, although near the end, she tired and might fall. She could climb steps slowly.

When she wasn't tired, Sarah could scoot across a room quickly on her Loftstrand crutches, which she called her "lofties." Her feet would move back and forth, with her good right foot giving momentum. Sometimes, she seemed to hop, pressing down with her crutches. When her energy flagged, Sarah would drag her left foot.

Sarah was seeing a physical therapist two times a week for thirty-minute periods. She took no daily medication and had feeling throughout her feet and legs. Her small-motor coordination was excellent.

Sarah had been attending a family day care program. The day care provider was a caring woman who enjoyed the four children with whom she worked. But Mrs. Schultz felt that by September, when Sarah was four, she would benefit from the stimulation of a larger group of children and a carefully planned educational program. Moreover, in September, Mrs. Schultz was starting graduate school full-time to get her M.B.A. and would need Sarah to be in full-day child care. This wasn't available through the family day care provider.

Because they lived in the neighborhood, Mrs. Schultz had often seen the children playing happily on the playground at the day care center. She had heard positive reports about the program from friends whose children had gone there. Now, after seeing for herself the warm interactions between the children and teachers and the many interesting activities, she felt sure that her daughter would benefit from this setting. She explained to Denise that Sarah could handle the physical setup at the school without major changes. It was on one floor, and there was a ramp already. "Would you be willing to accept Sarah in the program in the fall?" she asked. "We'd work with you in any way to ensure that this is a positive experience for both her and for your staff."

Denise liked the Schultzes already. During the meeting, they had been honest about sharing the ups and downs of parenting a child with special needs. They were proud of their daughter and her accomplishments but aware of the hurdles still to be overcome. They seemed to appreciate the center and its offerings but did not expect extraordinary treatment for their daughter. Yet

Denise wondered whether the staff would be able to meet Sarah's needs—and continue to meet the needs of the other children as well.

The Day Care Center

The Early Learning Center was a private, nonprofit preschool. Although it ran on a shoestring budget, as do most day care centers, it had an excellent reputation for its high-quality, developmentally appropriate program. The curriculum included a wide variety of carefully planned, play-oriented experiences in areas such as art, block building, music and movement, dramatic play, science, language arts, and outdoor activities. The teachers were responsive to the interests and needs of individual children, as well as of the group. If a child brought in tadpoles found in a local pond, this might stimulate several activities to learn about frogs.

In addition to Denise, who occasionally taught, the staff was composed of four highly experienced teachers trained in early childhood education. The class had twenty-seven children from three to five years old. There were twelve boys and fifteen girls, including five Asian children, one Peruvian child, two black children, and two biracial children. Three of the Asian children and the Peruvian child had been adopted as babies by Americans. The two other Asian children were new immigrants; they were just learning English.

The group size was large, but somehow it had always worked, which Denise attributed to the high teacher-child ratio. Still, the physical space, with only two moderate-sized rooms, was cramped. Although the center met the state guidelines for amount of space per child, in reality, children often flocked together. This situation could be cozy, but Denise wondered if the younger or smaller children weren't sometimes overwhelmed. The teachers were aware of the potential for confusion and worked to keep the atmosphere calm at these times.

The Staff Meeting

During naptime, the staff met to discuss the pros and cons of having Sarah in the program. The teachers related their observations of Sarah. She had stayed at the art table most of the time. Although there were four other children with her, most of her attention was directed to the teacher, Jean. As Jean wrote names on the children's artwork, Sarah peppered her with questions: "What kind of pen are you using? What color is it? Can you show me how it writes? What letters are you writing?" Jean had been impressed by how articulate and inquisitive Sarah was. She also realized that Sarah had been the center of her attention.

After the art activity, it was snack time. Sarah looked bewildered as the children raced to be first in line to wash up at the sink. "This is natural, everything is new to her," Jean thought. Jean helped Sarah gather up her crutches and maneuver herself through the maze of small tables in the art area over to the sink. Sarah insisted on turning on the water herself and then dallied a bit, enjoying the flow of warm water over her hands. When she finally got back to the snack table, several of the children had already finished snack and were starting to get ready to go outside.

By the time Sarah finished snack and put on her outdoor gear to leave with her parents, all the other children were already outdoors. As she helped Sarah, Jean worried that there were only two teachers outside with the large group but that there was plenty of ice for slips and slides. And suppose Sarah were out there—how would she fare if she hit an icy patch with her crutches?

Denise filled the teachers in on what she had learned about Sarah and her family. Then, the staff discussed whether to admit Sarah into the program. Denise encouraged her staff's active participation in decision making, although she knew that the final responsibility was hers.

Jean had liked Sarah. But she was concerned about both Sarah's well-being *and* the other children's. "I saw how much attention she needed, and I'm concerned that some of the other children will get short shrift. Also, I'm worried that she just won't be safe. Remember how crowded our space is. She could easily get bumped by other children, and then she'll go flying and really hurt herself. I think it would be in her best interests to attend a program with fewer children. There are many other good programs in the area that we could recommend to the Schultzes," Jean said. Denise listened attentively to her caring, thoughtful teacher.

"I know what you're saying," piped up Lisa. "I was worried when I heard that Sarah might be coming. I hardly know what spina bifida is—and certainly haven't ever taught a child with this condition. But I was impressed by her determination. Look how she insisted on turning on the water to wash her hands and tried to open the front door herself. She's an appealing, spunky child. I think she'd manage the hubbub of our group, and I think both we and the other children would benefit from living with and learning from a child with special needs. After all, we always talk about our commitment to diversity."

"Yet," Denise said,

> I'm concerned about her safety in this situation and the amount of staff time she'll require. I'm not sure we have the training to handle this situation well. Dr. Schultz said that Sarah does fall more often than most children her age, and her balance is shaky, especially without her crutches. However, he assured me that with the spinal fusion, she is no more at risk than other children. He says she knows how to fall so she won't hurt herself. But we personally don't know how fragile she is physically. And Mrs. Schultz did describe how both Sarah and her older brother like lots of adult attention.
>
> Still, I can also see Lisa's point that having Sarah at the center could be an enriching opportunity for everyone. I told the Schultzes that I'd call them in a week. Of course, we wouldn't reject Sarah because of her disability, but we need to consider what's in her best interests. The Schultzes seem to trust our

judgment, and I'm not sure what to advise them at this point. It's going to be a tough week.

Advance Study Questions

1. What is the dilemma that the director of the center, Denise, faces?

2. What are the underlying issues in this situation? What factors must Denise consider in order to make an informed decision?

3. How is the problem viewed from the perspectives of Jean, Lisa, and Sarah's parents?

4. What decision should Denise make and why?

5. If Denise decides to admit Sarah to the program, what, if any, special accommodations will have to be made for her?

CASE 4

Two Steps Forward, One Step Back

Robert Piazza

CHARACTERS

Student:	Phillip
Kindergarten teacher:	Cheryl Stone
Principal:	Dr. O'Brien
Parents:	Mrs. Short
	Mrs. Inzero
Students:	Karen
	Brian
Phillip's instructional assistant:	Judy Bradley
Phillip's previous kindergarten teacher:	Mr. Charles
Consultant:	Joan Rizzo

Part A

Just the Beginning

Cheryl Stone met her principal, Dr. O'Brien, in the corridor after the first day of school. "I've just received a strange call, Dr. O," she mused. "Mrs. Short called. It seems as if her daughter Karen came home crying today. She thinks that maybe she'll go blind."

"I wonder what makes her think that?" the principal asked.

"Don't pull my leg. You know as well as I do where that came from. However, I thought Phillip's first day in my class went smoothly. The other children seemed to respond warmly to him. His aide, Judy, was with him constantly and was a big help. She seems to really know what he needs. Even my anxiety level dropped when I saw him and realized how cute he was."

Cheryl continued that Karen's and Brian Inzero's mothers were going to be meeting with her after dismissal the next day to discuss why a boy who was blind was in her kindergarten class. Dr. O'Brien asked Cheryl if she wanted her to attend the meeting too. Cheryl replied, "No. I don't want to make a big thing of this. I'll just tell them that a boy like Phillip has every right to be in a regular class. I'll also assure them that I'll be sensitive to the needs of their children. Thanks for asking though."

Phillip

Phillip was a seven-year-old boy with short, brown hair and a round, cherubic face. He had no brothers or sisters and lived with his mother, who had divorced his father five years ago. Phillip's mother worked in a local plant that produced firearms and ammunition. His father still lived in the area and spent almost every weekend with Phillip.

Phillip's overall development was normal until he developed retinoblastoma, malignant tumors behind the eyes, at ten months of age. Shortly after that, his eyes were surgically removed, and prosthetic eyes were inserted. Radiation and chemotherapy were performed for approximately one year to arrest any further malignancies.

When Phillip was $4\frac{1}{2}$, however, more tumors were found, this time on his lower spine. These tumors were shrunk and then removed. To minimize further complications, Phillip also had his bone marrow removed, cleansed, and then reinserted two months later. During this period, he lived in a sterile, bubble environment.

Over the next year, immune system problems arose because of these medical interventions, and Phillip was quite susceptible to colds and other illnesses. When he was healthy, a tutor from the State's Office of the Blind provided him with homebound instruction in oral language, fine-motor, gross-motor, and other developmental skills.

When Phillip was six, his doctors finally gave him permission to attend school. He entered a regular kindergarten class during February. His tutor, Judy Bradley, accompanied him as his full-time instructional assistant to help with the educational portion of the day. The State Board of Education also assigned Phillip a movement coach to acclimate him to the physical surroundings of the school. He used a white cane for mobility facilitation.

Phillip reported that he did not feel comfortable in the class that year. Although the teacher and the children were receptive to his placement, he said he felt like an outsider. Friendships among the children in the class were already firmly established, and because of his illnesses, Phillip did not know any children from his neighborhood.

Mr. Charles, his teacher for the remainder of that year, used an open-space environment within the classroom. Furniture was often moved to different locations of the room, depending on the daily activities. Mr. Charles also allowed for a flexible schedule, so that if children were enthusiastic about an activity, they could continue working on that task. In addition, Mr. Charles employed a cooperative learning system within the class. Children were assigned a partner for all activities. This partner would be changed every other week, so that each child would get to work with a different classmate throughout the year. Because of Phillip's disability, Mr. Charles felt that Judy Bradley should always be Phillip's partner.

At a meeting during June, a Planning and Placement Team decided that despite his age (he would be seven in August), Phillip should repeat kindergarten the following year in a more traditional kindergarten class. He would receive special transportation to Fox Run School, and Cheryl Stone was assigned as his teacher. Mrs. Stone had not been invited to this PPT meeting. Judy Bradley agreed to work with Phillip during the summer months on readiness-level skills.

The Community and School

Plantsville was a large suburban community. It consisted of six elementary schools (K through 6), a middle school (7 and 8), and a high school (9 through 12). The school system educated approximately 5,200 students with a professional staff of 462 teachers and support personnel. It was widely acclaimed throughout the area for its special education department, and 15 percent of Plantsville's student population was receiving some type of remedial assistance.

Phillip spent his second year of kindergarten at Fox Run Elementary School, a school of 423 children. He attended the afternoon session of this class which had twenty-four students. The morning class had twenty-six children.

Mrs. Stone, the kindergarten teacher, had taught twenty-five years in the Plantsville School System as a primary-level teacher and over the last four years as a kindergarten teacher. She had a Master's Degree in Early Childhood Education, but had not received any formal training in working with children with disabilities.

Judy Bradley, Phillip's instructional assistant, did not possess a college degree. She became interested in working with handicapped children when her own son was diagnosed as having Prader-Willi syndrome. At first, Judy volunteered her services to the special education department within the Plantsville System. Later, when school officials realized Phillip was going to need special help within its schools, Judy was asked by the Director of Special Education to attend in-service sessions given by the State's Office of Education for the Blind. Judy agreed, and began working with Phillip when he was three years old. Judy met on a monthly basis with consultants from that office to discuss Phillip's progress and to determine his future educational goals.

Mrs. Stone's class was set up like many traditional kindergarten rooms. In the front right corner by the windows was a rug area where the children began their day. It was also used for lounging and rest time. Next to this carpeted space was a play area that extended along the side and back walls. There, shelves, storage boxes, and closets contained wooden and cardboard blocks, math manipulatives, Legos, stringing beads, parquetry blocks, and many other materials that develop fine-motor abilities.

Taking up a large portion of the back of the room was a housekeeping corner, with dolls, an ironing board, a play stove, and a miniature store. Next to this corner was the art center with easels, paper, crayons, paintbrushes of all types, different varieties of paint, and cut-and-paste materials. A wash area with a double sink was wisely located adjacent to the art center.

A supply storage area and the children's cubbies, where they hung up their coats at the beginning of each day, were on the far side of the room. Next to the cubbies was a large bookcase known as the library.

Mrs. Stone's desk occupied the front of the room. Behind her desk was a medium-sized blackboard that would lower to the floor so that the children were able to reach it.

The central portion of the classroom contained three octagonal-shaped tables that were, in effect, workstations. These stations helped structure the preacademic work sessions during the day.

A typical day began by the children viewing the calendar and weather charts at the rug area. A short language-development lesson followed, which usually tied into a theme or topic the class was studying. For example, if the topic were spring, a "think question" such as "Has anyone seen a sign of spring today?" might be asked and used to encourage discussion.

Thirty minutes was then spent on reading-readiness activities, such as letter-recognition exercises, rhyming games, and storytelling sessions that fostered and enriched the children's vocabularies. A fifteen-minute snack time followed during which the children would either listen to records or to Mrs. Stone reading a story. After snack time, the children engaged in independent work at various workstations or centers. They were expected to play at a different location each day. Mrs. Stone also made sure that the children were not in the same group each day, so that they would have to interact with all their classmates each week.

Math-readiness activities, such as shape cutting, estimation games, numeral identification lessons, and counting practice, usually concluded the day. Three days a week, the children attended special art, music, and physical education classes for forty minutes.

The Two Parents

Mrs. Short and Mrs. Inzero entered Cheryl Stone's classroom ten minutes after the afternoon class was dismissed. They looked around but did not notice Cheryl sitting in the corner behind a bulletin board and preparing materials for an art project the next day. Cheryl looked up and saw them first. She greeted the parents and suggested they move to the other side of the room where there was a large table to sit at and discuss their concerns. Mrs. Short spoke first.

> I'm almost embarrassed to be here so early in the school year, but my daughter Karen was really upset when she came home from school yesterday. She said

> she first noticed a child with a lot of adults around him, and then she saw that he had a white cane and that he was blind. As you'll find out during the year, Karen's a very sensitive child. She gets upset very easily. She also complains a lot. I bet she'll ask you if she can go to the nurse if she has a hangnail. She came home yesterday and wanted to know if she could go blind by being near or touching a blind person. Obviously, her concerns about going blind because she is near a blind boy aren't legitimate, but I have some concerns. Why is this boy here? It wasn't too long ago that I went to school, and I don't ever remember seeing a blind person in any of my classes, or any student with a physical handicap, for that matter. I thought they had special private schools for these kids that did wonderful things for them.

Mrs. Inzero just silently sat there, nodding her head in apparent agreement with her neighbor. Cheryl Stone replied:

> I don't know what to say to you exactly. I haven't had any kids in my class like this before either. And I've been teaching for a long time. The Director of Special Education told me last June that this boy, whose name is Phillip by the way, would be in my class. From what I've read in his records and from what his aide has told me, he seems to be a great kid who really wants to be here with normal children. I will observe things very carefully and watch how he performs in this class. If I don't feel like he belongs here, I'll let the appropriate school officials know. For Phillip's sake and for that of the rest of the class, I don't want to be giving him so much attention that the whole class suffers.

"Thanks, Mrs. Stone. That's all we're requesting," said Mrs. Inzero, as both parents stood up to leave.

As the mothers departed, Cheryl reflected on their mutual concerns. Phillip appeared to be a fine, well-adjusted child, but she really didn't know too much about him. She certainly didn't know how to teach him. Cheryl hoped that Judy would be a valuable resource. She had to be, or this placement would not be successful. Cheryl vowed to observe Phillip carefully and withhold judgment about his placement in her class for the next few weeks.

Watching Things Closely

Cheryl watched the art area as her students were cutting colored construction paper into different-sized shapes for a collage. They were all working in an independent manner, except Phillip. He and Judy were working at a corner table making the same designs, verbally interacting with each other, but saying nothing to any other children.

Their actions paralleled previous behaviors she had noted between the two of them in her class. Phillip was not truly integrated into the kindergarten classroom. Instead, he and Judy were creating their own classroom. Cheryl often overheard Judy echoing back to Phillip directions she had just given to the entire class. Simple statements, like "Get out your crayons and scissors," were repeated to Phillip, often twice. This child is blind, not deaf, Cheryl pondered.

During the first ten days of school I haven't seen Phillip engage in a meaningful conversation with another child. I've seen other children say "hello" to him, and he'll return their greetings, but that's about as far as it goes. Judy and I are basically developing the same kind of relationship. She's a very pleasant lady, but we aren't communicating either. She does her thing, and I do mine. Is this the way it's supposed to be with a child who is handicapped and an aide in your classroom? I'm glad Mrs. Inzero and Mrs. Short came in a few days ago. They helped to sensitize me to the potential problems of having a blind child in my class. But the problems I'm noticing are not the ones I anticipated. To make this class a better one for all the children, including Phillip, Judy and I are going to have to talk. I'll call her tonight and see if she can stay for awhile after the children leave tomorrow afternoon.

Advance Study Questions

1. What are the major problems facing Cheryl Stone in this case?

2. What underlying dilemmas have exacerbated the situation?

3. Does Phillip belong in a kindergarten classroom? Why, or why not?

4. What must be done to optimize Phillip's learning environment? How should his teacher be involved?

5. If another child who is handicapped is mainstreamed in Cheryl's classroom, what should be done before the youngster is placed?

CASE 5

A Matter of Perspective

Judith B. Buzzell

CHARACTERS

Regular education teacher: Mrs. Jacobs
Special education teacher: Ms. Winthrop
Classroom aide: Mrs. Melton
Principal: Dr. Cleary
Student: Peter Powers
Peter's parents: Mr. and Mrs. Powers

Part A

"I just can't work with Peter anymore!" exclaimed Mrs. Jacobs, one of the kindergarten teachers at Hightop School. She had grabbed Ms. Winthrop, a special education teacher, in the hall and was pouring out her frustration. "I've tried my best, but that child is driving me crazy. Every day he does something that gets under my skin. During seatwork time yesterday, the children were supposed to color pictures of objects that began with *m* on their worksheet. Each time Peter finished coloring one of the pictures, he called out, 'All done, all done, all done,' and continued chanting until either his aide or I got there. I couldn't concentrate on teaching the other children, and they couldn't concentrate on their work. Several children looked up, a few started giggling, and one child even started imitating Peter and chanting along with him! I really don't think it's fair to the other children to have Peter in the class. It's December, and we've tried him in my regular kindergarten for half a year now. I've given it a good shot, but enough is enough. I'd like you to call a Planning and Placement Team meeting to reconsider what to do with Peter. I wasn't trained to work with a child with a pervasive developmental disorder."

The School and Community

Hilltop was one of four elementary schools in the rural community of Lancaster. Residents of the town farmed the gently rolling countryside or worked in one of several defense plants a few miles away. The town strongly supported education; its teachers were among the highest paid in that part of the state. In the area of special education, it was generally understood that "whatever the kids need, they get." The decline in the defense industry, however, had begun to take its toll on the economic well-being of the town, and thus, on the monies available for the school system. One plant had closed. There was talk of rescinding the 3 percent raises promised to teachers this year.

Approximately 450 students from kindergarten to sixth grade attended Hilltop, a low, sprawling brick structure built in the 1970s. There were also two special education prekindergarten classes, one of which was taught by Ms. Winthrop.

Most of Hilltop's teachers had twenty or more years of experience. There was a full-time school psychologist, and other specialists were hired when needed. These consultants included a speech and language pathologist, a clinical psychologist, and an expert on autism and developmental disorders. There were four children with pervasive developmental disorders in the district, and last year, the consultants met with the teachers of these children for one hour a month per child. This year, there seemed to be less need, and the consultants were scheduled to come in September, December, and April.

The district prided itself on keeping up with innovations in education, and there was a lively in-service training program for teachers. For the past two years, kindergarten through second grade teachers had been participating in Least Restrictive Environment (LRE) training to help them to identify at-risk students and to work effectively with these children within their regular education classrooms. The goal was to keep the children in the mainstream. Some teachers grumbled about the LRE initiative because administrators had mandated the training without even consulting with the teachers.

The Teachers

Mrs. Jacobs was highly respected by the school staff, and each year several parents requested her to be their child's teacher. She had been teaching kindergarten for twenty-seven years. After majoring in early childhood education at the state university, she went on to get a master's and a sixth-year diploma. She had seen a variety of educational trends come and go, including the open classroom and the back-to-basics movement. At this point, she regarded new proposals with some skepticism and felt that her own experience was the best guide. Her goal was to ensure that the children had the skills they needed to succeed in first grade, and she felt comfortable with her personal approach. In the past, her approach had worked well for several mainstreamed students with special needs.

There were twenty children in Mrs. Jacobs's class. They sat next to each other at desks arranged in two long rows facing each other. Mrs. Jacobs's desk was at the head of these rows in the middle, and she was often seated there.

Around the perimeter of the room, there were various learning centers. There was a block area, with accessories such as toy dinosaurs and cars. The dramatic play area had a play stove, refrigerator, dishes, and dolls. There was also an indoor jungle gym and a computer. The bulletin boards were decorated with materials that Mrs. Jacobs had made or purchased. One of them sported a large snowman throwing snowballs with letters on them.

The children attended kindergarten from 9:00 to 11:30 A.M. When they first arrived, they had a puzzle time at their desks. After discussing the calendar and the weather, they had work time. At their desks, children completed worksheets designed to help them learn colors, shapes, letter names and sounds, and number concepts. They also used manipulatives, like Unifix cubes and parquetry blocks, to reinforce number concepts. The children left the class twice a week for gym and once a week for a library period. Outdoor time was infrequent. Mrs. Jacobs wanted to take the children out more but didn't feel there was enough time within the half-day format.

Mrs. Jacobs set clear expectations about behavior. The children had to be quiet and raise their hands before speaking. When leaving their desks, they lifted their chairs, without sliding them, and placed them under their desks. They walked to the library in single file with arms by their sides. Mrs. Jacobs prided herself on how well-disciplined her students were.

Ms. Winthrop, the special education teacher, had been teaching for four years. Although she had originally planned to be an occupational therapist, her work at her college's laboratory preschool sparked an interest in teaching, and she majored in special education. Now, she was taking courses to get certified in elementary education as well.

Ms. Winthrop's first job involved teaching severely and profoundly handicapped children in a self-contained classroom. She was committed to mainstreaming children with special needs into regular classrooms, and when she took the job, she said, "If I do a good job, I won't have this position in a year and a half." She did, in fact, facilitate the integration of her first students into the mainstream, and the self-contained program closed in two years.

Now, Ms. Winthrop worked with a special needs prekindergarten group of seven 5- and 6-year-olds. She expected that after a year with her the majority of these children would be mainstreamed. Another special education teacher worked with a group of 3- to 5-year-olds. Twice a month, the two special education teachers at Hilltop met with the two kindergarten teachers for about twenty minutes to discuss how the mainstreamed children with special needs were managing in their classes. Mrs. Jacobs came to these meetings with long lists of problems about Peter. Ms. Winthrop felt Mrs. Jacobs was not particularly interested in finding solutions to them; she could remember only one suggestion that Mrs. Jacobs had tried, and it was relatively easy to implement.

As a result, Ms. Winthrop wasn't surprised that Mrs. Jacobs no longer wanted to keep Peter in her class. However, there was no time built into Ms.

Winthrop's schedule for either ongoing consultation or in-class assistance to regular classroom teachers. Ms. Winthrop wondered whether that would have kept the situation from coming to a head. Furthermore, the consultants' December visit had been cancelled due to snow and rescheduled for January.

There was an aide, Mrs. Melton, in the classroom, but that hadn't seemed to help. Mrs. Melton worked with both Peter and another child, who had speech and hearing problems. She had been advised specifically not to shadow Peter because he needed to learn to interact more with children and become less dependent on adults. If Peter were having difficulty with a worksheet, Mrs. Melton would state the directions more simply to help him to understand. When he called for attention or chanted, "I'm done," she would redirect him to other work.

However, Mrs. Jacobs was responsible for guiding Mrs. Melton's work, and she had commented in the meetings with Ms. Winthrop that she felt that Mrs. Melton, although well-meaning, could be more of a hindrance than a help—one more person to be aware of and responsible for.

The Child

When Peter Powers was three, his parents, a librarian and a corporate executive, were alarmed by his severe temper tantrums and his inability to express himself through language. Although his pediatrician had considered this a temporary stage, he arranged for a battery of tests at a well-respected children's hospital. Peter was diagnosed as having pervasive developmental disorder (PDD), a severe brain disorder which generally results in impairments in social relationships, communication skills, and play patterns. The hospital staff considered Peter's PDD a form of high-functioning autism. Peter had normal intelligence.

Instead of talking, Peter, at age three, expressed himself mainly through gestures and facial expressions. His parents tended to anticipate his needs, so that if he motioned for a glass of water, they would get him one. Although many preschoolers talk to themselves as they play, Peter did not.

Peter had other behaviors characteristic of PDD children. Changes were difficult, and he had a need for sameness. For example, he liked his mother to put him to bed, and he insisted on wearing the same red T-shirt every night. Before his parents understood this need, if his father tried to put him to bed in other nightclothes, he would cry ferociously, flailing his arms and legs. One time, when he was $2\frac{1}{2}$, he and his mother were building stairs with Legos. The next day, he insisted on rebuilding the stairs in the same place and remembered the exact pattern of the colors and sizes of Lego blocks for each set of stairs.

Sometimes Peter enjoyed new situations, but many times he was unusually fearful of them. His parents thought he would enjoy visiting a nearby natural history museum, but, when they arrived, Peter refused to move from the lobby into an exhibit area where there were dioramas of woodland settings and creatures. He protested loudly when his parents gently encouraged him, and the family decided to leave the museum. He had avoided eye contact with any of the museum personnel.

Peter attended Ms. Winthrop's special needs preschool class for two years. His expressive language increased dramatically during this time, although he continued to have some speech disturbances. He repeated key words or phrases at inappropriate times ("Wash your hands. Wash your hands. Wash your hands." or "Want ice cream. Want ice cream.") He also took on the role of others in speech. For example, he would state to his mother, "Say 'time to go to bed,' " as if to direct her to tell him about bedtime. He also interpreted speech literally. Once Mrs. Powers lost control and shouted at him, "You're driving me up a wall." Peter looked very confused, as if he expected to see her in a car driving up a wall.

He liked to be with his peers in the neighborhood, and he tried hard to join in their play and to fit into their world. He had rollerblades and skated with the children in the neighborhood. The specialists at the children's hospital felt he would never be able to play soccer because of the need to integrate skills of spatial awareness, prediction, following rules, and personal safety. But Peter cried and begged his parents to let him try, and he succeeded and recently joined a team. Considering the growth in his skills and his motivation to be with his peers, Ms. Winthrop felt that he should be mainstreamed into a regular education kindergarten.

Back to the Discussion between Mrs. Jacobs and Ms. Winthrop

Mrs. Jacobs began to describe to Ms. Winthrop why she felt it was inappropriate for Peter to stay in her kindergarten. "He just doesn't listen! I can't tell you how frustrating it is when, at the end of playtime, I ask him to put away the dishes in the little kitchen and then line up for gym, and he completely ignores me," she said with obvious exasperation.

> During story time, Peter doesn't pay attention. He fidgets, gets up, sits down, and is so restless that the other children become distracted. Then, when I ask him a question to help him to focus, he can't answer it. The other day, we were reading *The Three Little Pigs*. When I asked Peter why the wolf blew the pigs' houses down, he had no idea. He doesn't have the comprehension skills that a kindergartner should have.
>
> At other times, when I ask simple questions, such as "What did you have for breakfast?" he either mumbles or says, "No, thank you." The other children laugh, and the flow of the discussion is broken. It disrupts their learning, and he's not keeping pace with them. Sometimes, I even think he's trying to be the class clown.

During seatwork times, Peter was unable to work independently. Every time he finished even a small part of the task, he called, "All done," and waited to be recognized. "He knows he has to write both his first and last name on his paper, but before he'll add his last name, he insists that I check his first name and tell him to go on. If I had only five kids in a class, I could take this time, but I have nineteen other children to teach, too," Mrs. Jacobs said.

Peter copied the other children's work and seemed unable to do anything on his own. His art work looked just like the work of the student next to him. When the class took the Metropolitan readiness test, dividers were placed between the children. Still, Peter knelt on his chair and leaned over the divider so he could copy from his neighbors. "If he can't do work like this independently, I'm afraid he'll never make it in a regular class. He has no idea how to respond to the test questions. Even when he knows the material, he can't understand the questions," said Mrs. Jacobs.

Peter's demand for routine had become difficult for her. During the morning exercises, she generally discussed the calendar before the weather. If, by chance, she reversed the two, Peter would protest, "Calendar, do calendar. No weather, do calendar." While Mrs. Jacobs felt consistency was important, she liked to have some flexibility and to be able to take advantage of "teachable moments." But then Peter became very upset.

Peter also had problems during playtime. If another child knocked over his block tower, either purposely or by accident, he would plaintively and persistently complain, "Scott did that," until Mrs. Jacobs came over. She taught all the children to talk through their problems with each other to come to some solutions, but Peter never tried to solve his difficulties with the other children in this manner.

Sometimes, Peter became overly stimulated and ran around the room. His excitement was contagious, and other children would begin to chase him. Mrs. Jacobs would have to ask Peter to stop many times before he complied. At these times, it was also hard to quell the other children's excitement and get them involved in more purposeful play or work.

After she had shared this information, Mrs. Jacobs told Ms. Winthrop that she would like a PPT meeting called to discuss placing Peter in a different class. She felt that by this point in the year, Peter should be functioning better and that he required more individual attention than she could provide, causing the other children's needs to be neglected. "I think Peter would do better in your class. He might really manage better in a smaller group," Mrs. Jacobs suggested. Ms. Winthrop agreed to arrange for the PPT meeting and asked whether she could observe Peter a few times in the kindergarten class before the meeting. Mrs. Jacobs readily consented.

Ms. Winthrop felt that there were three choices that had to be weighed carefully. First, Peter could stay in Mrs. Jacobs's kindergarten class, and Mrs. Jacobs could receive extra help in working with him. Second, Peter could be transferred to Mrs. Esposito's kindergarten class which was more play-oriented. Mrs. Esposito had some training in special education and seemed more comfortable working with children with special needs. Perhaps, because of that, she already had three children with special needs mainstreamed in her class. Third, Peter could be placed in the self-contained special needs prekindergarten program again. Then, it would be his third year in her program. She had a group of seven children with a full-time aide.

Ms. Winthrop felt some sympathy for Mrs. Jacobs's position. She knew how demanding Peter could be, and the concern about the other children losing their teacher's time seemed legitimate. Maybe her class would be the best solution. However, she remembered how proud Peter had been that day last May when she had explained to him that he would be going to kindergarten. He wanted so much to be like other children! Maybe he would manage better with Mrs. Esposito, who seemed more accommodating to individual differences. Yet, that would entail a major change in Peter's life and might strain Mrs. Esposito to work with four children with special needs. Although he was having difficulties in Mrs. Jacobs's class, he was familiar with the routine and considered a couple of the children his friends. In light of how difficult changes were for Peter, she wondered whether any kind of a transfer would be in his best interest. There was no easy answer to this dilemma, but she knew the principal would expect her recommendation next week.

Advance Study Questions

1. What is the problem that Ms. Winthrop faces?

2. How does the situation appear from Mrs. Jacobs's perspective? How does it appear from Ms. Winthrop's perspective?

3. How did this situation develop? What, if anything, might have altered the circumstances that produced this problem?

4. If you were Ms. Winthrop, what recommendation(s) would you make at the Planning and Placement Team meeting?

CASE 6

The New Child in My Class

Tracie-Lynn Zakas and Robert Piazza

CHARACTERS

Student:	James Krosek
James's mother:	Mrs. Krosek
Special education teacher:	Mrs. Terry Simpson
School psychologist:	Miss Finn
Preschool teacher:	Mrs. Vece
School social worker:	Mr. Drum
First grade teacher:	Mrs. Brower
Principal:	Mr. Osborne
Students:	Leslie
	Jill

Part A

A Messy Start

When Terry Simpson walked into the lunchroom at Mason Elementary School to collect her students, she was just in time to see James Krosek hurling his food-filled tray at Leslie, one of his classmates. Dripping with spaghetti, Leslie began to wail hysterically. James had wanted some of her potato chips, and when she politely refused to give him any, this was his response. Terry began to understand why James's first grade teacher had wanted him removed from her classroom. James had been referred for special educational services and placed in Mrs. Terry Simpson's primary level class six weeks into the school year, with the justification that her class provided better behavioral systems and more appropriate instructional opportunities for a child with orthopedic handicaps. In considering the situation, Terry thought:

> This might be true, but what this child really needs is an "attitude adjustment." I've had many unruly children in my class before, but none quite like this little boy. He really didn't think there was anything wrong with throwing that tray.

When I asked him what he could have done rather than throw his tray at Leslie he said, "I don't know. She wouldn't give me any chips. That wasn't nice of her." He accepted no blame for this incident.

The Child

A thin, wiry, six-year-old boy with a face full of freckles, James had Duchenne's muscular dystrophy (MD), a disease that causes the muscles of the body to lose protein. Muscle tissue is then replaced by fatty and other tissues over a period of time. Often, the onset of this disease is in early childhood, causing progressive muscle deterioration so that by the early teens, an individual may need a wheelchair. Death occurs in the twenties for many of those afflicted with MD.

James showed symptoms of MD at about three years of age. His difficulties with running, maintaining balance, and climbing stairs had progressively worsened over the past few years. Although not yet in a wheelchair, James moved slowly and at times appeared very lethargic. He had also experienced asthma and frequent bouts with pneumonia.

A thick file followed James to Mason Elementary School. Medical, psychological, educational, and social worker reports, as well as anecdotal information from his previous teachers were included in it. The findings revealed some contradictions. A recent assessment of James's intelligence suggested that he was within the high-average range (IQ 112). Early academic skills seemed to be developing nicely. James could identify and write all the letters of the alphabet and read some basic sight words. Some reversals and inversions of letters and shapes were noted in James's graphomotor work, but the psychologist indicated that James performed similarly to other children who were a few months shy of their sixth birthdays. Developmentally he was considered an appropriate candidate for first grade.

James did not attend kindergarten but received two years of instruction in a preschool class for children with handicapping conditions. This class emphasized the development of readiness and preacademic skills in the hope that some of the students would graduate to a regular first grade class. Observations by Miss Finn, the preschool psychologist, revealed that James had serious difficulties with peer relationships and also had problems accepting appropriate discipline from his teacher and other service providers. Temper tantrums seemed to be the rule rather than the exception. Mrs. Vece, James's preschool teacher, thought that the behavior observed by Miss Finn was typical of his day in, day out performance.

But observations conducted by Mr. Drum, the school social worker, during the latter part of the year had painted a different picture of James's behavior. He found him attentive and calm. In an interview, James was polite, compliant, and very verbal. He did express a wish to go to a school the following year where the work would not be so hard. A report written by Mr. Drum concluded that

James might benefit from a half hour per week of social work services, but that his behavior in no way met the criteria of a child with severe emotional difficulties.

After two Planning and Placement Team (PPT) meetings in mid-June of last year, the assessment team recommended that James be placed in a regular first grade class on a trial basis. Mr. Drum was assigned to closely monitor James's academic and behavioral activities. He would also work with James in a small group setting to improve his peer relationships. Physical and occupational therapy would continue for two 45 minute periods a week. Minutes taken at the final meeting indicated that James's mother strongly pushed for this regular class placement. She wanted James to be with normal children, and not in a special class for his entire life.

School and Community

Mason Elementary School was a K–6 school housed in a classic, two-story brick building built in the 1930s. It had undergone numerous renovations over the years to make it habitable for several generations of children. Still, its age showed, and there was a shabby, unkempt feel to it. The pale green classroom walls were graying, the outdoor play equipment was chipped and rusting, and the dull floors were in need of repair or polish.

Mason was one of two elementary schools in Delton, a moderate-sized town (population 12,500) nestled in the valley of the Pawcanak River. This town once thrived because of a local rubber-products plant, but when that company moved south, many people lost work, and the overall standard of living of the community declined considerably. Many families in town received federal or state assistance. Delton's population was composed primarily of second-generation Irish, Italian, Polish, and Slovak Americans.

Family

James lived with his mother and maternal aunt on the first level of a two-family home. This house was owned by his mother's parents, who lived on the second floor. James used to live on the second floor, but these living arrangements were changed a year ago because of the difficulty he had climbing the stairs. Two years ago, James's mother began studying nursing at a local community college. She also worked thirty hours per week at the local supermarket. His grandparents were retired, and his aunt was currently unemployed.

James had never had any communication with his father or his father's family. His parents were married for only one year, and his father left home when his mother was pregnant, which coincided with his father's layoff at the local rubber-products plant.

There were no other children in James's immediate family. Also, he had no close friends in the neighborhood.

A Much Needed Change

Five weeks into the school year, Mrs. Brower, James's first grade teacher had enough of this trial placement. "He's outrageous," she exclaimed to Mr. Drum. "He's always falling out of his seat to get attention from me and the rest of the class, and he never finishes his work; he just daydreams most of the day. And that's only a tenth of the problem. He doesn't fit in with the rest of the kids. He's got some pretty bad attention problems." Mr. Drum encouraged her to fill out a referral form so that the PPT could discuss the appropriateness of the current placement. On the form, Mrs. Brower offered a partial list of the incidents that she said were ruining the climate of her class, including the following:

> *September 5:* James insisted his assigned seat be next to the aquarium. When he didn't get his way, he yelled loudly that this wasn't a fun class. The next day, the fish were dead. The aquarium's thermostat had been increased to its maximum position by someone.
>
> *September 11:* The art teacher reported that James had spilled paint on the art room floor. When he was asked to clean up the paint, he said, "No, that isn't my job."
>
> *September 19:* A girl in the class was shoved to the floor by James as he rushed to the head of the line for lunch. He told her that she should never take his place in line again.
>
> *September 23:* I neglected to put a star on one of James's math papers which was very well done. I later found him searching through my desk drawer for the star box.
>
> *October 1:* James was drawing with a ballpoint pen on his desk top. I told him this was unacceptable behavior and he should wash the ink off. He said he always draws on the furniture at home, and besides, this was his desk.

A meeting on October 10 was attended by Mrs. Brower, Mr. Osborne, the school principal, Mr. Drum, Miss Finn, James's physical and occupational therapists, Mrs. Krosek (James's mother), and Terry Simpson.

Two hours of rather heated discussion followed. During the meeting, Mrs. Brower reiterated her concerns about James's behavior and attention to tasks. She acknowledged that she may have been partly at fault in being overindulgent because she had no idea how to discipline a boy such as James. Mrs. Krosek responded, "Why didn't you ask? I would have told you how to handle him." Mr. Drum apologized for having seen James for only two half-hour periods during the first month of school. He informed the group that the beginning of the school year was always hectic, and his schedule was now firmly set. Mrs. Krosek was silent, but her face reddened.

The team finally analyzed the two placement options for James. Either he would remain in Mrs. Brower's class with twenty-six other children who he would compete with academically or be placed in Terry Simpson's class. The only time Terry spoke during the meeting was when her principal asked her to describe her class. She informed Mrs. Krosek and the rest of the team that she currently had a group of nine students. Six children in her class had moderate-to-severe emotional difficulties. The other three were children with language-based learning disabilities. Her class also had a full-time aide. When Terry finished, Mrs. Krosek finally spoke up:

> You forgot to tell us that your class is on the first floor and Mrs. Brower's class is on the second floor. James comes home exhausted every day. Counting recess, lunch, specials, and other activities, he must climb those stairs five times a day. Did any of you consider that? For that reason and that reason alone, I think maybe Mrs. Simpson's class is the right one. I hope you'll now wake up to all of James's problems.

The professionals on the PPT looked sheepish after Mrs. Krosek's comments but quickly concurred that Mrs. Simpson's class was the best placement for James at this time. The following Monday, Terry Simpson's class would have ten children. The team agreed to James's mother's request not to label him emotionally disturbed but to continue to designate him orthopedically handicapped.

The First Day

Terry Simpson introduced James to the other children in her classroom during circle time. He reticently nodded his head in acknowledgment. After opening exercises, Terry began the alphabet game. When the letter *L* was reached on the ABC cards, it was James's turn. He burst forth with a long and rather involved story about a lake that he recently visited. Mrs. Simpson politely interjected, "James, during this alphabet game, we try to keep our stories short so that everybody can get a turn."

Terry's jaw dropped as the six-year-old sharply retorted, "Don't interrupt me when I'm talking. I'm not finished yet."

James was allowed to continue, but later in the morning, Mrs. Simpson took James aside and firmly reminded him who was the teacher and who was the student. Once again, she was bombarded with caustic comments about how he didn't like being interrupted when he had important things to say. This boy had been in her room for two hours, and Terry Simpson was emotionally already somewhere between flabbergasted and livid. Terry took a deep breath after James's last comments and suggested he return to his seat. He did so without delay.

Later in the morning, Mrs. Simpson told her children to line up for lunch. She was not surprised to see James rush to the front of the line. Leslie Connor was behind James, clutching her free lunch ticket in one hand and proudly holding a bag of potato chips in the other hand. Terry observed that this was the first time all year Leslie had brought a snack to school to supplement her lunch. As the aide left with the children for the cafeteria, Terry proceeded to the teacher's lounge. She entered the room as Mrs. Brower was leaving. Mrs. Brower asked, "How did the morning go with our friend?"

"That young boy has a lot of surprising things to say. I found his language skills quite good," Terry replied sarcastically.

At the end of the lunch period, Terry went to the lunchroom to collect her children. Having just completed his food toss, James was sitting stolidly, arms crossed, jaw firm, as Leslie wailed. The honeymoon, which never began, was over.

Advance Study Questions

1. What is Terry Simpson's major dilemma?

2. How did this situation develop?

3. What is Mrs. Krosek's view of the problem? Is she helping or hindering the situation?

4. What immediate steps need to be taken to help remedy James's classroom behavior?

5. Is the fact that James has muscular dystrophy a relevant issue in this case?

CASE 7

A Different Kind of Student

Loretta L. Rubin

CHARACTERS

Students:	Colleen Murphy
	Sara Moyer
Colleen's parents:	Mr. and Mrs. Murphy
First grade teacher:	Mrs. Sharon Lomax
Principal:	Mr. Dworski
Resource teacher:	Mrs. Jones

Part A

"Tell me, Mrs. Lomax, you're Colleen's first grade teacher—do *you* think that our daughter is retarded?"

As Sharon Lomax faced Colleen's parents, she considered Mr. Murphy's question. Did she think that their daughter was retarded? Certainly Colleen didn't learn in the same way that other children did. She was delayed in a number of areas, but perhaps she could find a solution to Colleen's learning difficulties. Or perhaps a more comprehensive special education placement would be in Colleen's best interest? Perhaps she would not fit there either? Could they find a more suitable program in a community such as theirs?

The Community

Middle City was a mid-sized, economically poor New England city with a population of over 100,000. Once a thriving industrial center, the number of factories and businesses had dwindled because of financial reverses or relocation. Now the city depended on the business generated by the prestigious university located there. The university provided cultural and academic assets, but its tax-exempt holdings drained the economically strapped community. The needs of the distinctive city neighborhoods were often at odds with the priorities of the university and its students.

This university community contained a cross-section of varied cultures, but the majority of its public-school population was African-American and Hispanic. Many of its impoverished students relied on the public schools for social or academic support services. But in this economically deprived school system, only those in the most distress were able to receive assistance. School administrators insisted that the district needed more money for services for its youth, while the city administration found it impossible to ask its hard-pressed citizens for more money for education.

The School

Parkview School was a small neighborhood school located at the eastern corner of the city. It had an older staff who had been teaching at the school for a number of years. They were proud of the school's long-standing reputation for fostering academic excellence. Unlike most of Middle City, the area around Parkview was lined with nicely maintained single-family homes. At one time, all the students came from that neighborhood. Now, some of the children who attended Parkview came from the neighborhood, but an equal number came from other parts of the city. Some were bused from nearby neighborhoods to achieve greater racial balance. Others were driven from neighborhoods farther away to attend Parkview because of its excellent reputation. Also, a number of parents from the Parkview area opted to send their children to a nearby magnet school because of its particular educational philosophy. The school, which had once been relatively isolated from the urban problems of Middle City, was now struggling to meet the needs of inner-city students while trying to retain the local population at the school.

The Teacher

Sharon Lomax had been a teacher for over fifteen years in Middle City. Most of that time had been spent teaching first through third grades in an urban school at the opposite end of town. She was beginning her second year at Parkview.

Sharon had not followed the teacher education route common among her colleagues. As a liberal arts major at a small New England university, she added student teaching as an additional course in her senior year. After graduation, she worked as a researcher for an educational evaluation firm, and she completed her remaining course work for certification. Although offered jobs in other communities, she had elected to return to her hometown of Middle City in order to make a difference to urban children there. Attempting to compensate for her scant background in elementary curriculum, she had taken a number of courses and workshops in alternative methods of teaching reading and language arts. She had earned a reputation for her stubborn determination to use alternative methods to teach her students to read and write.

The school district, however, was committed to a basic reading series organized around a developmental sequence of skills (a basal reader). The children's progress was evaluated based on the basal tests in this series, the results of which were reported monthly to Mr. Dworski, the principal. To meet this requirement, Sharon selectively used stories and skills from the city's basal reader. She integrated these with the teaching techniques that had proven successful for her in the past.

She relied primarily on her version of the whole language approach in which she used both children's literature and the students' writings based on their own experiences. She tried to construct a more meaningful path to literacy than she felt was offered by the basal series. She used student pieces and spelling lessons to teach phonetic word structure. Drawing and writing activities constituted a good part of her language lessons. One of her favorite activities was helping students write poems and stories and illustrate them. These were then bound into books for the class, which, along with other pieces of student work, were included as a segment of their reading instruction.

As the new first grade teacher at Parkview, she replaced a popular retiree who was known for pioneering the use of an innovative method of reading instruction using a phonetic approach. Sharon felt a tremendous pressure to establish a good reputation at Parkview and prove the success of her whole language techniques. Her upcoming class seemed the perfect vehicle to test her methods.

The Class

Many of the children in the incoming class seemed bright and motivated; several were in the gifted program at the school. There were also students whose backgrounds had not adequately prepared them for the first grade curriculum. There were children from homes torn by emotional and economic problems. Many of the children were from single-parent families. Some families were coping better than others. There were those who had support from grandparents and other relatives, but others were completely dysfunctional due to drugs and violence. One could expect that this class would contain several students with unidentified learning or emotional problems. Two of the students were to be mainstreamed from a special education class for children who had experienced severe delays in oral language.

The Student

Compared with many of the other children, Colleen had the benefit of a warm and caring family. Mr. and Mrs. Murphy had noticed that as a baby, Colleen had seemed a little slow to learn new things. She didn't walk until she was nearly two years old. Until that time, she had said only one or two words. She had some difficulty following oral directions, and she seemed confused about which hand to use. Her kindergarten teacher and parents had observed that she had difficulty with fine-motor and gross-motor coordination. During her kindergarten year, she was unable to use scissors properly and to copy simple geometric shapes. On the playground, her deficiencies in gross-motor coordination left her far behind the other children. She was unable to coordinate her body sufficiently to climb monkey bars or ride a bicycle. Her parents felt that special glasses and assistance from the physical therapist would help remedy the situation.

Mr. and Mrs. Murphy had enrolled Colleen, at the age of five years, one month, in the public school because they felt that her exceptional needs would not be met at the parochial school her two older brothers attended. During the kindergarten screening, a placement team had recommended a class for children with developmental delays. Colleen would have had to be bused to a school outside of her neighborhood. For this reason, in addition to their reluctance to label Colleen, her parents decided against the special placement and sent her to a regular class at Parkview instead. At Parkview she was placed in a regular kindergarten. Although not labeled a special education student, she was allowed to receive additional support from special education personnel.

Colleen's kindergarten year at Parkview had been mixed. She had seemed happy and socially well-adjusted, but her teacher felt that she wasn't as prepared for first grade as many of her classmates. Special support would continue in the first grade. An assessment performed at the end of the kindergarten year confirmed that a mild learning disability appeared to exist.

Mr. Dworski had told Sharon that Colleen would be coming to her room this year. Although a recent psychological test had indicated she was a child with low-average intelligence, he described her as a child who might require some extra help in small-motor coordination. She would work with an occupational therapist, and she had been referred to the resource room for thirty minutes a day for any needed academic support. That should have given Sharon Lomax a clue that this wasn't a simple case of a child with one isolated problem.

In her career in Middle City, she had never seen a case where a first grade child received any special services unless they were absolutely necessary. In her previous class, a child had waited three weeks after being identified as needing psychiatric placement. And here was Colleen, entering first grade and already receiving daily services from a resource teacher and weekly visits from the occupational therapist.

The First Day of School

When the first day of school arrived, Sharon understood what Mr. Dworski meant. Colleen was a sweet, amiable child, whom the other children seemed to like. Her long, dark hair neatly braided, she was all dressed up for the first day of school. She was cooperative and attentive, but it soon became evident that she was unable to do most of the tasks expected of a beginning first grader.

At age $6\frac{1}{2}$, she was still unable to write her name and was uncertain as to which hand to use. She was able to "draw" all the letters of her name (in capitals). However, the letters were all over the page; there was no attempt to write them sequentially from left to right. She had the same organizational problem drawing a face. The eyes, nose, and mouth were all there, but not in their expected positions, nor were they enclosed by a head.

Numbers were equally problematic. She was unable to identify numerals, except the number 1, and found it necessary to "touch count" even two or three objects. Even with manipulatives such as blocks or Unifix cubes, Colleen had difficulty understanding addition or subtraction. Her weaknesses seemed most apparent in prereading skills. Colleen couldn't memorize even the simplest sight words, like "stop" or "go." This inability presented difficulty in using the basal reader. Its preprimers relied almost exclusively on sight vocabulary, introducing only the consonants and a few limited phonograms.

First Term

As the term progressed through September and October, Colleen's problems became more pronounced. She was unable to produce recognizable illustrations of even the simplest stories. Her spelling and writing showed that Colleen had no understanding of underlying word patterns. Although she could learn some letter sounds in isolation, she had great difficulty remembering them in words. Sharon's attempts to connect reading and writing sounds as she said them didn't prove much help. Whenever Colleen created a piece of "writing," she would immediately forget what she had wanted to say with her pictures and her invented spelling. The sight words she had studied by rote for spelling would show little relationship to their actual letter configuration when she wrote them. At times, even the initial letters were incorrect.

Mrs. Jones, the resource teacher, came daily and assisted Colleen in the lessons that Sharon was teaching the class. Even with Mrs. Jones's assistance, Colleen had difficulty accomplishing the assigned tasks. She hesitated to attempt anything without individual help.

By the end of the first term, some of Sharon's alternative techniques began to yield limited effectiveness. By using mazes to help her track from left to right, Colleen learned to write her name sequentially. With direction, she began to draw a more complete picture of a face. In her drawings, figures began to be connected by a ground line, indicating that she perceived the relationship between the pictorial elements.

In other areas, Colleen was experiencing more substantial success. With Sharon's help, she learned how to use her arms to cross the parallel bars in the school yard. At home, she was beginning to ride a two-wheeler. The extra materials Sharon furnished for study at home provided some limited assistance in learning numbers and letters. But Colleen was still far behind most of her classmates.

School Team Meeting

Sharon realized she needed more information. It was obvious that Colleen's problems were more far-reaching than she had been led to believe. She asked to meet with Mr. Dworski and Mrs. Jones. As Sharon outlined her frustration, they discussed everything that had already been tried. To Sharon, it seemed as if she were quickly exhausting a fairly extensive repertoire of techniques. Both Mr. Dworski and Mrs. Jones were sympathetic.

At one point, Sharon said, "It's as if this child is a fingertip away. I feel that I can find a way to reach her, but she always seems to be just beyond my grasp." Mrs. Jones responded that there were some children that were just too difficult to instruct in the context of a regular classroom environment.

"I have never met a child that I couldn't teach. There are some that I haven't taught as much as I would have liked, but never one to whom I couldn't teach something," Sharon replied.

Mrs. Jones responded, "Then you're very lucky. As a special education teacher, I've met a number of children who couldn't be taught."

Sharon left the meeting unsatisfied. Colleen had made *some* progress already. She recalled several other children whom she had taught to read; they had also been labeled "unteachable." She was more determined than ever to find a way to teach Colleen to read. She decided to speak to Colleen's parents to discover the extent of her challenge.

Parent Conference

Mr. and Mrs. Murphy were very open to talking to Colleen's teacher. As a matter of fact, they expressed their pleasure that Sharon was working so closely with the resource teacher. Warming to their discussion, Mrs. Murphy told Sharon a bit about Colleen's history. In turn, Sharon discussed with Mr. and Mrs. Murphy the methods she had used and the limits to their success. She reiterated that although she was determined to find a more effective means to teach Colleen to read and write, that capability was still a long way off. Sharon looked at Mr. Murphy and thought again about his question. Was Colleen retarded? Would she ever find the means of reaching her, or would Colleen need to be placed in a different setting? How long should she persist in trying?

Advanced Study Questions

1. What is Sharon Lomax's dilemma? What are the underlying issues in this situation?

2. How did this situation develop?

3. If you were Sharon Lomax, how would you respond to Mr. Murphy's question about whether Colleen is retarded?

4. If you were Sharon, what action(s), if any, would you take with regard to Colleen's reading instruction? Colleen's placement? Why?

CASE 8

How Much Can You Expect?

Judith B. Buzzell

CHARACTERS

Teacher: Rebecca Charney
Audiologist: Dr. Corman
Speech therapist: Joan
Tutor: Maria
Student: Lesley
Lesley's parents: Anne and Stuart Wight

Part A

The In-Service Workshop

"Be sure you get to that workshop," Rebecca's principal insisted. A workshop was being held in May at Crestview Elementary School for all the teachers in the school to help them understand and know how to use Lesley's hearing equipment. Lesley, a kindergartner in the school, had a profound hearing impairment. From her principal's expression and pointed directive, Rebecca sensed that she would be Lesley's first grade teacher.

The workshop consisted of a brief fifteen-minute explanation of how Lesley's FM (frequency modulation) auditory trainer worked and how to put it on Lesley. The system seemed complicated to Rebecca. Both Lesley and the teacher wore the equipment. Her teacher wore a microphone/transmitter, usually clipped to her blouse or sweater, at a distance of about 7 or 8 inches from her mouth. When she spoke, it would always sound as if she were speaking directly to Lesley—the sound was constant no matter where the teacher was in the room. With the FM trainer, the signal of the teacher's voice would always be stronger than the background noise. Lesley wore an FM receiver and ear molds. The receiver was a box about $4 \times 2\frac{1}{2}$ inches worn in a denim bag suspended around the neck. She secured it at the bottom with a belt around her waist. Wires connected up from the receiver to her ear molds. Lesley always wore this equipment. If she were working alone silently at her desk, she could switch the trainer to "aid only" so she would no longer hear the teacher. Every day when school began, Lesley had to take out her own hearing aid, put in new ear molds, and then put on and connect the receiver. The teacher would need to help her.

Rebecca left the workshop with a queasy feeling. After this cursory introduction, she had no clear understanding of how the system worked. "How will I really use it?" she wondered. "How will I even turn it on? How will Lesley turn it on? Will it work?"

In May, Lesley was assigned formally to Rebecca's class. Lesley would be one of twenty-five children, several of whom had special needs. There were two children, an Italian and a German, who spoke no English. There was one who, for religious reasons, had severe dietary restrictions; he could not even use the water fountain. Another child had been in the transitional class and then failed first grade twice; this would be his third year in first grade. There was also a child who was born with only one ear. Rebecca had a reputation in the school as a very intelligent, energetic, and caring teacher. Still, while she was intrigued by the opportunity to work with Lesley, she wondered if she would be able to rise up to meet the challenges of this class.

The School and Community

Crestview Elementary was one of seven elementary schools in the town of Seneca, a poor town with little industry and a population of about 25,000. Although Seneca always provided the basic educational services, as mandated by law, it had stinted on its school funding for the last two decades. The recession of the early 1990s had put a further strain on the town's, and hence its schools', budget.

In an attempt to keep the tax rate low, few new schools were built. Some of the schools looked like odd architectural conglomerates, with added-on wings and separate trailer annexes. Often, the special education classes were held in these annexes.

The Teacher

Rebecca Charney had been teaching for sixteen years. She had attended a well-regarded, small liberal arts college and majored in sociology. When she decided that she wanted to become a teacher, she took additional courses to become certified. She began teaching in Seneca and stayed there. Because of her inquiring mind and strong commitment to good teaching, she avidly read about new strategies, took workshops, and tapped other able and experienced teachers as resources. Her skill was recognized in the system, and often she was asked to conduct in-service workshops for colleagues, particularly in the area of language arts. She juggled the demands of her teaching with those of her three children and husband, a physician.

Lesley

Lesley's mother, Anne Wight, was a small-boned, pretty woman. Her delicate appearance belied her strength in facing her daughter's difficulties and in making sure that she received the best possible health and educational services. Anne was an occupational therapist, and her husband, Stuart, was a middle-level manager in a business. She only worked part-time for the sake of meeting her four children's needs.

Lesley was born with a cleft palate. The doctors told Anne and Stuart only that they might expect Lesley to have chronic ear infections and a speech problem. They were not led to expect additional difficulties.

Lesley seemed inconsolable as a baby. She cried a great deal, and the cry had a peculiar, shrieking quality. Her parents assumed that she was suffering from colic. However, when Lesley was six months old, there were clues that more was wrong. For example, when Anne walked into the room after Lesley's nap to pick her up and said, "Lesley, I'm here," her daughter didn't respond as her three older children had. Facing the wall, Lesley would not even turn toward Anne.

By the time Lesley was eight months old, Anne *knew* there was a problem. Lesley had made none of the typical baby sounds to communicate. At this point, Lesley underwent five months of extensive testing. The brainstem testing revealed that the baby had moderate-to-severe sensorineural hearing loss. At a meeting with the pediatrician, the ENT (otorhinolaryngologist, commonly called an ear, nose, and throat doctor), and an audiologist from their health plan, the Wights were told that Lesley needed hearing aids in both ears. In addition, it was suggested that the child attend the state's school for the deaf. This was a residential school, located about an hour away, where both signing and oral communication skills were taught (a total communication program).

Anne was stunned. "The terrifying part was that we knew Lesley needed help, but we weren't sure how best to help her," she commented. "I had an older uncle who was deaf and only signed. I don't know if it was my experience with him or my sense about Lesley, but I was determined that she would speak." Furthermore, she had no intention of putting her young child in a residential program.

Yet, Anne had a nagging worry that she might not be making the right decision—after all, she was not the expert. What if she were depriving Lesley of the potential for more communication by not enrolling her in a total communication program?

The Hearing Aids

Soon after the testing was completed, when Lesley was fourteen months old, she became a client at the speech and hearing clinic at the local state university in a neighboring town. She was fitted with only one hearing aid to avoid overpowering such a young child with her first introduction to sound. "It was amazing to see her pay attention," said Anne. However, Lesley was now fearful of once comfortable experiences, like going to the beach with its crashing waves. The exuberant shouts of the older children now startled her, and sometimes she wailed and pulled out the aid.

Still, Lesley generally responded well to the aid. When she had surgery to correct her cleft palate during the summer of her second year, Anne and Stuart could console her with soothing talk.

By September, after further testing, Lesley had been fitted with biaural aids (aids in both ears). She was eighteen months old. It was wonderful for her parents to be able to really talk to her and to sing to her.

Anne expected to see fast growth in her daughter's language development. In fact, she expected an overnight miracle. Her daughter seemed very curious and bright. With biaural aids, Lesley could hear, and Anne did not think there were any other reasons for developmental delays. But, Lesley did not start talking immediately.

The same September, Lesley joined a rehabilitative play group at the university's speech and hearing clinic. Children and parents participated. Anne felt she was learning how to teach her child. The speech therapists explained that it was necessary to build Lesley's receptive language (her comprehension) before she could be expected to produce expressive language (that is, talk). Lesley began to be able to follow simple directions. If you asked her where her shoe was, she could point to it or go get it. She started to make some repetitive sounds, such as "Ma ma" and "Da da." Still, while it was clear that she was beginning to understand language, there were no words that were truly intelligible beyond those.

Another Piece of the Puzzle

Two months after Lesley got her biaural aids, her pediatrician gave her a developmental examination. When he showed her a picture book, she leaned over and pressed her face against the page to see it. This action was a striking signal to the doctor that Lesley might have poor vision, and he referred the child to an ophthalmologist.

Anne could not believe there was a visual problem. She had observed this behavior before, but she had been told that children with hearing impairments tended to be more visual as a way of compensating for their other sensory loss. Moreover, Lesley was a highly physical child with intact motor skills. Anne believed that there was no way that Lesley could run and climb with such agility if she were visually impaired.

After testing Lesley, the ophthalmologist was astounded by the degree of myopia he discovered. (Later, Anne learned that Lesley had severe congenital myopia; the charts only tested as high as 20/400, and Lesley could not see even that well.) Yet he, too, felt that her active physicality was inconsistent with this degree of difficulty. A second opinion, however, confirmed the diagnosis. "I just felt so badly that she had not been able to see for so long," said Anne, "but that was the turning point."

On her second birthday, Lesley got her glasses. "I think it was the most amazing day I've ever spent with anybody," exclaimed her mother. Lesley noticed absolutely everything. She sat in her stroller and stared at her shoes. She touched people's faces as they spoke to her—as if she never before had any idea where sounds came from.

From this day forward, Lesley's behavior changed dramatically. Before, in the play group, she was easily distracted when objects were pointed out to her. Now that she had images to associate with words, such as "doll," "crib," or "mother," she was very attentive. Within two weeks, she began imitating sounds, and within two months, she had a vocabulary of thirty words. Although her language development continued to be slow until she was four, it developed steadily.

Schooling for Lesley

Dr. Corman, the audiologist at the university's speech and hearing clinic, urged Anne to enroll Lesley in a preschool program. She felt Lesley, now age three, needed the stimulation of being with children with normal hearing. Anne, though, did not want to send Lesley because she felt that she was home for Lesley, and the young child was already going to the rehabilitation program twice a week. But, because Anne had great confidence in Dr. Corman and respected her judgment, she enrolled Lesley in the university's laboratory school for preschoolers. This proved to be a positive experience for Lesley. One of Lesley's preschool teachers can still remember how quickly Lesley seemed to map out the setting and know where particular toys and materials were kept, despite her visual impairment. She was obviously a curious, bright child. During this time, Lesley also continued with the rehab program.

When Lesley turned four, Anne and Stuart faced another decision. Dr. Corman informed them that the public school system was legally obligated to provide services for Leslie. Leslie was eligible to attend a class for children with hearing impairments, but after visiting the class, Lesley's parents decided against it.

The class had seven or eight students with hearing impairments who both signed and spoke. Anne and Stuart felt that these children, who were not as verbal as Lesley, would not be as good models for Lesley as a class of normally hearing children. Also, the teacher used both oral language and signing. Anne and Stuart did not want Lesley to use sign language and felt that this would be confusing visually for her.

They decided to keep Lesley in a mainstreamed preschool program. Anne later reflected:

> Maybe it was a little denial on our part. It was comfortable working with people who had known Lesley a long time, and it would be hard to start sharing information about her with new people. You get so comfortable with your child's limitations. You begin not to see them as handicaps. When you have to look at a class like that, filled with wonderful, wonderful children but, nevertheless, children who all have the same problem your child has, it's an awfully big reminder. I had decided that the only way I could survive was to focus on the normal things about Lesley. Of course, I had to deal with her hearing aids and her corrective lenses, but I really tried not to make those my only focus on her. I felt that putting her in a class like that would be hard for me, even if not for her. Yet, we still toss around the idea that if she were in a classroom with a teacher for children with hearing impairments, maybe we wouldn't have to be troubleshooting for her and maybe there would be supports that are not available in a mainstreamed setting because there not everyone knows about the problem.

Public School—Kindergarten

When Lesley turned five in the spring, Dr. Corman felt she would be ready for kindergarten in the fall and would need a five-day-a-week program—although Anne considered delaying for another year. The Wights again visited the school system's class for students with hearing impairments and again decided against it. They enrolled Lesley in the public school that their older children had attended.

Anne believed that the auditory trainer would be crucial for Lesley's functioning in the mainstream. Unfortunately, Lesley's kindergarten year was not the best because the town didn't have an FM system available until February. At that point, it was hard to convince Lesley that she needed the trainer because she had been managing without it. So if Lesley didn't want to use the trainer, the teacher didn't make her. Although the teacher felt warmly toward Lesley, Anne felt that the teacher was addressing Lesley's emotional needs at the expense of her hearing needs.

Also, the kindergarten teacher chose not to have the system's teacher of children with hearing impairments demonstrate the use of the trainer to the other pupils, although this could have been done fairly easily. She felt that would put Lesley on the spot and make her feel self-conscious. In retrospect, Anne was regretful. She believed that this would have been a valuable learning experience for the other children.

Speech Therapy

In kindergarten, Lesley started speech therapy. Joan, a warm, lively speech therapist, met with Lesley two times a week for a half hour each time. Lesley went to an afternoon kindergarten program and received speech therapy in the morning, so that she wouldn't be pulled out of class. In therapy during kindergarten and first grade, the emphasis was on articulation, sound discrimination, and resonance.

For example, because Lesley had difficulty discriminating sounds in high frequencies, she lisped on some of those sounds, such as /*s*/ or /*z*/. Discrimination difficulties also affected related consonant clusters in the middle of words, so that she had difficulty articulating a word like "misty." She also had trouble with plurals. She would say "brush" for "brushes," for example. It was particularly hard for Lesley to pronounce the *th* sound. She'd even joke about this hurdle. Joan decided not to push the *th* issue, because Lesley's articulation was not that poor (she could always be understood), and Joan didn't want therapy to become a chore for her.

For sound discrimination, the tasks included distinguishing between words in pairs, such as "sick-thick," "fink-think," "pat-back." These activities would focus on Lesley's ability to detect differences in words based on sound differences.

As often happens, even following surgical repair of a cleft palate, Lesley experienced hypernasality (too much resonance in the nasal cavity) and audible nasal emission (emission of air from the nose). Articulation therapy was used to improve resonance.

Lesley always scored well in language. Her vocabulary and language were average to superior. She had a large vocabulary and used varied sentence structures. Joan attributed this to Lesley's early intervention experiences.

The Problem with Mainstreaming

Anne was led to believe that Joan would be a resource to the classroom teacher. Although she felt very positively about Joan, Anne felt that Joan's training wasn't what the teacher needed—she was neither an audiologist nor a teacher of children with hearing impairments. Anne believed that it would have been helpful for a teacher trained to work with students with hearing impairments (who had extensive experience using auditory trainers with children in the classroom) to observe Lesley in the classroom and to give the teacher some pointers on how best to use the equipment—rather than letting the teacher decide *not* to use it.

At the end of kindergarten, Anne requested a Planning and Placement Team (PPT) meeting. At the PPT, the Wights asked for an in-service workshop for the upcoming first grade teacher on how to use the trainer. It was obvious to Anne that she couldn't supply enough information, nor was it necessarily appropriate for a parent to be instructing the teacher. The audiologist from the university had volunteered to do the in-service, but this was flatly turned down by the school system.

At this point, Anne did not feel confident about Lesley's program. She also felt a little anxious that her role seemed to be the coordinator of all Lesley's services. She wasn't sure she could do that, nor did she know how to, and she really didn't feel that it was right for a parent to be in this position.

> She commented: "My biggest problem with mainstreaming is that the teachers don't receive the in-service training that they need. I've been lucky to have good rapport with them, and they've accepted the information I've provided. But, really, this information should be shared among professionals. Information should be supplied to the teacher, so that she knows what she can reasonably expect from the child, as well as how to use the equipment.

The In-Service Workshop—Again

Although Lesley's audiologist from the university did not conduct the in-service workshop, one *was* held. The leader of the workshop was the teacher of the students with hearing impairments in the system. She described how the FM auditory trainer worked. The principal required all the teachers in the school to attend (although many of them had not and would not have any contact with Lesley). Rebecca attended, as did Anne.

As Anne observed the reactions of the teachers attending the workshop, she sensed that they were not happy. And, in fact, Rebecca was among them. Rebecca felt the fifteen-minute workshop was much too short to give her the background she needed to understand Lesley's hearing impairment and to know how to use the equipment to help Lesley best. Moreover, she knew that this bright, engaging child also had severe visual problems. Kindergarten offered a play-oriented curriculum with hands-on experiences and little emphasis on reading and writing. First grade was much more demanding academically.

"How," Rebecca thought, "can I best teach a child with these special needs to learn to read and write? How should I adapt the classroom, the curriculum, and my strategies to help her to be successful in those areas?" As a committed professional, Rebecca intended to do her best.

Advance Study Questions

1. What is Rebecca's dilemma?

2. What are some underlying issues in this situation?

3. Describe the history of the diagnosis and treatment of Lesley's disabilities.

4. If you were Rebecca, how would you adapt your classroom, the curriculum, and your strategies to help Lesley to learn to read and write?

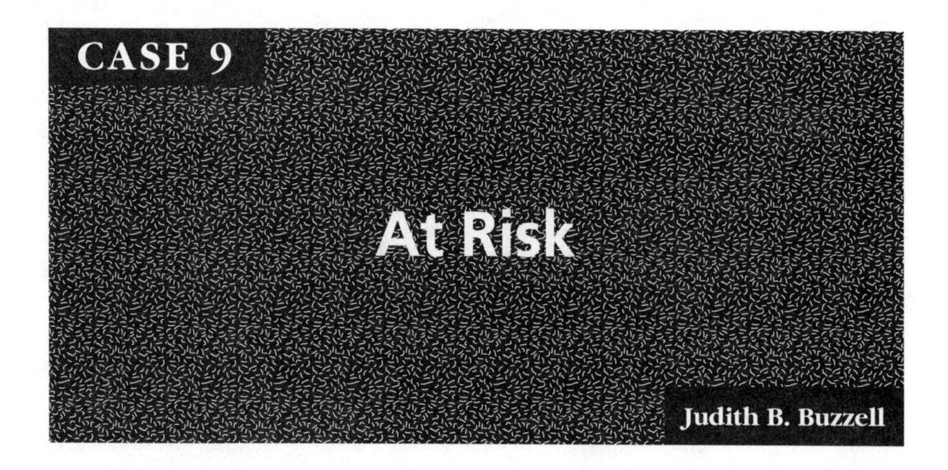

CHARACTERS

Teacher: Ellen Green
Principal: Dr. Johnson
Students: Derrick
Sharon
Luis
Tyrell
Jerome
Maria
Martin
Jamal
Josephine

Part A

It was a balmy June day, and Ellen Green, a second grade teacher, was relaxing in her backyard with her best friend, Lisa. The day before, Ellen had finished her last day of her fifth year of teaching at Horace Mann, an urban elementary school, and she was just beginning to catch her breath. She always found the transition to summer hard because her teaching concerns lingered. She started to review her past year with Lisa. Although Lisa had heard some of what Ellen was saying before, she began to understand why the combination of events was devastating for Ellen.

"We've been haunted by a series of deaths this year," Ellen began. Then she described how the year started—the deaths of Derrick and his father in late August had shocked the entire school. Derrick had been trapped in a house fire, and when his father rushed in to rescue him, he, too, had succumbed to the flames. Ellen couldn't believe the news when she first heard it.

A handsome, sparkly eyed child, Derrick was friendly and outgoing. In kindergarten, he had come to Ellen's first grade for advanced work in reading.

The next year, Derrick, as a first grader, was in her class full-time. He was intelligent, well behaved, and filled with a zest for life. He came from a model family. Both parents volunteered frequently in the school. His mother headed the Parent-Teacher Organization; her energy and enthusiasm were admired by all. His father, a hospital administrator, conducted health education workshops with the children. Derrick was a child who had every chance for success, the kind of child about whom teachers said, "I want him in my class."

The entire school was reeling from the loss. Ellen had been scheduled to have Derrick again in second grade, and she wondered how she could return to the classroom without this wonderful child there. She described how, during subsequent months, she was periodically washed by waves of pain. But, as she said to Lisa, "I felt I had to use all my energy and strength for the kids." They talked about Derrick and his death and read stories, such as *Freddy the Leaf*, about cycles of life. The school provided special support services for both the children and its staff. Still, as Ellen commented, "That was a tough beginning, and I don't think I've gotten over it."

Then, shortly after Derrick's death, Sharon's mother was killed in a car accident. "This little girl just lost her mom . . . " Ellen's voice trailed off as she described the unimaginable.

As if all this weren't enough, her class experienced a third death in one year. Luis's mother recently died after a long illness.

> This has been my hardest year teaching. In other years, there's always been a sense of accomplishment at the end of the year and an excitement about the year to come. This year, having to deal with the children's pain and my own, has really challenged my professional abilities. And I think these tragedies have made me more vulnerable to feeling stress over the more typical kinds of things that happen in urban schools. I find it hard to feel any successes in the year. Although I try to remember that this was an exceptionally difficult year, and I know intellectually that I've done a good job, I just don't feel it.

Ellen paused and looked toward the nearby woods behind her yard, as if looking for a refuge in their beauty. Her small, rural community seemed so removed from the city of Yorkville, seven miles away. "I'm at the point of making a hard decision. I feel such a commitment to these children and to the school, but the stress is starting to affect all the other aspects of my life. Frankly, I'm not sure I'll go back in the fall."

The Teacher

Ellen was the only member of her family who had gone to college. Her family was poor and moved often. For a while, she lived in a housing project, one of the few whites among predominantly African-American families, and shared a bedroom with her mother.

Although education was not emphasized in her family, she always had a sense of broader horizons, of wanting some growth-producing experiences. At age fifteen, she started working to support herself. She worked at a variety of jobs—managing a food co-op, waitressing in a fancy restaurant, making electronic parts in a factory, driving a camp bus.

Ellen had always enjoyed working with children and, thinking she might wish to open a nursery school, at the age of twenty-two, she went to a community college to study early childhood education. After receiving an associate's degree, she went on to the state university. Although she majored in education, by that time she had no intention of teaching. She was excited by learning and focused on gaining as much as she could in a wide variety of areas. But she didn't want to be part of the public school educational system that she felt hadn't worked for her. She felt that schooling, at all levels, had been a grinding out of products—vocabulary words, multiplication tables, historical dates—and that teachers had failed to nurture her own thirst for understanding and deeper knowledge and imbue her with a sense of learning as a critical lifelong process.

After finishing her B.S. at age twenty-six, Ellen married and eventually had three children. Her husband was an electrician. Following a period of successfully selling children's toys, Ellen decided she needed to make more money. While she was looking for child care, a director of a small, home-based day care center invited her to teach at the center. Ellen joined her staff and, eventually, bought the home and business.

Ellen threw herself into her work. She designed a new curriculum and renovated the children's play areas. There was always a waiting list of children to enroll. Ellen developed strong relationships with the staff, and many kept in touch with her long after they left.

However, Ellen's job was basically administrative. She missed working closely with children and other adults and wanted a new challenge. By this time, she also was feeling more confident that she could accomplish her educational goals in a public school setting without being compromised by the bureaucracy. She started looking for a teaching position in March and had landed a job by September. It was ten years since she had been certified to teach, and she was thirty-six years old.

Ellen's classroom reflected her belief in experiential, process-oriented learning. Desks for the twenty children were grouped in two concentric squares. Around the perimeter of the room were art, science, math, and reading learning centers. The reading corner had a homey feel with its Oriental-patterned rug, lamp, pillows, appealing display of books, and poster that beckoned, "Come to the World of Books."

In the science area, trays held collections of shells and rocks, and several aquariums were filled with toads, frogs, an iguana, and fish. There was a rabbit, too. The animals provided an opportunity for writing experiences, discussions about change and death, and study of the environment and conditions for creature survival.

The walls were plastered with posters, photographs, messages, and children's art. An exhibit of photographs of faces of children with varied expressions asked, "How Do You Feel?" A poster on discipline listed class rules, rewards, and consequences. A sign exhorted the children, "Do Your Best Work!"

Ellen sought to inspire a love of learning in children, which she felt teachers had failed to nourish in her. It was gratifying to her to hear a child who struggled with math enthusiastically comment, "I love math!" Insofar as possible, Ellen tried to integrate subjects and develop conceptual understanding so that learning would be more meaningful for children.

She felt, however, that you could not ignore skills development. Skills were crucial, but they should be presented as *tools* you use. For example, writing skills were tools for expressing yourself.

Now, in her fifth year, Ellen continued to develop new ideas for her teaching. She worked in the after-school program, teaching drama to children. She and a colleague wrote the plays, which they tried to relate to the children's lives. Ellen enjoyed interacting with the children in this more informal way.

The City

Yorkville was the sixth poorest major city in the country, even though it was in one of the richest states. It had approximately 140,000 residents. Unemployment was high, and at about 50 percent among young people. The once-thriving tool and die trade had died, and now there were few unskilled jobs available. Two hospitals, a utility company, and a private university were the city's major employers.

Eighty percent of Yorkville's public school students were minorities, mostly African-American and Hispanic. Over 50 percent of the families of the children were receiving some form of public assistance. The superintendent of schools had instituted a free breakfast program because so many children were coming to school hungry.

Yorkville ranked last of all districts in the state in per-pupil spending. The state was pressuring the city to increase its school funding, but city administrators countered that there were no monies to do so. In 1991, the richest district in the state spent approximately $9,000 per pupil; Yorkville was spending less than $4,000. Its pupils scored lower on statewide reading tests than students in any other district in the state. The high school dropout rate was the highest in the state.

In the late 1980s, the drug trade burgeoned. About 10 percent of the population was estimated to be drug abusers. Yorkville had the highest number of AIDS cases of any city in the state. Moreover, in 1991, the city had a dozen more homicides than did the entire state of Vermont, largely related to drug crimes and gang violence. There had been nine killings in one 2-month period. Guns had flooded the city to the degree that mothers told of young children sleeping in bathtubs to hide from stray bullets ricocheting through their apartments.

The School

Horace Mann Elementary School was housed in a former junior high school in one of the poorest sections of the city. Built in the 1940s, the old, brick, two-story structure had rain dripping in places through its ceilings, and tiles peeling off floors. Its old-fashioned window shades were so grimy that, Ellen said, you didn't want to start cleaning because you'd never get to the bottom of the dirt.

Horace Mann was a community school. Almost all the children walked to school. There were about 30 staff and 600 students, of whom approximately 35 percent were Hispanic and 65 percent were African-American. Although the teachers were from racially and ethnically diverse backgrounds, it was rare to see a white face among the children.

The school had adopted a nationally recognized program, developed by Dr. James Comer, an eminent African-American child psychiatrist and a professor at Yale University, to improve the education of poor children.

Dr. Comer wrote that children from poor families lived largely outside of this country's social mainstream and were likely to be unprepared for school. They may not speak standard English, the language of schooling. They may not have been read to at home, and yet they were expected to appreciate books at school. They may not have learned social skills of negotiation and compromise. School and home expectations may be in conflict: a child who has been taught at home to fight back may get into trouble in school for doing so. Comer believed this lack of preparation for school was more characteristic of children who came from minority groups which had been historically discriminated against and still did not participate fully in the educational, political, and economic opportunities of this country.

He proposed a school improvement plan that would help parents feel part of the school and form an alliance with its staff to support the educational mission of the school. At the same time, parents and their children would receive support and guidance from school personnel to face the stresses in their everyday lives more successfully. The healthy psychological and social development of children would form the foundation for academic success.

The Horace Mann School had been chosen as a model for the Comer plan. As Comer recommended, it was governed by a School Planning and Management Team (SPMT) headed by the principal and including representatives from the parents, teachers, and mental health professionals (a social worker, school psychologist, or special education teacher). This group focused on developing and carrying out a yearly plan for the academic program, the school atmosphere, and the professional development of the staff. It met once, and sometimes twice, a month.

There also was a mental health team consisting of the social worker, the school psychologist, and the special education teacher. It often focused on the needs of individual children and their families. One child, for example, was misbehaving and seemed to need a stronger sense of belonging and community. After brainstorming ways to help him, the team suggested that he help the janitor for a short while in the early morning. The child liked the personal relationship with the janitor and seemed to feel pride from doing real work and genuinely contributing to the school; his behavior improved.

There was also a Growth Center for kindergartners and first graders who needed one-to-one attention. Perhaps they were either unusually shy or so active and unfocused that it was hard to reach them. They would be linked with volunteers, often college students or retired persons, for a half hour of play and unpressured conversation. Normally there were about three children per class in this program; Ellen said kids asked to join it.

The Planning and Placement Team (PPT) consisted of the school psychologist, the social worker, the assistant principal, and the teacher who was referring the child for an evaluation. The team might also include the speech pathologist, the special education teacher, and even a medical doctor. This team focused on children with academic problems; children with social or emotional problems more likely would be referred to the mental health team.

The special education teacher worked with children with identified learning disabilities and with social or emotional problems. She acted as a resource to the classroom teacher and also pulled out individual children for an hour a day of intensive services.

The curriculum integrated the teaching of social skills, academic skills, and the arts. Social skills were taught in the areas of government and politics, health, economics, and recreation. For example, as part of a unit on government, children might write letters to mayoral candidates inviting them to speak at school. They would learn how to be good hosts, how to formulate questions about issues they had studied, and how to ask the questions respectfully. After the candidate visited, they would write thank-you letters. Thus, they were learning critical thinking skills, writing skills, public speaking skills, and good manners.

This team approach and concern with the social, emotional, and academic development of children matched Ellen's personal philosophy of teaching. She found the school environment stimulating.

The Stresses

Still, Ellen found working with urban children enormously stressful.

Last year, she had asked to follow her first grade class to second grade. Although not usual in the school, her principal flexibly agreed to this request.

Ellen saw several advantages to this. Once she knew, by the middle of the first grade, that she would keep the class, she found that she was challenging the children more. She moved those who were ready for second grade work right into it, rather than stopping with the first grade books.

There was also a difference at the start of second grade. She didn't have to spend six weeks getting to know the strengths, weaknesses, learning styles, and temperaments of the children. Although the children had developed over the summer, she already had a good grounding. From the first day, for example, she knew which children were competent calculators but needed work on their reasoning skills, and which children had good decoding skills but needed to develop their comprehension abilities.

She found that the work of the poorer performing children clearly improved and that, among all students, there was less absenteeism. She thought this might be related to the consistency these children were experiencing—same teacher, same teaching style, same peers—and the strength of their bond to her and one another that had developed over time.

Although their mutual attachment was helpful, Ellen found that it created problems for her as well. She became more concerned about where their lives were going and just what would happen to them. The dark sides of their lives became even more upsetting to her.

As Ellen put it, "Every day, you witness fallout from the most negative aspects of this country in your classroom." And it was no longer a question of children being simply exposed to upsetting experiences; rather, horrors shaped their lives.

There was Tyrell, whose father had been trying unsuccessfully to find work. The family had been evicted from their apartment and then moved from one shelter to another. Tyrell came to school dressed in mussed clothes and ravenously hungry for the school's free breakfast.

Jerome had been born prematurely to a drug addict and had spent the first six weeks of his life in an incubator in the hospital. His grandmother had gained legal custody of him and was raising him. He had difficulty following directions and paying attention and was receiving special education services. Maria, a frail, easily frustrated child, had been in several foster homes after her mother abandoned her and before her aunt started caring for her.

Martin's older brother had been killed recently. They lived in a desperately poor neighborhood. On a walk to the store, his brother had been caught in the line of fire during a dispute between two drug dealers. Martin complained frequently of bad dreams and headaches. Ellen thought his mother seemed severely depressed.

The children's journals reflected their concerns. Amid stories of birthday parties, bicycle rides, and a Thanksgiving celebration, one child had written, "I rember when Derrick was alive. He had a lot of friends. . . . I was there when he was crying and sad. . . . I get mad then I just snap out of it. And he will feel better because of me."

In their conversations, the children revealed other experiences. During a discussion about keeping healthy and not smoking, a child told of his dad smoking "white stuff," and the child said he had tried it once. Ellen responded by emphasizing the dangers of drugs and the way people lie to themselves by saying they'll try them just once.

After a child had taken another's dime, the class had a discussion about stealing. They ended up talking about jail, and one of the girls commented, "My cousin's in jail because he shot somebody in the head four times."

Ellen's response to the children's upsetting experiences was a profound pain, a biting anger and sadness which threatened to overwhelm her and prevent her from functioning effectively. She felt that her sensitivity was a strength in working with children. It added to her warmth, caring, and insight, making her more aware of the children's needs. Ironically, however, it also made her more vulnerable, more responsive to their distress. She could not let her sensitivity and involvement become a liability. She felt she needed to maintain some degree of objectivity and emotional distance in order to make sensible educational decisions. For the most part, she felt she did.

However, there was a disparity between her intellect and her emotions. Intellectually, she knew she was doing her best. But emotionally, she had begun to lose hope. Perhaps the deaths this year had made it especially hard for her to stay hopeful. She had entered the profession with high ideals; now, she wondered whether even her best efforts would have success with children facing such desperate circumstances.

Just recently, one of her boys, Jamal, had been transferred to a self-contained special education class. He was an overly active child who had difficulty staying on task, and this had begun to affect his reading achievement. Sometimes arrogant and rude, he caused conflicts with other children regularly. Ellen had tried some behavior modification strategies with him, as well as working individually with him. After she initially referred him and he was tested, he was given resource help part-time, then half-day, and now he was to have special services on a full-time basis.

Ellen was worn down by the continual breaking up of fights and conflicts among some of the children and by their often disrespectful behavior toward her and each other. It upset her that these children took so much time and attention away from other children who were ready to learn. So, in some ways, it was helpful to her and the class for a highly disruptive child to be removed. "Yet," she commented, "as much trouble as Jamal was, and he was an enormous handful, both his eyes and mine welled with tears when it was time to say goodbye." She had begun to realize that she couldn't save all the children, but she still felt guilty over those she lost.

She was haunted by the children's difficulties and questioned how long she could continue to absorb the pain. She wondered how other teachers managed to maintain some detachment in order to protect themselves. She didn't think they referred children for special services as much as she did. Were they less aware or less caring? Perhaps they were more effective because they didn't get emotionally entangled with the kids.

Once, during a school vacation, she was in the pediatrician's office, grading papers while her son was having a checkup. A fellow teacher came in with her child and noticed what she was doing. She couldn't believe Ellen was correcting papers during her vacation. Her comment was, "I give the kids board work and then grade the papers while they're working."

Because of the intense social and emotional needs of the children, Ellen felt torn between addressing those needs and sticking to the curriculum. Children often spoke in class about upsetting events in their lives. Should she allow time to discuss those or move on because it was math time? Their personal issues were important, yet wasn't she failing them if she didn't review regrouping in addition? The day was only so long.

Besides the issues that children brought up spontaneously, the school was required to formally teach social skills that had once been taught at home. And this wasn't true of just the urban schools. Concern about AIDS and drug abuse had led the state to mandate education for all students to promote self-esteem, decision-making skills, and awareness of chemical abuse.

Thus, teachers faced the problem of these add-ons to the traditional curriculum. Ellen was directed to teach two to three half-hour lessons a week focusing on social development. She tried to meet the spirit of these directives by integrating the lesson objectives into her usual curriculum. One of the reasons she loved to teach literature was because it enabled her to focus and reflect naturally on human needs and relationships. Also, it provided escape to other worlds for these children who faced grave threats in their own. But it was not always easy to integrate the mandated objectives into the regular lessons, and if she couldn't, she had to find the extra time.

Sometimes, Ellen wondered whether the school day should be lengthened. But she thought to herself that administrators and legislators would probably just keep adding more to the curriculum. She felt insecure and worried about accountability. How could she make sure that she had accomplished everything that she was supposed to? And, she thought, what really should be the scope of the curriculum?

A related problem was the frequent comings and goings of children in the class. This year alone, Ellen lost three children whose families had moved because of neighborhood gunfire. Two new children arrived in March. Another child had missed two weeks, and the state child welfare department had to be called to get his parents to bring him to school. Ellen was constantly trying to fill kids in and catch them up.

The contrast between what the teacher was trained to deal with and what she really should deal with also became an issue. Her children shared stories of family turmoil daily, but she wasn't their mother, nor was she even trained to counsel children, as was a social worker or psychologist. Basically, the kids came to her with seemingly limitless needs, and, even though she had no special competence and was "only" their teacher, she listened to them and did what she could.

Ellen found herself becoming angry with some of the parents. When she looked at Josephine, with her burn marks and distorted arms that had once been broken by an abusive mother, she felt furious. When a father with bloodshot eyes and alcohol on his breath came to pick up his son, it was as if she were placing her own child at risk. Yet, teachers *can't* be judgmental, Ellen thought. You have to make parents feel welcome and part of the school.

The violence in the neighborhood permeated teachers' lives in other ways. Some had had car windows bashed in. Ellen was holding her breath, hoping hers wouldn't be next.

The Satisfactions

Despite the many stresses, the Horace Mann School held Ellen like a magnet. She had done her student teaching at an innovative, well-endowed private school in town that served primarily upper-middle-class children. She preferred Horace Mann because she felt a greater sense of accomplishment; the kids at the private school did not need her the way her kids did. Because of their social circumstances, children at the private school were at the right place at the right time and would probably make it no matter what.

The kids at Horace Mann did not have the same advantages. The odds were against them. If they were going to make it, they might have to do it on their own and would need an inner strength to do so. She felt that if she didn't help them gain the academic and social skills they needed, there was a chance they wouldn't get them at all. She wanted to strengthen them, make them more resilient, so they could survive and succeed.

Although it happened infrequently, she felt needed when parents showed their appreciation. One parent had told her that her daughter would never again have such a good teacher. Ellen believed that wasn't so and wanted the parent to expect more. At the same time, she was gratified by the comment.

Ellen felt she was fortunate to have Dr. Johnson as her principal; she had rare talents. Supportive of her teachers and concerned about their professional development and their emotional well-being, she recognized the stresses of urban teaching and tried to alleviate them whenever possible. "I can go to her," Ellen had said to her husband. One day, Dr. Johnson and Ellen were discussing whether she should keep an unusually active and inattentive child in her class. Dr. Johnson commented to Ellen, "I'm so glad I've got teachers like you here," taking time briefly to appreciate Ellen's dedication to the child before returning to the issue.

Ellen learned from Dr. Johnson. In considering a problem, Dr. Johnson looked at the whole picture and balanced the needs of all members of the school community. If there was a child with a behavior problem, she'd consult with the child's teacher, other teachers who'd had the child, and the child's parents. She'd consider whether the teacher needed a break and the child should be transferred to another class. Perhaps the parents could benefit from a parenting class or other forms of social support.

When teachers disagreed, Dr. Johnson modeled problem-solving strategies for them. She raised problems for discussion, listened impartially to teachers, and helped them develop negotiating skills. Ellen respected her approaches.

Dr. Johnson didn't expect perfection from her teachers, but she helped them to strive for professional excellence. Ellen remembered an incident from her first year of teaching. Eating lunch with some other teachers, she had expressed her frustration about a parent who kept neglecting to take her child, whose head was crawling with lice, to the doctor. Just as she was speaking negatively of the parent, Dr. Johnson walked in. Recognizing that her attitude was inappropriate, Ellen later apologized to the principal. Dr. Johnson accepted the apology graciously and gently warned Ellen against falling into the trap of being negative about parents.

Ellen felt that Dr. Johnson nurtured her as a professional, just as Ellen nurtured her students' development. She was taking a group of teachers to visit an innovative school in New York. However, if she offered you opportunities and you were stretched thin, you could always say no and she'd understand. She did it with parents, too. "She's taken parents and moved them up through the Parent-Teacher Organization, and now many of them have important citywide responsibilities."

Finally, Dr. Johnson always asked about Ellen's personal life, showing concern for her kids. She and Ellen enjoyed going out for a glass of wine occasionally and just chatting.

Ellen also felt support from a group of colleagues at Horace Mann who shared her perspectives on teaching. In fact, they were developing plans for a "school within a school" to try out some of their ideas. Dr. Johnson was encouraging this experiment. Their sharing of ideas would become more formalized through a regular planning time. They were already discussing having a special room for kids where they could work on long-term projects, like building a house model, conducting an electrical experiment, or making a sculpture.

The Decision

Ellen's backyard visit with her friend had been a relaxing start to the summer, but the question of whether she would return to Horace Mann in the fall continued to nag her. Although she felt a strong commitment to the children and to her principal, the stress had begun to pervade her family life.

A few weeks ago, she'd had a particularly rough day and had said "No" to the children many times. Later, driving home after picking up her children at their sitter's, her son asked, "Mom, I learned a new song in school today. Do you want to hear it?" Without thinking, she said, "No." She realized that, for that day, that response had become almost automatic. She was so tired and preoccupied that she hadn't heard her own child's question. "Oh, oh," she thought to herself.

At the end of the day, she found it hard to leave the school day's experiences behind. While she tried to focus on the family's casual conversation at dinner, she thought, for example, of the funeral that day in Horace Mann's neighborhood. One of the parents had been shot; the school community was again mourning.

Her energy and drive, while helpful to her class, could be counterproductive to her family. Some evenings, she tried to watch TV with her family or share their few hours together in another way, but as she thought of new school activities she wanted to develop, her work lured her. She had to sit on her hands to stay put.

Thus, she felt constant demands to give of herself. The children at school needed, wanted, and required her to be giving to them. When she got home, her own children needed and deserved her attention. And she still had work to do. Her strength was being sapped, and she felt guilty that she was unable to meet everyone's needs in the way she felt best. She wondered if all teachers who were serious about their jobs felt this way.

The job demands created tension with her husband. Generally supportive, he had commented that she spent more time giving to other people's children than to their own. He believed that urban teaching was probably too stressful. Perhaps, after five years, he was right, or maybe this had been an exceptional year because of the many deaths. She couldn't afford not to work, but should she return to Horace Mann in the fall? A suburban position might be less stressful. To be fair to the administration, she would have to decide soon. The newspapers had been full of news of cutbacks in the city, including the school budget. Pink slips, announcing layoffs to teachers, would be sent out soon. Maybe she'd get one of those, and then the decision would be made for her.

Advance Study Questions

1. What is Ellen's dilemma?

2. How did this problem develop? What is the nature of the stress that Ellen experiences? In what ways does she like her job?

3. Who, if anyone, is at risk? If so, how might this risk be lessened?

4. If you were Ellen, what would you do?

Additional Readings

Anson, A. R., Cook, T. D., Habib, F., Grady, M. K., Haynes, N. and Comer, J. P. (1991). The Comer school development program: A theoretical analysis. *Urban Education, 26*(1), 56-82.

Comer, J. P. (1988). Educating poor minority children. *Scientific American, 259*(5), 42-48.

Elam, S. M. (1989). The second Gallup/Phi Delta Kappa poll of teachers' attitudes toward the public schools. *Phi Delta Kappan, 70*, 785-798.

Engelking, J. L. (1986). Job satisfaction and dis-satisfaction. *Spectrum, 4*, 33-38.

Feinman-Nemser, S., & Floden, R. E. (1986). The cultures of teaching. In M. C. Wittrock (Ed.), *Third handbook of research on teaching* (pp. 505-526). Chicago: Rand McNally.

Haberman, M., & Rickards, W. (1990). Urban teachers who quit: Why they leave and what they do. *Urban Education, 25*,(3), 297-303.

CHARACTERS

Student:	Mark J.
Mark's parents:	Brian and Ann Jones
Advocate:	Dr. Lewis
Second grade teacher:	Miss Dale
Math teacher:	Mrs. Kay
Mark's brother:	Jeff
Principal:	Mr. Capasso
Social worker:	Mrs. Nolan
Resource teacher:	Miss Schultz
Language clinician:	Mrs. Ellis

Part A

Help!

Mrs. Jones met Dr. Lewis at a Fourth of July barbecue hosted by a mutual friend. "I understand you're a special education professor at the state university," she said.

"That's right. I'm just returning from sabbatical," replied Dr. Lewis.

Mrs. Jones confided that her son had had a very difficult time in kindergarten and first grade. "I feel he has a learning disability. In August, Mark is going to be diagnosed by a psychologist from outside the school system. The school system personnel said they were going to test him last year, but they never got around to it. I don't trust the system anymore, Dr. Lewis. Can you help me get the proper services for my son? I need some help! A friend of mine said you often serve as an advocate. Perhaps you could help us when we have our Planning and Placement Team meeting."

Dr. Lewis told Mrs. Jones to call him when the independent evaluation was completed.

The School System

Brownsville, a small suburban town, houses mostly professionals who have a high regard for education. The two K–6 elementary schools are organized with low pupil/teacher ratios. The system is proud of the high percentage of children who pass the statewide comprehensive mastery test. At a recent board of education meeting, the superintendent of schools informed those present that the average IQ of children within the school system was 116, well above the regional and national averages.

The School

Mark attends second grade in Thomson Elementary School, which has 400 children. The three second grade teachers group all their students homogeneously for reading and math. It is not uncommon for children to have different teachers for these subjects. Miss Dale, Mark's teacher for all subjects except math, has taught in the school system for twelve years. Certified in elementary education, Miss Dale also holds a special education certificate. Mrs. Kay, Mark's math teacher, has just begun her first year of teaching. Two resource teachers, a psychologist, a social worker, a speech and language clinician, the school nurse, and the building principal compose the school's Planning and Placement Team (PPT).

The Family

Mark, the younger of two sons, is eight years old. His older brother Jeff is an eleven-year-old sixth grader who also attends Thomson School. Mr. Jones, the vice president of the Rotary Club, is a prominent business executive in town. Mrs. Jones is not currently working, but she has a master's degree in elementary education and taught fourth grade for three years before her children were born. Mark's brother, Jeff, is in the high reading and math groups. His IQ is reported to be 133.

Ann and Brian Jones are heavily involved in the education of their children. They regularly attend PTA meetings and parent conferences, and they read education journals usually reserved for academics. Mrs. Jones visits the school often to observe Mark and Jeff working in their classrooms, and she closely monitors their homework. If either of their children has difficulty with any work, both parents provide intensive and usually immediate assistance.

Late in the Summer

Mrs. Jones called Dr. Lewis six weeks after their initial discussion.

"Dr. Lewis, we just got Mark's test results from the psychologist. They're horrible! It's worse than I suspected. A WISC-R was given, and he received a full scale IQ of 96, a performance IQ of 107, and a verbal IQ of 86. The examiner also gave the WRAT, and his scores for reading, math, and spelling were all well below average. My son didn't learn anything last year! Over the past year, my husband and I have spent at least an hour a day tutoring him in reading and math. If it weren't for us, Mark wouldn't know anything. Is Mark ever going to learn? Is his learning disability so severe that he's going to have to go to a special class? The psychologist suggested that we might want to put him into a private school. She said we might also want to get a lawyer. What should we do?"

Dr. Lewis asked when Mark was evaluated, and Mrs. Jones replied, "Last Tuesday. It was so hot and humid. Mark wasn't feeling that well, but it was the only time the psychologist could test him before school begins, and we wanted our independent evaluation ready before September so that we could meet with the PPT before Mark started school. I called the school today, and Mr. Capasso, the principal, said he could schedule a PPT on Monday to discuss Mark's program. Can you attend this meeting with me and my husband?" Dr. Lewis said he'd be glad to.

The PPT meeting was held the following Monday. The team had a copy of the independent evaluator's report. Everyone agreed that the school's learning disabilities resource teacher and speech and language clinician should conduct a thorough educational and language assessment during the first two weeks of school before a program could be discussed. Another meeting was scheduled for September 25.

The Big Day Arrives

Dr. Lewis and Mark's parents entered the school foyer. They were greeted by Mrs. Nolan, the school social worker who was also the chairperson of the PPT. All members of the PPT were present. In addition, Miss Dale, Mark's second grade teacher, was in attendance. After formal introductions and informal pleasantries, Mrs. Nolan began the meeting:

"We are here today to discuss the diagnostic results gathered over the last couple of weeks. If it's okay with everyone, I would like Miss Schultz, our resource teacher, to begin."

Ann and Brian Jones nodded in nervous agreement.

Miss Schultz began by briefly describing the Woodcock-Johnson Psycho-Educational Battery and the Key Math Test, the two diagnostic devices she had administered (Exhibit 1 shows the results). She indicated that both tests were norm-referenced and revealed standard scores, percentile rankings, and grade-level scores. Their major purpose was to compare a child's performance with the performance of other children who have taken the test nationally.

Miss Schultz summarized the data by stating that Mark was within the average range in most areas. She did note that although Mark was able to read a number of one-syllable words, his word attack skills were poor.

Mark couldn't decode simple nonsense syllables such as *nan* and *tiff.* He is also unsure of his long and short vowel sounds. He appears to rely heavily on his sight-word ability to read. I should mention that while Mark does read very slowly, he comprehends what he is reading.

All Mark's knowledge of basic concepts, his calculating skills, and his application abilities fell at the average or lower end of the average range. Since he often relied on his fingers while performing simple addition and subtraction problems, it does not appear that his math facts are at an automatic level of functioning.

I must reiterate that all his abilities are close to what might be expected of a child in the beginning of the second grade.

EXHIBIT 1

Woodcock-Johnson Psycho-Educational Battery (achievement section)

	Grade Scores	*Percentile*	*Standard Scores*
Reading cluster scores	1.9	38	95
Math cluster scores	2.0	43	97
Writing cluster scores	1.8	30	92
Knowledge cluster scores	1.7	21	88

KEY MATH TEST

	Scale Score
Basic Concepts (S.S. = 98)	
Numeration	10
Rational Numbers	9
Geometry	9
Operations (S.S. = 87)	
Addition	9
Subtraction	7
Multiplication	—
Division	8
Mental Computation	—
Applications (S.S. = 95)	
Measurement	9
Time and Money	11
Estimation	8
Interpreting Data	8
Problem Solving	9
TOTAL TEST STANDARD SCORE	94

GRADE SCORE = 1.9

Mr. Jones interjected, "Why are these results higher than the testing data we received last month from our private examiner? I don't believe Mark is performing like other second graders. Especially not second graders in this system." After a few minutes of silence, Jones threw up his hands, "Will somebody tell me what's going on?"

Dr. Lewis answered, "In all likelihood, the school's testing would not have shown Mark to be functioning close to an average level if he wasn't getting so much extra help. Remember, Mr. and Mrs. Jones, you work with Mark almost every day. This might have an effect on Mark's scores. Also, Mark has received therapy from a trained language clinician over the last year and a half."

All members of the PPT looked up in surprise at this last statement. Mrs. Nolan said, "We didn't know Mark was getting this kind of extra help. I think we should now hear from *our* language clinician, however. She tested Mark last week."

Mrs. Ellis, the language clinician, stated that she administered the following tests: the Peabody Picture Vocabulary Test, the Boehm Test of Basic Concepts–Revised, the Test of Language Development, and the Expressive One-Word Picture Vocabulary Test (Exhibit 2 gives these scores).

Mrs. Ellis began her discussion of the results by indicating that Mark was very attentive and cooperative during the testing situation. She continued, "Many of Mark's responses were very slow and calculated. I don't think that Mark ever responded using a complete sentence with a subject and a predicate. His grammatical functioning, especially in the receptive areas, appears to be at an average level. I have more concerns with his expressive skills. He had difficulty giving definitions of simple words. For example, when I said 'ice,' he

EXHIBIT 2

Test of Language Development

Picture Vocabulary	9	Spoken Language	87
Oral Vocabulary	7	Listening	94
Grammar Understanding	11	Speaking	80
Sentence Imitation	4	Semantics	88
Grammar Completion	9	Syntax	87
Word Discrimination	9	Phonology	91
Word Articulation	8		
($\bar{x}$ = 10)		($\bar{x}$ = 100)	

Peabody Picture Vocabulary Test—(S.S. = 89)
Boehm Test of Basic Concepts—(percentile rank = 18th)
Expressive One-Word Picture Vocabulary Test—(S.S. = 84}

said, 'It's hard,' rather than saying, 'It's frozen water.' A zoo was described as a place you can go to, like a circus. Even after some prompting, he could not state that it was a place you go to see animals. An igloo was a house. Such answers were correct but not complete. Sentence imitation tasks required Mark to repeat dictated sentences back to the examiner. He was very frustrated with this task. Mark's understanding of some of the basic concepts we use in everyday situations was also poor."

"Overall, I see Mark as a child with a moderate language disorder. This disability is predominantly seen on tasks that require him to express information in complete thoughts."

At this point, Miss Dale interjected that although Mark was very quiet in her second grade class, he appeared to be appropriately placed. "I think he fits in well with the other children. He is in group B, the lower reading and math group, but this doesn't seem to bother him. He is not the lowest performing child in class. Also, his behavior is quite good."

It was now time to determine whether Mark should receive any special education services. Everyone attending the PPT meeting agreed that Mark should see the school's language clinician for an hour a week. Goals were quickly established to increase expressive skills and semantic development. Discussion concerning Mark's need for academic remediation was not as amicable.

Mr. Capasso, the principal, said, "I think we can all see that Mark has specific deficits in language, and those deficits are going to be addressed. He does not qualify as a child with a learning disability in reading or math, however. According to state guidelines, a significant discrepancy should exist between his academic achievement and his ability. Test scores don't show this."

Dr. Lewis responded, "I agree that *test scores* don't show a significant deficit. However, I must remind you that Mark has been getting a lot of extra help outside of the school system. I also feel that the IQ results from one month ago are a low estimate of Mark's true potential. I feel he should be seeing the resource teacher once a day for at least thirty minutes."

Mrs. Jones quickly added, "I agree. You overlooked Mark's problems for two years. We have gone to considerable expense to provide Mark with the help he needs. It is time this school helps him with *all* his problems. I'm not leaving here until he gets what he needs. If I have to, I'll get a lawyer and begin due process."

Heated discussion continued, but a compromise was reached. Mark would receive learning disability resource instruction three times a week for a total of ninety minutes. Goals in the areas of decoding and mastering the basic facts in addition and subtraction were written. A statement was also included in the minutes that the program established for Mark was to be reviewed at a formal PPT in December. Mr. and Mrs. Jones also asked Dr. Lewis to monitor Mark's program over the next three months.

EXHIBIT 3
Individualized Education Program

Student's Name: Mark J. **Date of Birth:** 4-30-84 **Date:** 9-19-92
School: Thomson Elementary **Grade:** 2

Members of the P.P.T.

Name	Title
Mr. and Mrs. Jones	Parents
Dr. Lewis	Advocate
Miss Dale	Teacher
Mr. Capasso	Principal
Mrs. Nolan	Social worker
Miss Schultz	Resource teacher
Mrs. Ellis	Language clinician

I. **Present Level of Performance**
   A. Academic Achievement:
      Woodcook-Johnson Psycho-Educational Battery
         Reading cluster—1.9 grade equivalency
         Math cluster—2.0 grade equivalency
         Writing cluster—1.8 grade equivalency
         Knowledge cluster—1.7 grade equivalency
      Key Math—1.9 grade equivalency
   B. Social Adaptation—age appropriate
   C. Prevocational/Vocational Skills—not applicable
   D. Psychomotor Skills—not applicable
   E. Self-Help Skills—not applicable
   F. Medical Information—not applicable
   G. Speech/Language Hearing:
      Test of Language Development
         Spoken Language—S.S. = 87
         Listening—S.S. = 94
         Speaking—S.S. = 80
         Semantics—S.S. = 88
         Syntax—S.S. = 87
         Phonology—S.S. = 91
      PPVT—S.S. = 89
      Boehm Test of Basic Concepts—18th percentile
      Expressive One-Word Picture Vocabulary Test—S.S. = 84
   H. Psychological—*WISC-R*
      Full-scale IQ = 96
      Verbal IQ = 86
      Performance IQ = 107

EXHIBIT 3—cont'd
Individualized Education Program

II. **Student Eligible for Services and/or Instruction:** Yes
  A. Primary Diagnosis: L.D.

III. **Goals and Objectives**
  Goal 1—Mark will improve phonic skills
    Objective 1: Mark will decode closed syllables—90%
    Objective 2: Mark will decode silent *e* syllables—90%
    Objective 3: Mark will decode open syllables—90%
    Objective 4: Mark will decode vowel *r* and vowel team syllables—80%
    Objective 5: Mark will decode words with easy endings—60%
  Goal 2: Mark will improve calculation skills
    Objective 1: Mark will state all addition facts correctly—100%
    Objective 2: Mark will state all subtraction facts correctly—100%
  Goal 3: Mark will improve language skills
    Objective 1: Mark's vocabulary will improve
    Objective 2: Mark will express himself more fluently

IV. **Personnel Responsibilities for Goals**
  Goal 1: Miss Schultz, Special Education
  Goal 2: Miss Schultz, Special Education
  Goal 3: Mrs. Ellis, Speech and Language

V. **Statement of Justification of Placement/Services**
  There appears to be a discrepancy between Mark's aptitude and his achievment levels. Language processing is interfering with learning.

VI. **Special Instruction/Services Needed:**

Service	*Hours/ Week*	*Direct/ Indirect*	*Date of Implementation (Month/Year)*
Special Education resource	1½	Direct	10/92
Language/speech/hearing	1	Direct	10/92
Regular education	27		10/92

VII. **Program Monitoring**
  A. Personnel Responsible: Planning and Placement Team
  B. Date of Review: 6/93.

Mr. Capasso emphasized the need for exit criteria to be written into Mark's Individualized Education Plan (IEP). He was not pleased that Mark was going to be labeled learning disabled. When Mark met the specific objectives outlined in his IEP, Mr. Capasso wanted his special education services terminated. (Exhibit 3 shows Mark's IEP).

Advance Study Questions

1. What is the dilemma in this case?

2. How did this situation develop? Discuss the underlying problems.

3. Is Mark a child with a learning disability? Support your argument.

4. What kind of services do you feel Mark needs? Do you feel the PPT conducted Mark's assessment properly?

5. How can the educational services available to Mark be improved?

A Question of Ownership

Sally Francia and Robert Piazza

CHARACTERS

Student:	Sam Grady
Sam's parents:	Mr. and Mrs. Grady
Teacher of the hearing impaired students:	Sara North
Second grade teacher:	Lisa Weeks
Instructional assistant:	Merle Evans
Speech and language clinician:	Lori Nolan
Resource teacher:	Louis Morrisey

Part A

A Quiet Decision

February break had just ended, and most of the school was settling back into its usual routine. It was going to be a long time until the next vacation, but many teachers felt this was the time of year when children learned the most. In Sara North's afternoon therapy session, Sam Grady and another child with a hearing impairment were busy practicing their grammar drills. Merle Evans, Sam's classroom assistant, was helping to set up the language experience program as she did every afternoon, when she candidly remarked, "Sara, did you know that Sam's reading group has been changed?"

"No," replied Sara. "What has it been changed to, and when did this occur?"

Merle indicated that Sam had been moved from the top reading group to the middle one and that she thought it had happened the Monday before the vacation. "At first, I assumed you knew about it and approved of the decision. But since you haven't said anything to me about it, I thought I would ask you."

Concern appeared on Sara's face as she quizzed Merle to find out if she knew any substantial reasons for the change. Sara asked if Sam's parents had been notified.

"His teacher, Lisa Weeks, said he didn't do well on the midyear test, and he wasn't keeping up with his peers in the group. I don't know if his parents know about this. I do know both groups use the same book, but the higher group is about seventy-five pages ahead of the middle group and is moving at a faster pace," responded Merle.

Sara North labored over what to write in Sam's communication log that afternoon. This log book had been specifically established to increase daily communication between all professional staff and Sam's parents. She searched this parent-team notebook for any entry by Lisa Weeks to either Sam's parents or the team concerning Sam's progress in reading, but found none. Sara decided to include only information about the skills Sam was working on in her class, but was determined to take the other matter up with Lisa directly.

The School and Community

Clement Hiller School serves 650 students, grades K through 5, in the rural community of Walton. Despite its pastoral setting on a former onion patch, the elementary school boasts technically advanced educational hardware and software and fosters high competitive academic standards. Inscribed in the doorway of Hiller School is the motto, "Taking Students As Far As They Can Go." The 55-member faculty consists of 33 classroom teachers, 7 specialists, 2 psychologists, 1 guidance counselor, 2 speech and language clinicians, 6 special educators, 1 reading consultant, one teacher for the students with hearing impairments and a teacher for children who are gifted, and 1 school nurse. The district administrator for special services is also housed at Hiller.

Located approximately ninety minutes north of New York City, Walton is a rural community of 6,500 people. Devoid of industry or commercial shopping, Walton has retained its historic, colonial appearance. Many of its large and well-maintained homes are set on three to four acres of property surrounded by woodlands. There are few clustering neighborhoods; instead, most homes are set off singularly on meandering roads. The community is largely composed of professionals, with both parents actively engaged in careers. While the town supports its own elementary school (Hiller), it shares the cost of a regional middle school and high school with two neighboring towns.

Sam and His Family

Sam is a 9-year-old boy with a severe to profound bilateral loss of hearing. He has recurring episodes of otitis media and concomitant allergies, which complicate his performance.

Sam predominantly employs oral communication, using total communication (a combination of oral and manual communication) as an assist whenever necessary. He is currently mainstreamed in a second grade class at Hiller School with support services from a resource teacher, a teacher trained to instruct the students with hearing impairments, and a speech pathologist.

Although Sam remains with his peers for most of the day, he misses science, art, and music to attend his pullout classes. Sara North helps Sam work on concepts in the third grade reading and math texts. All second grade curriculum material was pretaught by Mrs. North during Sam's first grade year and the summer before second grade. During the current year, this material is also reviewed and supported by the resource teacher and the speech pathologist.

Beginning in the first grade, Sam has been given preferential seating in front of the teacher. He also has a classroom assistant to facilitate receptive and expressive speech. At all times in school, he uses a Phonic Ear FM Auditory Trainer bilaterally.

Sam's mother, Jan Grady, is an occupational therapist employed by a large, university-based hospital. His father, Bob, is a high school principal in a nearby town. Sam was born in northern New England where both of his parents worked in their respective fields. The pregnancy and delivery were normal and without event. Sam was a healthy child with expected developmental responses.

At seventeen months of age, Sam received a routine measles, mumps, and rubella inoculation from his pediatrician. That evening he ran a high fever and was in great discomfort. The fever persisted, but the Gradys were told by their doctor that it was a typical reaction to the shots. After several days, the symptoms disappeared, but Mrs. Grady noticed that Sam did not turn his head when his name was called. He also no longer noticed telephone rings, doorbells, or door slams. Sam stopped making verbal utterances. His mother's work with people who were disabled quickly alerted her to a problem. A return visit to their pediatrician and an extensive audiological examination confirmed the Grady's worst suspicion: Sam was hearing impaired.

The etiology of Sam's hearing loss was listed as unknown, because of the difficulty within the medical community of proving that an inoculation caused deafness.

Sam's parents immediately tried to learn as much as they could about their son's condition. After much research, they chose to follow an aural program for toddlers suggested by the John Tracy Clinic in California. The premise of this system is to get the child to listen first. Then all remaining residual hearing is utilized to encourage babbling and sound production. Finally, lip movements and facial expressions are attached to vocalizations.

The Gradys religiously practiced this method and, as a result, Sam was using the initiating sounds again by $2\frac{1}{2}$ years of age. When he was $2\frac{1}{2}$, the Gradys also traveled almost one hour twice a week to take him to a speech pathologist who provided two hours of therapy weekly during two separate sessions. Three mornings a week, Sam attended a preschool special education class in the town in which they resided.

Sam's progress was quite satisfactory. Although his language age was delayed one year behind his chronological peers, he was naming objects and turning toward familiar sounds such as vacuum cleaners, car horns, and radios.

A year later, the Gradys both accepted positions in southern New England, where they were raised and had worked in the early years of their marriage. They settled in Walton because of its fine reputation for providing special educational services. Sam was enrolled in a preschool special education program five mornings a week and received daily speech and language services from Lori Nolan. Sara North was the preschool teacher of the hearing impaired class.

By the summer of his fourth birthday, Sam had begun to read some basic sight words typically found in a preprimer reader. He could organize these words in correct syntactical order and generate complete sentences.

When Sam was almost five, he was attending the preschool class for a full day and was put in a preteaching program. This program introduced language material months ahead of when it was going to be presented in the regular curriculum so that Sam could become quite comfortable with it. The Planning and Placement Team (PPT) also decided to have Sam remain in the preschool class one more year to improve his social skills, gross- and fine-motor development, and language ability. Since Hiller School had an academically oriented kindergarten, Sara North would have additional time to preteach the beginning reading and math skills.

At age six, Sam was mainstreamed into a regular kindergarten class. That year Sara North moved to the elementary school to serve children with hearing impairments at that level. She gave Sam five hours of private instruction, and Lori Nolan continued to offer support in speech and language. Sam's parents communicated closely with his teachers and reviewed his skills at home, cheering his accomplishments. Sign instruction was begun late in the kindergarten year. The Gradys wholeheartedly supported his acquisition of sign language at this time. Sam's kindergarten year was deemed a success by all who worked with him. A psychological test that year placed Sam within the high-average range of intellectual functioning. Reasoning and memory skills were found to be especially strong.

First grade was very successful. Sam was placed in the upper groups in both reading and math, achieving at a superior level in these and other subjects. The strategy of preteaching skills one-on-one well before they were introduced in his mainstreamed class was paying large dividends. That year, Sam also received two hours of instruction per week on visual integration and fine-motor skills by Hiller School's resource teacher, Louis Morrisey. Sara continued preteaching skills and language that would be confronted in the curriculum in the months ahead, and Lori Nolan continued providing speech services.

The Team

At a PPT meeting at the end of Sam's first grade year, the decision to place him in a mainstreamed second grade class was unanimous. Sam's parents suggested, however, that more formal communication occur among the professionals working with him. It was decided that a communication log book would be kept and that brief statements about Sam's performance would be recorded each day by each teacher. These entries could be read by anyone working with Sam. The log book would be sent home every day and read by Sam's parents. In addition, all those working with Sam would meet at least once a month to discuss his progress and any concerns.

Sam's program for the second grade looked like this:

Merle Evans continued her assignment as Sam's classroom aide.

Sara North continued her assignment as teacher of hearing-impaired students at Hiller and saw Sam for five hours a week.

Lori Nolan continued to give Sam speech and language support, but her therapy sessions with Sam were reduced to two 30-minute periods.

Louis Morrisey continued to support Sam in his resource room for visual-motor development, but this service was also reduced to one hour per week.

Lisa Weeks was assigned as Sam's second grade teacher. She had twenty-two years teaching experience, all at Hiller School. Because the philosophy of integrating children with hearing impairments within the regular class was new at Hiller School, she had little previous experience with children like Sam. However, she had been quite successful over the years working with specialists when children with learning disabilities were mainstreamed in her class.

Lisa accepted the assignment to have Sam in her class with some reservations. She had questions about equity between Sam and the other students, especially for grading. She wondered how she could treat all students fairly with Sam in her class. Lisa did attend the year-end PPT meeting when Sam's second grade program was developed, but she said very little.

Talking to Lisa

The day after Merle told Sara about Sam's reading group change, Sara put a note in Lisa Weeks's school mailbox indicating that they needed to talk about him. Lisa was curious about a midweek meeting, but the next day she greeted Sara cheerily in the small planning room that adjoined her classroom. "I just learned that Sam's reading group was changed a week and a half ago. Is that true?" Sara cautiously asked. Lisa nodded in confirmation, and Sara asked if Sam had shown a behavior or academic problem of which she was unaware.

Mrs. Weeks answered that there had been a definite problem. "First of all, Sam was not comprehending the lessons on prefixes and suffixes. He's also disruptive in the group. He always has to get out of his seat to get a tissue or something, and he often loses his place when asked to read aloud. He also scored only 76 out of a possible 90 on the midterm basal reading test. The passing score was 72, but I feel that children in the top group should be doing much better than that. Sam needs more review. That's why I decided to put him back in the middle group. He'll get the review there."

When asked who administered the test, Lisa replied that she had given it to the entire group. Sara reminded Lisa of the IEP recommendations that reading tests be previewed and/or administered by the speech pathologist or the teacher of the hearing-impaired students, to monitor sections that might require aural ability. Lisa became visibly irritated. "That's just it. I don't agree with that procedure. If a child is in the top group, he must conform to the group standards. And furthermore, how can I continue to give a grade in reading to a child and have no control over his education?"

Sara understood Lisa's dilemma. Lisa was a fantastic teacher and had very high standards. But Sara had her own dilemma: how to ensure an appropriate education for Sam. Sara politely asked Lisa to bring her concerns and Sam's midterm test to a team meeting that was going to be held the next day. She reassured Lisa that they would try to come to a reasonable resolution.

Advance Study Questions

1. What is the dilemma faced by Sara North?

2. What are some of the underlying issues in this case?

3. How is the central problem viewed by Lisa Weeks, other team members, and Sam's parents?

4. What decisions need to be made? Who should make them?

5. If disagreements exist among team members, how should they be resolved?

CASE 12

Case of Inclusion

Deirdre Peterson and Robert Piazza

CHARACTERS

Students: Lisa
John
Lisa's parents: Steve and Jill Wilson
Special education teacher: Susan Johnson
Third grade teacher: Mrs. Sarah Hill
Paraprofessional: Mrs. Carey

Part A

Early October

Susan Johnson, the special education teacher, took a sip of her morning coffee. "Yuk, cold coffee!" No time to grab a hot cup, she was running behind schedule. She put down the cup, left her resource room, and hurried down to the third grade to pick up two students for a reading group.

As she walked quickly down the corridors of Pleasant View Elementary's open-space school, the echoes of teachers' voices filled every empty space. She turned the corner toward the third grade area and noticed that the classrooms were filled with work samples, which had impressed many parents last week during open house. Susan smiled proudly as she glanced at Lisa's story about herself. She entered the third grade area to pick up Lisa and John from Mrs. Hill's class. It was 10:30 A.M., and she'd have to wait a few minutes until the students finished their morning snack breaks. She immediately located John, who was gabbing with a friend sitting next to him. She hoped to find Lisa sharing experiences or playing with a friend, too.

Just last week at open house, Lisa's mom approached her with concerns about Lisa's placement into Mrs. Hill's third grade class. At last year's annual review, while Susan Johnson was on maternity leave, Lisa was placed in Mrs. Hill's class, and two close friends she had known for three years were placed in another class. Lisa's mother was concerned about whether Lisa would be able to interact with these friends during the day. She also realized how reluctant Lisa was to make new friends. Susan Johnson assured her that before November Lisa would have a handful of new friends, and she would see her old friends at lunch and recess. Susan hoped she was right.

As Susan Johnson looked across the room, she spied Lisa in the back, finishing her snack and coloring alone. "Oh, no!" she thought. She asked Sarah Hill, "Lisa isn't sitting with anyone again?"

Sarah replied, "I know, she doesn't want to play with the other kids . . . she prefers to play alone. I've rearranged her desk three times, and she won't have anything to do with them. They just don't seem to have anything in common. Lisa likes to color, and the other students are into crossword puzzles and other word games."

Susan wondered to herself, "Why don't they have anything in common? They've been in the same school for years. What can I do to get Lisa more involved with her classmates?"

The School and Community

Pleasant View was an open-space elementary school made up of two buildings. One building housed the cafeteria, office, and gym; the other contained classes from kindergarten to fifth grade. Pleasant View, one of eight elementary schools in Fairheights, served approximately 280 students. It was not your typical open-space school. Over the years, teachers had slowly barricaded themselves off from each other using bookcases, cabinets, dividers—anything that worked. However, the teachers continued to interact with one another as in an open-space environment. They team taught, sharing activities, lessons, experiences, and students across grades for all academic subjects.

Pleasant View was located in a suburban part of Fairheights County, nestled in rolling farmland and freshwater ponds. Fairheights lay in the Manaset River Valley. In its early years, it was a medium-sized industrial and boating town. Today, it was a large city, made up of both rural farm country and urban city dwellings.

Lisa and Her Family

Lisa Wilson was a petite ten-year-old with beautiful blue, almond-shaped eyes, blond hair, and a wonderful smile. When she was a baby, she was diagnosed as having Down's syndrome, a genetic chromosomal disorder which usually was accompanied by mental retardation. Lisa's syndrome was trisomy 21, 47xx, +21. Psychological testing indicated that Lisa was a child with moderate mental retardation and an IQ of 53.

When Lisa was born, her parents were excited to learn they had a new baby daughter. As Steven and Jill Wilson gazed down at their beautiful newborn, they felt blessed with such a wonderful, precious child. Later, this excitement was tempered by their apprehension when they realized the demands of raising a child with Down's syndrome. Steven, thirty-three, a dentist, and Jill, twenty-seven, an elementary school teacher, wanted to give Lisa only the best. During Lisa's first years of life, the Wilsons worked every day to provide her with meaningful experiences. From her infancy, they received special education services for Lisa and looked toward her educational needs in the future.

Lisa was never isolated in their family. She went everywhere with Steven and Jill—shops, restaurants, family and friend gatherings, and vacations. As an only child, Lisa was an integral part of a loving and caring extended family. The Wilsons believed her education should be similar, filled with rich experiences and many friends. Since Lisa did not have brothers or sisters, it was even more important that the Wilsons see Lisa flourish in an environment with close peer relationships.

Lisa and Her Early Education

The Special Education Preschool Program Lisa began her formal education in a preschool, self-contained special education class at three years of age. She was placed in a class with five other students who had moderate to severe disabilities. The class was highly structured, using time-out areas and behavioral management techniques. Lisa's peers were considered lower-functioning intellectually than she. The classroom was segregated from other nondisabled preschool classrooms, in an isolated wing within a regular education elementary school.

The Wilsons hesitated at first about the placement. They had hoped Lisa would be placed in a class where she would have to strive to fulfill expectations higher than her own ability level. Reluctantly, Steven and Jill Wilson left the decision of Lisa's placement to the education professionals and hoped for the best. This attitude changed quickly, however.

Within a few days of Lisa's placement into the special education classroom, Lisa began exhibiting behaviors at home which were not normal for her. She would throw tantrums for no apparent reason. She had "accidents"—regressing in her toileting skills. The Wilsons believed, after several weeks of these unusual behaviors, that Lisa was trying to tell them that she was unhappy in her new classroom. Lisa's actions appeared to be lowering her to the ability level of her classmates.

At a meeting with her teacher, the Wilsons were told that Lisa was put in a time-out room frequently for not following directions and that she was acting aggressively toward the other children. Lisa's parents could hardly believe what they were hearing. Lisa had always been a very happy, quiet, well-behaved child; yet now that she was three years old, the Wilsons were dealing with behaviors they had never seen before. They felt Lisa needed an environment with appropriate role models and higher expectations. Sensing that the educational standards were too low for their daughter, the Wilsons asked for a Planning and

Placement Team (PPT) meeting to discuss Lisa's placement. At the meeting, the team discussed all aspects of Lisa's education and decided to place Lisa in a regular preschool Montessori program. The public school system paid the tuition for this placement.

The Montessorian program educated young children by individual guidance rather than by strict control over their behavior. Lisa's behavior changed within days of being placed in the regular preschool program. She no longer had tantrums or toileting accidents. The Wilsons reported that she was also much happier at home.

The success of the Montessori program was inspiring to Lisa's parents. They kept her in this program until she turned six years old. Lisa's parents and her preschool teachers were all concerned about the transition from preschool to the public elementary school program. The Wilsons did not want to place her in another special education class. They believed that a placement similar to her preschool special education class would set her back academically and socially, but that placing Lisa in a class with her nondisabled peers would stimulate her emotional and cognitive development. After several meetings with school staff, the Wilsons decided to try a pilot integration program at Pleasant View Elementary School, their neighborhood school. Lisa would attend this school, and Susan Johnson, the special education teacher from Pleasant View, would consult with the staff on a regular basis.

The Special Education Teacher Susan Johnson was just beginning to feel comfortable with her new responsibility as an integration consultant. This was her second year in the role, which had consumed much of her professional life during the last seventeen months. She attended three comprehensive workshops given by a local learning resource center that the state Department of Education had sponsored. Susan had also visited integration programs in bordering states. Full administrative and financial support had been given to Susan to build and enhance the program at Pleasant View Elementary.

> I never really believed that any youngster with a handicap needed to be placed full-time in a special education class. During my first three years as a teacher, I often felt very frustrated in my efforts to educate children who were classified as retarded in my cloistered classroom. My typical class had a very low student/teacher ratio, often with only five or six children. This lent itself to limitations such as lower expectations, inappropriate role models, and a lack of stimulating natural experiences. Children in regular classrooms have ample opportunities to share experiences with a normal peer, and to participate in group activities that are difficult to do in a small class, such as put on plays and run book fairs.
>
> My administration has been very supportive over the last two years, allowing me to run in-service sessions with the regular education staff and encouraging me to take risks and be creative with programming my students into the regular primary grades.

My responsibilities as a consultant have brought many new challenges. I've met with regular educators to plan and adapt curriculum, supervised three paraprofessional staff members who have helped me with the integration programs, team taught with the kindergarten through third grade teachers, and managed time schedules of many children and classes.

One of the most difficult things that I've done is to allow the regular educator to take over the primary role as teacher for the disabled child. However, if I didn't let that happen, I think this program would have failed in the first month.

Although I received my Master's degree in Special Education last June, I don't think my professional training helped prepare me very much for what I'm doing now. I even had many arguments with some of my professors about whether I was doing the right thing including my children in regular classes. I guess you have to be right on the firing line to really know if something works or not.

Kindergarten–First Grade–Second Grade

Lisa's integration into the regular classroom from kindergarten through grade two had been a relative success. She was able to adapt to most of the kindergarten and first grade curriculum with little trouble. Lisa's most difficult areas were her fine-motor skills and her ability to interact with her peers. In kindergarten, Lisa would become distracted very easily during story time or any other structured periods. She had difficulty with cutting paper and writing the letters of the alphabet. Mrs. Carey, a paraprofessional, assisted Lisa during these activities. The regular education kindergarten teacher set up a buddy system to encourage Lisa to play with others. During both play time and center time, all students would have a buddy with them. This system enabled Lisa to interact with others, but it did not call attention to her, as a separate strategy would have.

Although the kindergarten experience had been positive, the PPT at the end of the year decided that Lisa should be retained. Her parents agreed, and by the end of her second year in kindergarten, all those who worked with Lisa felt that she should be promoted to first grade.

Lisa's first grade experience was also positive. She still needed paraprofessional support for all fine-motor activities, but she learned to write her first name quite early in the year. Lisa read in a preprimer, allowing her to be a part of a first grade reading group, which the regular educator instructed. Lisa also attended a regular math group, since math lessons were taught with manipulative, hands-on materials. The spelling program was adapted for Lisa. She was given five spelling words a week, while her peers had twelve, and she was allowed to spell these words orally to Mrs. Carey, while the other students had a written test. During the summer, Lisa's parents sent her to a summer school run by the town to solidify her academic skills. She also attended a swimming class to improve her gross-motor ability.

By second grade, though, Lisa began to fall substantially behind her peers in the academic subjects. Lisa was unable to compose a complete sentence or to complete simple addition and subtraction problems. She was only reading at a first grade level with moderate success. However, Lisa was not removed from the regular second grade classroom. She continued to be involved in many activities with her peers. For example, during social studies, Lisa participated in the drug and alcohol curriculum and learned about family dynamics. The lessons were given orally, and her testing was modified by giving her fewer questions.

Mrs. Carey instructed her in spelling within the regular class. While the other students worked on their second grade spelling assignments, Lisa learned three new Dolch words per week. Second grade math activities were again presented with manipulatives, allowing Lisa to participate in the low math group without adaptations. She was pulled out to Susan Johnson's resource room for reading lessons only. Susan instructed Lisa in reading, using a linguistic approach which capitalized on Lisa's strong rhyming abilities.

Moderate success was achieved in second grade, and Lisa entered third grade on a low second grade level in most academic areas. She was still reading at a first grade level, however. Steven and Jill Wilson were thrilled about the friendships Lisa was developing. She played with children throughout the neighborhood and, although shy, was accepted by her peer group.

Third Grade–November and Still No Friends

For the first time, Lisa was placed into a regular classroom with another integrated student, John, who was severely language impaired. Lisa began relating to John as her best friend and seldom played with her friends from the previous year. She played with John on the playground and sat with him during lunch. There was some comfort in spending so much time with John. Lisa realized they had much in common. They were in the same reading group and on the same level in many academic areas. In fact, Lisa was stronger in math than John, which pleased her.

At the same time, Susan Johnson was beginning to feel anxious about the amount of time she was pulling Lisa from the regular classroom. Since the gap was widening academically between Lisa and her classmates, Susan felt the need to work with Lisa in her own resource classroom, without distractions, for two hours per day. Lisa and John made up a small group for reading, writing, spelling, and math. Lisa spent another forty-five minutes in a small group learning functional community living skills.

One week John came down with a severe cold and was out of school for seven days. During that time, Lisa ate lunch by herself and stood alone talking to the duty aides during recess time. She realized that John was her only friend and came home crying one day telling her parents that none of her friends liked her anymore. The next day Susan Johnson received a phone call.

The Phone Call

Jill Wilson had noticed that Lisa was constantly talking about John. She was also disturbed that Lisa did not mention her old friends from second grade who were presently in her third grade classroom. She was beginning to feel that Lisa's relationship with John was isolating her from her peers. "John's a nice boy," Mrs. Wilson explained to Susan on the phone one day, "but it's now November, and Lisa is still not interacting with other third graders, or any new friends." Mrs. Wilson explained that Lisa might feel more different now that she was in a class with another child who had a significant disability.

Susan Johnson sensed that there was much truth in what Mrs. Wilson was saying. There was nothing wrong with Lisa and John's friendship, but because it separated them from interacting with others, it was a problem. She told Lisa's mother she would meet with Mrs. Hill to discuss the situation and to develop strategies to include Lisa more with her third grade peers.

Susan did not know where to begin, but she knew that this situation was not caused entirely by Lisa's friendship with John. In the back of her mind was her concern over the widening academic gap between Lisa and her nondisabled peers and its negative impact on her developing friendships. "Because she functions on a first and second grade level in almost all academic areas, does this isolate her from her peers? How can Lisa feel a part of the third grade class when the other kids are reading and functioning on a much higher level and she is not with them for a large part of the day? Does this play a role in her difficulty to make and keep friends, or am I overreacting?" Susan wondered.

Lisa could easily fit back into a second grade class both physically and socially, but she had already been retained. She was two years older than her third grade peers. And just last month she had her first period! Since she started kindergarten a year later than most children, she should actually be in fifth grade. Susan Johnson contemplated how she could make Lisa an integral part of the third grade class without sacrificing Lisa's individual needs.

Advance Study Questions

1. What is the major dilemma in this case?

2. What are some underlying causes of this dilemma?

3. Who should be involved in finding solutions to Lisa's programming difficulties within the third grade?

4. Discuss some options available to Susan Johnson and Sarah Hill.

CASE 13

A Child's Disability—A Teacher's Handicap?

Barbara Heinisch

CHARACTERS

Students:	Hallie
	Maria
Hallie's parents:	Mr. and Mrs. Berman
Teacher:	Ann Jackson
Principal:	Ms. Copeland
Aide from previous school:	Mrs. Horan
Occupational therapist:	Larry Jones
Computer coordinator:	John Watson
Evaluator at computer lab:	Linda Hope

Part A

A New Student—Mid-October

The day was already chaotic; nothing had gone smoothly. First one of the boys had become sick and had to be sent home, and then the music teacher was called away on an emergency. Ann not only lost her free period, but she had to teach music for that period. Music was not one of her strong points, but she thought the children would benefit from the change of pace that singing provided. Ann had just collapsed into her chair when she heard a humming sound. A child in a motorized wheelchair was at the open classroom door. "Oh, no!" Ann thought. "This can't be Hallie. She's supposed to come tomorrow!"

Ms. Copeland, the principal, was right behind the child, who was concentrating on maneuvering her wheelchair into the classroom. Hallie's mother and father were also with her. Ms. Copeland, sounding overly cheery, explained that since the Bermans were already at school to meet with the social worker, they had decided to meet Ann before Hallie's first day tomorrow. While the principal was answering some questions about the inclusion of children with disabilities at the school, Ann observed Hallie. She was slightly built, and tilted over to one side in her small wheelchair. Her blond hair was meticulously arranged into two neat braids, and she had a cute, crooked smile. Ann could see that one hand was tucked up against her chest with the wrist bent down, but Hallie had enough control of the other to use it to work the joystick that controlled her chair. Ann squatted down to talk with the child at her eye level.

"Hi," she said. "I'm Ms. Jackson. I wish we had some more time to get to know each other before you start here. You'll have to tell me when you need help."

Hallie smiled shyly and spoke in a quivering, soft voice. "Thanks. In my other school, I had Mrs. Horan with me all the time. She helped me do things."

Hallie's speech was slow and slurred, but Ann found that she had no trouble understanding her. She wanted to ask more about Mrs. Horan's role in Hallie's last school. She knew from the start that there was no money available in the current year's budget for classroom aides. Just then, Ms. Copeland said that it was time for the Bermans' appointment. "Why don't you stop by my office at the end of the day, Ann?" she asked. "We can discuss the accommodations for Hallie." Ann smiled and nodded, feeling overwhelmed, and said good-bye to Mr. and Mrs. Berman. "See you tomorrow," she said to Hallie.

Somehow Ann got through the rest of the day. The children were restless. It was an uncharacteristically cold and windy November, and it looked like it might snow. As the last of the children filed out of the room at the end of the day, Ann thought about Hallie again. As she gathered her books together, she sighed heavily. "Twenty-two children already," she thought, "and now one more who will need a lot of attention."

School and Community

Hallie and her parents recently moved to Oakmont, a town in the northeastern United States, with a population of approximately 22,000 people. Hallie's father, worked for a large manufacturer of jet engines, was transferred to Oakmont from another facility of the same company that was 175 miles north of their present residence.

In addition to the jet engine company, Oakmont also had numerous other midsized and large companies in the defense, pharmaceutical, and building construction industries. It possessed one of the largest tax bases in the state, and its residents enjoyed a relatively low rate of taxation on their personal property, such as homes and automobiles. Oakmont's high school, middle school, and four elementary schools were looked upon throughout the state as providing superb and exemplary programming in both regular and special education.

Citizen support for education appeared to be changing, however. Because of the recent imposition of a state income tax and a townwide property re-evaluation that caused a significant increase in the tax rate on homes, many people were more critical of how the municipality was spending tax dollars. Oakmont's residents had defeated the board of education's budget in four referendums. Despite moderate increases in teachers' and administrator's salaries, Oakmont's education budget was 2 percent lower this year than last year. Music, art, and sports programs had been severely slashed by the board of education, and all teacher's aide positions had been eliminated.

Hallie's new third grade class at Green Farms School had twenty-three children. Two boys in this class received remedial instruction from a learning disability resource teacher, but during her four years of teaching within Green Farms School, Ann Jackson had not encountered a mainstreamed child with Hallie's level of physical involvement.

Later That Day

When Ann arrived at the principal's office, she was pleasantly surprised to see Larry Jones there. Larry was an occupational therapist employed by the district. Last year, he had worked briefly with a student who had had some fine-motor coordination problems resulting from a head injury. Larry had helped them work out solutions to the problems this student was experiencing with writing. Ann liked his easy personality and the gentle manner in which he encouraged the children.

When they were settled in Ms. Copeland's office, Ann jumped right in. "I really feel unprepared to deal with this child. I only found out last week that she was coming, and I haven't even seen any records on her. I have no training in special education! There are so many things I need to know. Can she do the work the other students are doing? What is her cognitive level? Does she need help doing things? Can she write independently?"

She turned to Larry. "Will you be there to help?" With each question, Ann's voice was getting higher. She was filled with anxiety. Larry raised his eyebrows and deferred to the principal to answer the questions.

"From what I have been told by her parents, Hallie can do schoolwork on the same level as other third graders," said Ms. Copeland. "We haven't received her school records yet, so I guess we'll have to meet her to see what the situation is."

Larry finally spoke up. "Cerebral palsy can be severe or mild," he said. "Until we get a chance to evaluate her, we really won't know what her needs are or how much extra assistance she'll need. Some children with CP are mentally retarded; that doesn't seem to be the case here. Some children with cerebral palsy can walk; obviously Hallie can't. My big question is how she uses her hands."

They discussed some of the necessary accommodations, such as making things accessible to Hallie within the classroom. It was arranged that Hallie would use the bathroom in the nurse's office, so someone would be there to assist her.

As they got up to leave, Ms. Copeland touched Ann's arm. "When we first talked about Hallie, I told you we would do all we could to help you. I chose to place this child with you because of your sensitivity to children with differences. I remember how well Jeffrey did with you two years ago. Even though it was only your second year teaching and you really weren't prepared to work with a deaf child, you made him welcome and learned what you had to do to ensure his success. I know that you will do the same for Hallie."

Ann left the office in a daze. She was preoccupied with practical issues: What would it be like to teach a child like Hallie? How much assistance would she need? How would the other students react to her? How often would she need to have therapists visiting in the classroom? If Hallie wasn't able to walk, what else couldn't she do? As she drove home, Ann realized that she was jumping to conclusions; she needed more information.

Hallie's First Day

The next morning, Ann arrived at school earlier than usual. She knew that the classroom was not set up to accommodate a child using a wheelchair. Hallie needed the freedom to move around without difficulty. Ann moved some chairs to create wider aisles. As she worked, she was thinking about the "Kids on the Block," the national puppet troupe that had visited the school last year. "Kids on the Block," sends local troupes to visit schools, using puppets with disabilities in short skits with nondisabled puppets. The nondisabled puppet interacts with the puppet with the disability, asking the kinds of questions a curious child might if given the opportunity. After the skit, the nondisabled puppet leaves, and the puppet with the disability answers questions from the children in the audience. It was a wonderful way to introduce the concept of children with differences into a school which, until recently, hadn't had many such children. Ann wished it hadn't been so long ago since they were at the school. She wished she had time to somehow prepare the children for a child with a disability. She wished she herself felt prepared to teach such a child!

Ann was standing in the center of the room surveying the new furniture arrangement when Hallie and her mother arrived.

"Well, hello!" said Ann. "Welcome. I'm glad you're here." Hallie gave her a shy smile. Ann smiled at Hallie's mother. "I'm glad you came early," she said. "You can fill me in on any special needs Hallie has. Please come sit down."

Sitting on the small student chairs, they were now both eye level with Hallie, who continued to smile shyly whenever Ann caught her eye.

"What would you like to know?" asked Mrs. Berman.

Ann wasn't sure where to start. Glancing quickly at the clock, she realized that in only a few minutes the other children would be arriving. "Well, we haven't received any records from Hallie's other school," Ann said, "and I don't really know how much help she will need. What can we do to make this a good experience for her?"

Mrs. Berman smiled and said, "I'm glad you're Hallie's teacher. Hallie can answer your questions herself, though."

Ann glanced doubtfully at Hallie. "Okay, then, Hallie," Ann said, "suppose you tell me what you like best about school."

"Snack!" Hallie replied in a soft, barely audible whisper.

Just then the first of the children came bounding into the room. Mrs. Berman stood up to leave. "I'm sure you'll do just fine," she said. "I'll be in the office for a while if you need me for anything."

"Bye, sweetie!" she said to Hallie. Ann wasn't sure, but she thought she heard Hallie say, "Bye, Mom."

Mrs. Berman backed out of the room, looking reluctant to leave. The child had stopped smiling, and was watching the other children's surprised reactions to her.

Ann's teaching style was one of organized chaos. She seemed to be in several places in the room at once, and although there was a high level of activity, all the children knew what they were supposed to be doing, and there was a correspondingly high level of learning. Hallie seemed to be enjoying the activity, and since she and Maria seemed to be getting along well, Ann just watched her from across the room. Ann had introduced Hallie briefly, talking about why some people with disabilities have to find other ways to accomplish tasks. She had placed Hallie next to Maria because she thought they would get along well.

It was when the children were at their seats writing their papers that Ann realized that Hallie wasn't writing. She crossed the room toward her, stopping to touch the shoulders of several children along the way, and giving them words of encouragement.

Ann spoke to Hallie. "Can you write at all?" she said.

Hallie spoke softly, "Not too well. In my other school I told Mrs. Horan what to write, and she wrote it down for me." Ann nodded, thinking, "What am I going to do with this child? I need help!"

For the rest of the day, Ann juggled her usual teaching duties with spending time with her new student, who, she discovered, was really very sweet. Most of the children were curious about Hallie but were keeping their distance. Some of the bolder children had asked her questions about the power wheelchair, and she answered them shyly, but with a smile. Some of the girls were vying with each other to help Hallie, and she seemed to enjoy their attention. As her mother had promised, Hallie communicated her needs clearly. She had waved her good hand to attract Ann's attention and then had asked to go to the nurse's office to use the bathroom. She hadn't participated in class discussions, but she did seem to understand the content of the classwork. The major problem seemed to be with Hallie's writing. Her printing consisted of letters over an inch high, written faintly. Hallie did not have the strength in her hand to press down hard with the pencil. It took her an inordinately long time to write a simple sentence.

Ann ended her first day frustrated. What could she do with a student who couldn't write? She herself didn't have the time to do Hallie's writing for her.

Maria had offered to write for Hallie, but she wasn't a strong student, and needed to devote the time to her own work. So much of the day in Ann's third grade class was spent on writing-related activities. In addition to workbook pages and board work that had to be done, there was a writer's workshop that Ann conducted three days a week. Many of her children in the last few years had improved their writing abilities with these thorough lessons on prewriting, outlining, and editing skills. Ann knew that the chances of getting an aide to assist Hallie were slim. Just this year all the classroom aide positions had been cut from the school budget.

Advance Study Questions

1. What are the major dilemmas in this case?

2. What kinds of support might have made Hallie's entrance into Ann's class more successful?

3. Does it appear that Ann's class is an appropriate placement for Hallie?

4. What are some of the pros and cons of using computers as a classroom tool for students with writing disabilities?

CASE 14

The First Mistake

Robert Piazza and Judith B. Buzzell

CHARACTERS

Student: Emily
Emily's parents: Mr. and Mrs. Kelly
Teacher: Ms. Berlein
Principal: Mrs. Roderick

Part A

Early September

Ms. Berlein was completing her second week of her first year as a teacher. She recognized already that her fourth grade class would be a challenge because of the many and varied interests and abilities of the children. She felt quite alone in this situation. Unlike her student-teaching experience, there was no master teacher to provide constructive criticism and reassuring support on a daily basis. Yet she also felt secure in the knowledge that her class size was relatively small, with twenty students, and that her supplies were plentiful. Her room was well stocked with two Apple computers, new science kits, and many high-interest stories which the children avidly read.

The children noisily filed back into her room after their vigorous outdoor play. It was a beautiful late summer day, and math was the first subject on the agenda. The three math groups that Ms. Berlein had established earlier in the week moved to their appointed workstations. She explained the seatwork for two of the groups, so that she could directly instruct the other group for the first part of the designated sixty-minute period.

Midway through the math class, Emily, one of the students in the top math group, tugged at Ms. Berlein's sleeve and said, "I think I'm really going to like this school year. I like you, too."

"Thank you," Ms. Berlein replied, smiling at this ingenuous expression of affection and feeling pleased. "Why do you think this year is going to be so good?"

Emily enthusiastically exclaimed, "Well, one reason is you put me in the top math group with Jason, Kevin, Traci, and all the others. I've never been in the top group before. I've always needed extra help, and you probably know I had to stay back in second grade. My mother and father have often told me that I'm smart, but I never believed them. Now I do."

Ms. Berlein tried to conceal her surprise. She had not expected such a strong reaction from a child simply because of her grouping. For Emily's sake, she hoped the math book's placement test really assisted in making accurate grouping decisions. (Exhibit 1 describes the test).

The School and Community

Sachem School was a large, well-equipped, and modern elementary school serving approximately 600 children in grades K–6. It was the only elementary school in Chalfont, whose school system was renowned as one of the best in the state.

A suburban community of about 8,000, Chalfont seemed almost rural, with its wooded landscape and winding country lanes. Set back from the roads were handsome homes on $1\frac{1}{2}$-acre lots. The residents were primarily successful businesspeople, doctors, lawyers, and professors who taught at the three universities in the city, only four miles away.

Emily Kelly and Her Family

Emily was a slender, blond fourth grader. She had been retained in second grade because of a need to improve her reading and spelling. Testing indicated that, although her intelligence was in the superior range, she was a child with a mild learning disability in reading, spelling, and organizational skills. Her teacher and parents hoped that the extra year would give her the time to strengthen both her language arts and organizational skills. She had

EXHIBIT 1

The inventory/placement test attempts to determine the skills a student has mastered. It is a 50-item, multiple-choice test. Twenty percent of the fourth grade placement test problems are keyed to objectives at that grade level. Fifty percent of the questions assess skills that were to have been taught in the third grade, and 30 percent of the problems are keyed to second grade material. The test assesses calculation skills, money skills, and basic geometry abilities, with time, measurement, place value, fractions, and word problems. The test is administered in a group setting with a fifty-minute time limit.

difficulty copying neatly from the blackboard and remembering homework assignments. Somewhat flighty, Emily had trouble keeping her attention on a task. Although she listened when the teacher began to present a lesson, she soon became distracted by such things as children's laughter in the hall or the bubbling of the fish tank.

By fourth grade, Emily had grown more confident. She had a large group of friends and a lively social life. She busied herself with many activities after school and on the weekends, including tennis and horseback riding lessons. With forty minutes a day of extra support from the resource teacher in the language arts, she was able to maintain her reading level in the middle group. Her reading was not fluent, however. As she struggled to decode each word, her comprehension suffered. She was having more success in math. She had no difficulty solving simple problems in addition, subtraction, multiplication, and division.

Although initially apprehensive about Emily's retention, Mr. and Mrs. Kelly were pleased that it had seemed to work. Mr. Kelly, a tall, muscular jogger, was a partner in a prestigious law firm. Mrs. Kelly had been trained as an elementary school teacher, but choosing not to work after Emily was born, instead took an active role in community affairs and volunteered at the local hospital. The Kellys had one other child, Jeffrey, Emily's younger brother. Jeffrey was in second grade. He was in the highest achieving groups and seemed to master new skills and concepts almost effortlessly.

Although the Kellys accepted Emily's learning disability, they were determined that Emily would not be hampered by it. They spoke regularly with the principal and special education teacher to monitor her progress and to ensure that she was receiving the services she needed. Mr. Kelly conscientiously attended all the meetings at school along with his wife.

The Teacher

A new teacher, Ms. Berlein had been a student teacher at Sachem School and had been hired by the school system because of her outstanding performance. Her master teacher considered her one of the best student teachers she had ever had. Ms. Berlein graduated from the local state university with a 3.7 cumulative average. She had a calm demeanor and a degree of maturity unusual in a novice. She seemed challenged but not overwhelmed by her new position.

> I decided to stick with three math groups in the class; each group works at a different pace as well as at a different level. I could form other groups because there are several students in the upper group who are ready for more advanced work—I call them my whiz kids. That top group could be subdivided into two groups, but I don't know how I could handle all those groups at once. Although I know it might be ideal to individualize more, I feel comfortable with what I'm doing.

November Report Card

Emily Kelly

Reading	B	Social Studies	A
Spelling	B	Math	B+
Composition	B+	Science	A

Emily's parents were delighted with her first quarter report card. Because of Emily's placement in the top group, they had some doubts about how she might be doing in math and were relieved to see the B+. Yet, this grade seemed to reflect accurately the work she had done at home and the paperwork she had brought from school.

Although Mr. and Mrs. Kelly were not aware of it, nearly two-thirds of the math instruction during the first few months of school was review for most of the students in the top group. For Emily, however, it wasn't review; she needed to relearn previously mastered material. As a result, Emily completed her worksheets more slowly and deliberately than the others. Yet, at the end of the math periods, she seemed composed. When her quizzes were returned with Bs on them, she smiled with quiet pleasure.

Three Weeks Later

It was the Wednesday after Thanksgiving, and students and teachers alike were knuckling down to work before the next vacation. Ms. Berlein was circulating around the room checking the seatwork of her students. She had just finished teaching Emily's group math reasoning skills involving pre-algebra problems. (Exhibit 2 shows the exercise). Emily looked stumped, so Ms. Berlein wandered over to her desk. "What's wrong, Emily?" she asked. With a choked voice, Emily replied:

> I don't know. I don't understand this stuff. It seemed really clear when you explained it, but it doesn't now. Things are getting tough in this class. All the other kids are done with work, and they're playing on the computers or reading their library books, and I'm still trying to figure this out. I'm also taking home a lot of work that I don't finish during class time. Can you help me with this page?

Ms. Berlin put a hand on Emily's shoulder. "Even though this is the first time you've had to do problems with letters in them, they're really not different from the problems you've done before," she explained reassuringly. Then she spent about ten minutes working individually with Emily. She told Emily to treat the letters like an empty space and not to be confused by them. Then, they set up the equations using small blue chips. Emily seemed to do well with these concrete aids. Ms. Berlein thought to herself, "None of the other children in this group needed so much individual attention from me."

EXHIBIT 2

Find the number that would be represented by each letter in the following equations.

1. $H + 1 = 4$
2. $15 - N = 12$
3. $F + F = 10$
4. $L + 2 = 7$
5. $H + 7 = 17$
6. $M + 10 = 19$
7. $A \times A = 9$
8. $C \div 2 = 3$
9. $D \times 4 = 20$
10. $M + 17 = 20$
11. $9 \times B = 18$
12. $B - 7 = 13$
13. $G - 10 = 15$
14. $25 \div H = 5$

When it was time for the class to get ready for social studies, Emily had eight more problems to solve. She took these home for homework.

That Evening at Home

The Kellys were finishing dinner when Emily's father asked her if she had any homework. Emily said, "I had some math to do, and I did it when I came home. Ms. Berlein explained this new kind of math with letters and numbers in class today, and I think I understand it. It's pretty easy."

Mr. Kelly checked her work, which included the problems done with Ms. Berlein's assistance, and found that there were only three problems done incorrectly. He assumed that she must have gotten careless, since most of the beginning equations were solved correctly. After he explained to Emily why her problems were wrong, she promptly corrected them. Emily spent the rest of the evening reading a library book.

Time for a Change

During the Christmas break, when she could catch her breath, Ms. Berlein stopped to consider her nagging sense that the grouping of children in reading and math was no longer working as well as she wanted. Although the original groups had been effective earlier in the year when there was a great deal of review of the previous year's instruction, now some of the children were not keeping pace. She felt they would be more comfortable in a lower group. Other children were not being stimulated enough, and they needed more advanced work. She decided to switch four children in reading and five children in math. Emily was to be moved to a lower math group.

During the afternoon math class on the Monday after the Christmas vacation, Ms. Berlein announced the regrouping. All the children seemed to accept the changes with equanimity. That is, all except one.

Ms. Berlein did not notice Emily at first. Then, as her eyes glanced to the back of the room, she saw Emily, her shoulders hunched and her hand brushing away a few tears. Emily seemed to sense that she was being observed. She looked up with a forced grin on her face.

At dinner that night, Emily explained what had happened in math. Her parents calmly reassured her that she was doing the best job she could and that she should be pleased with her efforts. But anger simmered beneath their composed facade.

The Meeting

Early the next morning, Mrs. Kelly called the principal to arrange a meeting. While the Kellys were troubled by how the news of Emily's "demotion" was presented to her, they were equally concerned about ensuring that their daughter was in the appropriate math group.

Mrs. Roderick (the principal), Ms. Berlein, and Emily's parents attended the meeting. It was held during Ms. Berlein's lunch break. Since this was not an issue directly related to Emily's Individualized Educational Program (which focused on her language arts needs), the resource room teacher was not present.

Ms. Berlein began the meeting by apologizing to Mr. and Mrs. Kelly for the way she had handled the regrouping situation. "I'm a new teacher," she said. "I knew how much it meant to Emily to be in the top group. I should have spoken to her privately. I just didn't think it through well enough."

Although still upset, the Kellys accepted Ms. Berlein's apology. Their primary concern, after all, was to determine the best instructional setting for Emily. Actually, they had been baffled when Emily was placed in the highest group at the beginning of the year. They knew many of the children—these were highly intelligent kids who grasped and mastered new skills and concepts quickly. Although Emily was bright, it often took her a little longer to learn new material. And she did have a learning disability.

In the meeting, a written statement from Emily's resource room teacher was read. She believed that Emily might have trouble keeping up with the children in the top group. Ms. Berlein reiterated her judgment that a middle group placement would be more instructionally sound at this point. The higher group would be moving at a faster pace from this point on, with far less review and higher expectations.

Mr. and Mrs. Kelly felt torn. On the one hand, in the strong current of the advanced group, their daughter might flail and possibly drown. On the other hand, they were worried that this "demotion" might cause her recently acquired self-confidence to sink. When they expressed these feelings, Mrs. Roderick, the principal, asked, "What would you think about including Emily in this decision-making process? Let's find out what she feels would be best." When the others agreed, the school secretary hurried to get Emily from recess.

Emily listened intently as her options and the concomitant concerns were presented gently but forthrightly to her. Her cheeks, already rosy from the brisk January wind, grew redder. After a lengthy pause, she responded with determination, "I really think I can do it. I want to stay in the top group."

The adults assented to the child's wishes. Now, Ms. Berlein would have to figure out other ways to meet Emily's academic needs.

Advance Study Questions

1. What is the major dilemma faced by Emily's teacher in this case?

2. What other problems must Ms. Berlein deal with?

3. How are these problems interpreted by Emily's parents and the principal of the school?

4. Who should be involved in making the appropriate decisions about Emily's programming in mathematics?

CASE 15

Chen Yang

Judith B. Buzzell

CHARACTERS

Teacher: Jim Shannon
Students: Chen Yang
Ming Lo
George
Lamar
Sam
Chen's mother: Mrs. Yang

Part A

The First Day of School

Jim Shannon and Joan Greer, a fellow teacher, watched Chen Yang with concern. Their two fourth grade classes were on the playground, enjoying recess on their first day of school. Children were climbing on the jungle gym, swinging, and playing tag and touch football. Many of the children knew each other, having been together in classes in previous years at the school. They seemed eager to renew their relationships after the long summer.

In contrast, Chen, the new Chinese boy, paced the perimeter of the expansive yard. Always on the sidelines of the children's play, he spoke to no one. He moved in a slow gait, his arms swinging aimlessly by his sides and his shirt tails hanging out. As Joan watched this solitary figure, she observed, "He looks so out of it." Jim nodded in agreement.

The writer gratefully acknowledges the invaluable contribution of Michael Zito to the writing of this case.

The Community

Benton was a city of about 700,000. It sat on the edge of a large lake that provided natural beauty and recreation for its citizens. After a deep recession in the early 1980s, the city reorganized its manufacturing base, and had been able to maintain financial stability since then. During the transition, many highly paid, skilled, unionized blue-collar workers lost their jobs or were forced to take lower paying jobs, relocate, or join the ranks of the unemployed. The minority community was hardest hit by these changes.

The city was known for its ethnic and racial diversity. Immigrants had flooded in from Europe during the mid-1800s and through the early twentieth century. Blacks moved up from the South in the 1940s and 1950s. Now immigrants were coming here from Asian countries. The city celebrated this diversity with its renowned summer fests which were well attended by people from many different backgrounds. Each weekend of the summer, a different ethnic group sponsored a festival, with representative foods, crafts, music, dances, and more. However, there had also been some tensions and strife between the ethnic groups.

In the 1970s and 1980s, magnet schools were started in Benton. These drew children from neighborhoods all over the city. Parents had to apply to the magnet schools, and a lottery was held to determine which children would be accepted. The lottery's careful design ensured that there was a balance of ethnicity, gender, and family income level in the schools' populations.

The magnet schools were created, in part, to encourage white, middle-class families to keep their children in the public schools and, therefore, to desegregate the schools through voluntary means. In the 1970s and 1980s, the growth of the suburbs and the development of a major transportation system made it easier to commute, and more and more white families had abandoned the city. Generally, the magnet schools were considered successful in promoting integration, parent involvement, and high-quality education.

The School

Washington Elementary School, with approximately 600 students, was one of Benton's magnet schools. Most families chose the school for the diversity of its student body and its approach to teaching, which emphasized recognizing the developmental needs of children. Administrators and teachers in the school believed that children learn at different rates and in different ways, so teachers tried to individualize instruction as much as possible.

The curriculum integrated subject areas. Classes in each grade used a broad social studies theme as a framework for integrating language arts, science, math, the arts, and so on. Because of the focus on experiential learning, children were actively involved in hands-on activities like conducting science experiments, making dioramas, or taking field trips.

Although class size was large, as in all the city schools, Washington had been fortunate to secure extra funding through grants, and all classes had aides for at least part of the day. In addition, there was a firm commitment to parent involvement in the school, so frequently parents helped out in the classroom, listening to a child read, supervising a child's work at a computer, or conducting a small group activity. Parents also advised in the governance of the school and raised funds.

The Teacher

Jim Shannon, age thirty-four, had been teaching for two years. He was a six-foot, four-inch tall, muscular man, with dark hair and a full, reddish-brown beard. Despite his imposing stature, he spoke softly. His wife, whom he recently married, called him the "gentle giant."

When he went to college, in the early 70s, Jim majored in theater. After graduating, he became involved with a group, sponsored by an environmental organization, that presented performances all over the country to show people the global dangers of pollution. Later, he worked in improvisational theatre.

Although he was not interested in a teaching career at that time, he decided that he wanted to "break into the schools." He created a show for schools to educate and delight children with the wonders of science. The success of his performances sparked his interest in teaching. He took courses to get certified at the local state university and considered himself lucky to land a job at Washington Elementary School.

At Washington School, there was the freedom to try different approaches and the expectation that teachers would experiment. "I'm devoted to teaching. I want to be there for the kids, and I want to be real good. I'm very self-motivated," he said. As one of Jim's former professors commented, "You can drop into Jim's class at any time, and you'll know he's a natural as a teacher. It's obvious."

Jim's classroom was square, with six computer stations along the wall. The walls were painted pale blue and decorated with samples of the students' work. Students sat in groups of six around several rectangular tables. Jim emphasized to his students that the classroom was small and, while they didn't need to be best friends, they did need to cooperate.

One regular feature of the weekly cycle symbolized this focus on community. The previous year, the students had suggested that they have something like a "Kid's Court." Each Friday, students brought, to the court, concerns or complaints that they had had about other students or about the functioning of the class during the previous week.

The court had evolved from one that focused on punishment of offenders to one that emphasized mediation and group problem solving. Jim found that students more comfortably raised issues when they weren't worried about enraging their fellow classmates, who might get punished. During these sessions, students spent an hour and a half actively discussing topics such as how to prevent students from insulting each other.

It was typical of Jim's style that the process of Kid's Court was continuously scrutinized. In one session early last year, Jim raised the question of whether he should continue to be the judge or whether the students were ready to take over. The students evaluated the pros and cons of both sides of the issue and then voted to rely on his fairness for a while longer. Jim believed that if students learned to be more effective problem solvers, they would be more likely to take responsibility for their own behavior.

When teaching academic subjects, Jim also treated his students with respect. He wanted them to approach each subject as a scholar would. He treated them like serious, committed mathematicians by giving students opportunities to grapple with complex mathematical problems, not just to develop computational skills. He treated them like writers by teaching them a process for drafting, peer review, and revision of their writing. He took the doors off his cabinets and stocked them with a variety of paper and writing tools. For the reading program, students chose novels to read instead of basal readers (reading textbooks with a structured sequence of vocabulary and skills). In all areas, he tried to avoid busywork. In every possible way, he emphasized that what he asked his students to do was important and, if they weren't sure why they were being asked to do something, they should ask.

Back to the First Day

Jim's class of twenty-seven gregarious fourth graders finally settled into their seats. There were fourteen boys and thirteen girls, including eleven blacks, thirteen whites, one biracial child, one Pakistani child, and Chen.

There was a tone of eager anticipation, and a few children commented to each other that they were happy to get Mr. Shannon as their teacher. They had heard other students speak positively about Kid's Court and other intriguing experiences that went on in Jim's class.

Jim opened the year's first group discussion by telling the students a little about his background and interests. Then the students had an opportunity to talk. During the course of their years at Washington Elementary School, they had participated in many group discussions. Waving their hands vigorously, they vied to share their summer experiences first.

After several children had spoken, Jim directed a question to Chen, who had been watching him intently. Jim was aware that Chen was new to the school, but there had been no records available to learn more about him. "Chen," Jim gently asked, "can you share a special experience from this summer with us?" Chen sat still, looked toward Jim, and seemed attentive, but he did not respond to his teacher. Thinking that perhaps he had spoken too softly, Jim repeated,

"Can you tell us something about your summer?" Again, Chen looked blankly at Jim. There was a long pause, and then the loud voice of another boy punctuated the silence.

"Hey, what's the matter with him? Can't he talk?"

Advance Study Questions

1. What problem(s) does Jim, the teacher, face in this case?
2. What are some underlying issues in this situation?
3. How might the situation be viewed from the perspectives of Chen and the other students in the class? Why?
4. If you were Jim, what action(s) would you take? Why?

CASE 16

True Assessment

Joseph Amato and Robert Piazza

CHARACTERS

Resource teacher:	Tony Jackson
Psychologist:	Ronald Bates
Fourth grade teacher:	Jane Matthews
Student:	Yuri Bendrosian
Special education supervisor:	Sarah Howard
Interpreter:	Mrs. Yanosh

Part A

The Day Begins

"How's your day going so far?" asked Ronald Bates, the psychologist at Canton Elementary School.

"It was all right until you showed up. You always bring trouble. So why should I expect anything different now when I'm eating lunch," replied Tony Jackson, the school's resource teacher.

"You must be psychic. I want you to look at this referral form and tell me what you think," said Mr. Bates as he pulled up a seat and nibbled on some of Mr. Jackson's potato chips.

The referral form indicated that Yuri Bendrosian, a student with limited proficiency in English, was having difficulties in language arts, despite unspecified attempts by his fourth grade teacher to modify his assignments. Mrs. Jane Matthews, the fourth grade teacher, wrote on the form that she perceived a learning disability to be a contributing factor to Yuri's classroom performance. She felt he could no longer function adequately in a regular fourth grade.

Tony Jackson was bothered by this referral. "I don't know if I can touch this one. This kid's from another country and speaks very little English. Can we test reliably with the assessment devices we have? My training in special education never told me what to do with this kind of a situation. Anyway, he's probably not learning disabled; it sounds like he's having problems with the English language. Sometimes I feel like the teachers in this school think that everyone who doesn't get As or Bs in their classes must have a learning disability."

Mr. Bates stood up and countered, "So non–English-speaking fourth graders can't have learning problems. I know you don't think academic difficulties and learning disabilities are only confined to English-speaking kids."

"You know that's not what I mean! It's just harder to assess this kind of problem with a kid with this type of language barrier. I am never comfortable with our placement decisions regarding these youngsters. But I guess we both know that we're the only people around here who are going to test Yuri, right?"

Bates just smiled and said, "You got it, Tony. Either we do this assessment, or it doesn't happen. Let's just follow the established procedures and see what happens. When can you observe him?"

Tony Jackson told Ronald Bates that he would observe Yuri in his class the next morning and get back to him. This was always the first step in the assessment process. Often an observation would yield information so that recommendations could be made to the regular education teacher and further testing would not be necessary. As the psychologist left the lunchroom, Mr. Jackson threw the referral form into his folder labeled *THINGS TO DO.*

The School System

Bennington was a large manufacturing urban center with a population of 115,000, composed of heterogeneous racial and cultural groups. There were three high schools, three middle schools, and twenty-six elementary schools.

The school board was actively looking to reduce services and personnel substantially, due to pending cuts in funding. Bennington currently had a $17 million dollar budget deficit. The Director of Special Services had asked the special education teachers to look carefully at their caseloads to see if any students could be dropped from services at their annual reviews, which were typically held in May and June. The teachers had also been instructed to use more pre-referral procedures in order to reduce the amount of time they spend formally evaluating youngsters within the system. Special education personnel had been asked to, in the future, provide careful documentation that regular education interventions were tried unsuccessfully before discussing a child at a Planning and Placement Team (PPT) meeting. At the current rate of identifying children with handicaps, at least ten new special education teachers would be needed to avoid violating state special education guidelines and current contractual limits set for teacher caseloads. Fewer and more valid assessments were being sought by the administration.

The School

Canton School had an enrollment of approximately 675 students. There were five kindergarten classes, and either four or five classes in grades one through five, including one bilingual class for Hispanic children in grades four and five. A vice principal, a speech and language clinician, two Chapter One teachers, Mr. Jackson, and Mr. Bates made up Canton's PPT.

The school's enrollment through third grade was composed of students from Canton's own geographical district, which was primarily white and middle class. In addition to its district students, the fourth and fifth grades had pupils who were bused in from other districts throughout the city. Most of these fourth and fifth graders were racially and culturally different children from lower socioeconomic backgrounds. This school reorganization was the result of a recent court order after Bennington was found to be in violation of federal and state integration laws. The entire school system had been redistricted last year in compliance with a court order. Five fourth and fifth grade teachers at Canton asked for transfers in the last two months.

Ronald Bates was in his third year as a school psychologist and his first year at Canton School. He had completed his M.S. degree and was currently finishing his few remaining courses required for permanent certification in the school psychology program at a local state university. Prior to coming to Bennington, he had worked at a state institution for the mentally retarded.

Tony Jackson was in his second year of full-time teaching, although he had substituted within the Bennington system for three years while he was earning a B.S. degree in special education. He was presently pursuing a master's degree in the same field.

Yuri's teacher, Jane Matthews, was certified to teach kindergarten through eighth grade and had a master's degree in remedial reading. She had taught in the Bennington system for the past fourteen years in four different schools. Before returning to a regular fourth grade class last year, she was a Chapter One remedial reading teacher for three years.

Yuri and His Family

Yuri Bendrosian, a fourth grader, was the older of two boys in his family. A younger brother attended the second grade in another elementary school within the system. The Bendrosian family had moved to Bennington two years ago from Albania. Since there were no bilingual classes for children of his nationality in Bennington, Yuri was placed in a regular second grade. Although he was not proficient, his facility with the English language had been improving.

English was not spoken within the home setting. Yuri's father was a mason by trade and had been able to find ample work despite the hard economic times. His mother was not currently working, but was actively seeking employment.

Despite encountering a myriad of academic and language-related difficulties in second and third grade, Yuri was promoted. His second grade teacher had been able to converse with Yuri since she was a second-generation Albanian and had a moderate knowledge of the language. He was characterized by both of his previous teachers as "hard working and industrious." Neither his second nor his third grade teacher brought concerns about Yuri's learning difficulties to the attention of the school's PPT.

Mrs. Matthews wasted little time, however. In early November she referred Yuri for a formal evaluation. On the referral form, she estimated his reading achievement to be two years below his present grade level, and suggested that this was also severely lowering his performance in content subjects such as science and social studies. Recently, Mrs. Matthews had noticed a regression in his behavior, both in the classroom and in the schoolyard. This behavior had led to two probation slips and an in-school suspension. Although he had earned a grade of B in math and in penmanship, Ds were recorded in science, social studies, reading, and spelling.

The Observation

Mrs. Matthews was expecting Mr. Jackson. She knew it was rather routine that a PPT member would have to conduct an observation before a referral went anywhere. "We're just doing a social studies lesson. Is that all right?" she asked when she saw Tony Jackson appear at her door.

"That's just fine. I'll sit at the back table and watch. Just go about the lesson like I'm not even here," replied Mr. Jackson as he took his seat and tried to ignore the fifty-two eyes staring at him.

Jane Matthews led the class through a lesson on the southwestern part of the United States. The Mojave Desert and the irrigation canals, strip mining, and minerals of that region were the focus of that day's oral discussion. Children also read aloud from the social studies book and had to answer questions posed by the teacher. When Yuri was asked to read, Mrs. Matthews needed to provide assistance with over half of the words. He was also unable to answer questions asked after he read. Yuri's body stiffened after each incorrect response. When the next child in the class was called upon to read, Yuri put his head on his desk and exhaled a deep breath.

Later in the lesson, a discussion started concerning desert tourism. Yuri's face brightened and he frantically raised his hand. "My uncle. He just gone to Arizona. He saw Grand Canyon and he go on big balloon over the desert. I want to go there too sometimes." Mrs. Matthews thanked Yuri for his participation and told him and the rest of the class that she would like to visit the Grand Canyon also.

As the lesson concluded, Mr. Jackson prepared to leave. As he passed Yuri's desk, he knelt on one knee and whispered to him, "Great job! Keep up the good work!" Yuri glanced back and said, "Thanks."

Tony Jackson headed back to his room to complete the observation form and develop strategies for Mrs. Matthews to try with Yuri in her classroom.

Let's Try This

After school that day Tony Jackson walked into Jane Matthews's classroom. She was sitting at her desk quietly engrossed in correcting students' papers, unaware of his presence.

"Hi, Jane! How's it going?" he asked, nearly sending the fourth grade teacher into cardiac arrest.

"Jeez, don't do that!" she smiled, placing her hand over her heart and gasping for air.

"Sorry 'bout that. Do you have a few minutes to talk? I've got a few ideas that might help you with Yuri," said Mr. Jackson. Without waiting for a reply, he pulled up a chair and opened his leather portfolio.

> From my observation, it's obvious that Yuri's reading skills are very poor, and as a result, his reading comprehension is terrible. His comprehension abilities appear much better, however, when he listens to other kids read. It looks like his language skills are coming along, but I can see that he is still struggling to understand everything that is being said in class. School must be very frustrating for him. I haven't tested him yet, but it seems like his auditory memory is pretty much intact, and he's relying on it quite a bit. Try to optimize that and teach in that channel as much as possible. Also you might want to try peer tutoring if at all possible, if you think he can handle it. You could team him up with a responsible student who can read the social studies and science texts to him while Yuri follows along on the page. That person could also help him study for tests. I think it's only fair that you give him tests orally; that way he won't be penalized because of his reading problems. Maybe you could—

Jane Matthews interrupted Mr. Jackson at this point with an unbelieving look on her face. "You're kiddin', right? You really expect me to try all that stuff. You specialists are amazing. Do you know how many kids I have in my class? Twenty-six! It's impossible to individualize for everyone. Now when are you going to test him and get him out of here?"

Tony Jackson politely explained that before any child can receive special help, pre-referral strategies have to be attempted, even if they fail. After a brief silence, Jane began to speak in a low voice that escalated as she went on.

> Listen. You guys did this to me last year. Remember James? I was stuck with him all year. He never did get into a self-contained class like you promised. You're not going to do it to me again. I have too many other kids that need me to spend a lot of time with Yuri. Four other kids in my class have English as a second language, but Yuri's problems are the worst. He just doesn't seem to be with us most of the time. Just test him and see if he qualifies for help. Come on! Give me a break!

Tony jumped back in at this point and attempted to get things under control. He reminded Mrs. Matthews that the interventions she used with James the preceding year were quite successful and allowed him to get through the year with just Chapter One support. "You should be proud of yourself for what you accomplished. And James is doing quite well this year also," he indicated.

"Good for James, but last year was hell for me, and I don't want a repeat of that. Now get him tested. You're wasting valuable time. I'll do my best with Yuri while I have him, but you know where I stand on this matter." Jane Matthews picked up her pocketbook and walked toward the door. "I know you mean well, but just walk a mile in my shoes. You might see things differently."

The resource teacher followed his colleague out of her room and headed in the opposite direction to his own classroom. He mumbled to anybody who would listen, "Why should I even bother trying to do a good job? Thank God, tomorrow's Veteran's Day!"

Advance Study Questions

1. What dilemmas are faced by the diagnosticians in this case?
2. What are some of the underlying problems influencing the situation?
3. How is Yuri's current placement viewed by his teacher?
4. What should be done to decide upon an appropriate placement for Yuri?
5. How should Yuri's assessment be conducted?

CASE 17

The Performance

Denise LaPrade Rini

CHARACTERS

Teacher:	Christina Ray
Audiovisual specialist:	Marc Davis
Students:	Matt Andrews
	Paul
	Alexandra
	Sandy
Speech-language pathologist:	Mrs. Ruby
Matt's mother:	Mrs. Andrews

Part A

Christmas vacation had ended, and students and teachers had readjusted to their school schedules. Christina Ray watched the clock as she waited for the audiovisual specialist, Marc Davis, to arrive and demonstrate use of the equipment for the civics project scheduled in three weeks. This was always an exciting time of the year for Mrs. Ray, since she took great pride in her students' efforts and achievements with this project, considered one of Kennedy Middle School's more innovative curricular efforts. The children studied their local government for the first half of the academic year. In late January, their studies culminated in a mock "Town Meeting" focusing on a specific issue during one afternoon. Students assumed the roles of the government officials, and parents and other interested persons could attend as citizenry. This year, the local public access television station had asked Joseph Lewis, the school principal, whether they could televise part of the process, and he had agreed. Mrs. Ray thought how this situation alone would have been sufficient to increase her anxiety, but this year she had a particular concern: what should she do about Matt?

The Child

This was Matt Andrews' first year in the middle school as a fifth grader. He was a delightful young man with blond hair and baby blue eyes which made him appear younger than his ten years. He had proved to be a bright and eager student, as his elementary teachers had said.

However, no one had really prepared Mrs. Ray for Matt's speech pattern: he stuttered. At first, Matt had appeared somewhat shy in class as he adjusted to the new school and fifth grade. Apparently, in his previous school, the teachers and other students had grown accustomed to Matt's speech difficulty since they had all been together since kindergarten, and Matt had not been particularly self-conscious. With the move to the middle school, however, Matt was meeting new children from two other elementary schools. In addition, middle school kids were expected to be "cool" and act more grown up. Many of the children in Matt's class appeared uncomfortable with his speech behavior and made assumptions about his personality or intelligence based on his "goofy" speech. Christina recalled the first time that Matt's speech problem became obvious to his classmates.

It was late September, and the class was discussing a popular television program. The children became quite noisy and Matt shouted out his comments. This was the first time he had actively participated in a class discussion. Matt's face was flushed with excitement, and he was eager to state his point of view. He quickly said a few words, stuttering on several of the first sounds. The children giggled, apparently thinking Matt was purposely acting funny. As he prepared to continue, his eyes closed, he threw his head back, and his jaw became fixated. No sound came out, and a tremor appeared in Matt's face and neck. The other children were suddenly silent.

Alarmed, Christina went toward Matt, calling his name. Was this a seizure? As she touched his arm, Matt threw his head forward and emitted an explosive sound as he poured out the remaining words of his sentence. Christina commented on his statement and quickly moved the discussion along, deflecting the focus from Matt. The other children seemed subdued, and she noticed whisperings among the children in the corners of the room. Matt seemed oblivious.

At lunchtime, Christina held Matt aside. "Matt, are you feeling all right? You looked like you were choking when you were speaking in class just now."

Matt looked at his teacher with some surprise. "I get stuck when I talk, especially when I get excited," he replied. "Everybody just usually waits 'til I'm done."

The Community

Lovell was a relatively new community which had grown from a rural area of 3,000 to a well-established suburban town of 15,000 within the past ten years.

The community was largely populated by working class tradespeople and middle-class white-collar workers and their families. Increasing numbers of families had moved to Lovell because of its nearby state parks, its proximity to the center city ten miles away, its excellent choices in reasonably priced housing and property, and its low taxes.

The town officials and the local Board of Education were mindful of the need for a strict budget in order to preserve the modest property tax which was so appealing to community residents. The Board of Education was concerned that special education expenditures had increased dramatically during the past five years, in part because families with special-needs children had moved to the community knowing that it had a good reputation for providing required programs and services.

Consequently, requests both for positions and for additional services in special education were being scrutinized, with an emphasis on providing as many special services as possible in the context of the mainstream classroom, using a consultation model. This concept presented particular challenges for the director of pupil services and the special education staff, who had to deal with an increasing caseload size, and for the classroom teachers, who were expected to accommodate a greater number of children with special needs in their classes.

The School

Located in a beautiful new school building, Kennedy was the only middle school for grades 5–8 in the town. Fifth and sixth grades were self-contained, although the teachers often collaborated for various presentations and projects. The upper grades were departmentalized.

There was a strong sense of family in the school promoted by frequent assemblies and theme days in the school. Through a mentor program, eighth graders tutored lower grade children and gave other special assistance. The principal took pride in carefully overseeing all aspects of the school's operation.

The Teacher

An experienced teacher in her early forties, Christina Ray had taught for twelve years. She returned to teaching seven years ago when her younger child turned five, and she felt she could attend to both professional and maternal duties. Christina was a nurturing, caring teacher who was low-key and positive with her students.

In many ways, Christina was considered to be a traditional teacher: neat rows of desks, tidy work, organization, and quiet were generally the hallmarks of her room. However, Christina also enjoyed introducing unusual projects or materials to explore various curriculum topics in social studies, math, and science. She had a rare ability to understand each child's point of view and feelings, and worked to match teaching experiences to each child's needs as much as possible within the context of the classroom.

Perhaps these concerns for individualization and innovation came from Christina's own parental experience; her older child had been born with a birth defect. Although the specific genetic cause had not been diagnosed until her son was seven years old, from infancy he had exhibited severe developmental problems in communication, learning, and social and emotional growth. He also had a seizure disorder. Christina had frequently been on the other side of the special education issue, fighting for special services and placements that she hoped would make a positive change for her child.

Christina had a cordial relationship with her colleagues at Kennedy Middle School and was a volunteer for many extracurricular activities. Although her principal and most of her co-workers knew of her own personal difficulties, she generally kept her private life separate from her professional life. Keeping them separate was made easier since she was a resident of another town and her children did not attend Lovell's schools.

Matt's Adjustment to Fifth Grade

By October, Matt was a frequent participant in classroom discussions, which affected the progress of those discussions. Matt typically repeated or prolonged the beginning sounds or syllables of sentences, often tripped up on other words which followed, and demonstrated "blocks" similar to what had happened in September. Even his name was difficult for him to produce. When asked, he would generally reply, "MMMMMatt AAAAndrews." Whenever the class was actively involved sharing information, Matt's participation either slowed things down or stopped them dead. Christina noticed that the children did not approach Matt for conversations; he was left out at the lunch table, and no one asked for Matt as a partner in class study assignments.

One day when she was assigned to recess, Christina observed a group of the boys playing kickball. Matt had run up to join them, and there appeared to be some quarrelling. She then heard Paul, who often was difficult to manage, yelling, "We don't need the Porky Pig soundalike messing up our game!" Christina removed Paul from the game and had him sit the rest of the time out for breaking the rule of "good friend" behavior. Rather than continuing the game with Matt as a participant, however, the boys terminated their play and went off in different directions.

As the month of October went by, Matt's classmates continued to avoid him. Christina overheard several of the girls in class discuss a Halloween party which was being held in the school gym on Halloween night. The girls were making a list of the boys whom they wanted to ask to join the group that night. Alexandra asked, "What about Matt? He's cute."

"No way—he's such a dumb jerk! And he probably won't even be able to talk straight!" exclaimed Sandy, who was the "leader" of the girls.

Matt became much more self-conscious of his speech during class. He flushed, cleared his throat, and took deep breaths when preparing to speak. To Christina's distress, Matt also exhibited his blocking behavior more frequently. All these behaviors accentuated his differentness and perpetuated a cycle of rejection from many of the other children.

Of equal concern to Christina was the effect that all this was having on Matt's schoolwork. Part of the grade allotted for spelling, geography bees, and dramatic readings was based on quickness and accuracy of verbal output. When Matt repeated syllables or words, some of the children complained that Matt was using a ploy to give himself another chance—something the other kids didn't have. How could she be fair to everyone but still attend to this child's particular needs in the context of the classroom, Christina wondered.

Christina frequently pondered the differences among children in her class, particularly those who exhibited academic or behavioral difficulties. Now, with Matt in her class, she analyzed her reactions to him. Did his overall challenges seem so mild to her that she believed he could overcome them himself? Did Matt's behavior sometimes remind her of her own son's seizures and lack of control so that she overreacted to it?

Now that it was obvious to Christina that Matt stuttered, she approached the speech-language pathologist who worked at Kennedy Middle School for information and advice. Mrs. Ruby was a dynamic woman who often seemed harried. Of the approximately 1,200 children in the school, she provided direct speech-language therapy to fifty-eight, both in groups and individually. In addition, she evaluated children who were referred and was responsible for triennial review evaluations. Mrs. Ruby also functioned as a consultant to teachers and other specialists in the school, and, like other teachers, was in contact with families of children she saw.

When told about Matt, she recalled:

> Last June, I received the list of children PPT'd for speech-language services who were moving to the middle school so that I could begin to plan my caseload for this year. I remember that Matt's name was on the transfer list of kids who had been referred for therapy at the elementary school. Services weren't recommended for Matt because his speech difference was not affecting his academic performance. He received A and B grades through the fourth grade. How's he doing now?

Christina sighed and responded, "I'm not sure if what I'm observing is just Matt's temporary adjustment to fifth grade, or if this is his typical behavior. I also don't know what his first marking period grades will be like."

"Well, if you need me to observe him in class or the lunchroom, let me know," Mrs. Ruby said, and waved as she hurried to her next group of students.

The Civics Project

Marc Davis arrived with the remainder of the recording equipment, including monitors, hooker cables, and recorders. "Well, I guess this TV broadcast gives the whole project a new dimension!" smiled Marc as he began hooking things up to assess their placement in the room.

"Marc, I need your help on a filming and editing problem," Christina replied. "Is there any way to temporarily block out a speaker or pass over his part so that any problems that appear could be removed during taping?"

Marc frowned slightly. "What's up, Christina? This kind of issue never came up before."

Christina explained Matt's speech problem and her immediate concern about how to set things up for the civics project. Although children were encouraged to select the roles which interested them, and Matt had really wanted to be mayor or town manager, Christina had managed to redirect him to a role which required less speaking. She wondered how she could best prepare him to fulfill even this assignment. How could she minimize his self-consciousness and avoid the overflow effect his fumbling speech might have on the other children? If her civics project collapsed on television, how could she avoid the embarrassment to Matt, as well as to the principal, other school personnel, the class, and herself?

Marc nodded in understanding. "You're trying to figure out how Matt can do his part without losing face or messing up the whole presentation."

Christina sighed, "I've got to think of how to get Matt through this project."

Silently, Christina determined to pin Matt's parents down to an appointment date for a conference. She had tried a few times earlier to arrange a conference, but it had been difficult to find a mutually agreeable time. Once the project was over, there would be time to thoroughly discuss Matt's stuttering.

Although the civics project was the immediate problem, Christina was even more concerned about how Matt's stuttering was affecting crucial aspects of his life: his relationships with his peers and his academic performance.

Advance Study Questions

1. What problem(s) does Christina face in this case?

2. How did this situation develop? What are the underlying issues?

3. How do you think the problem(s) appear to Matt?

4. What immediate actions, if any, should Christina take with regard to the civics project? What long-term actions, if any, should Christina take to help Matt?

CASE 18

Pandora's Box

Susan Dimond Block with Judith B. Buzzell

CHARACTERS

Teacher: Ann Sorkin
Students: Monique Edwards
Linda

Part A

The Introduction

Ann Sorkin was in her third year teaching at City School, an alternative public school for at-risk teenagers. As she was walking toward her door, the guidance counselor stopped her to introduce a new student.

"Ms. Sorkin, this is Monique Edwards. She's just come from Bates High School and will be in your homeroom and health class."

"Hello, Monique. I'm Ms. Sorkin, your liaison teacher. Have a seat anywhere in the room. Class will be starting soon."

The counselor moved down the hall leaving Monique in Ann's charge. "It must be hard," thought Ann, "coming here in December. I wonder why she was referred now." Turning around to face Monique, Ann smiled and put her hand on Monique's shoulder to encourage her into the room.

Monique snapped back and lifted her arms. "Keep your hands off me, lady, and get out of my face."

The Students

Teenagers who couldn't "make it" in regular high schools because of behavioral problems or high absenteeism were sent to City School. Some also came from detention centers, group homes, or special programs. The "last hope" in the school system, it was believed that if you couldn't make it at City School, you wouldn't make it anywhere. The goal was for students to improve their behavior and attendance enough to return to their referring schools the following year.

City School had a student population of seventy-five predominantly African-American and Hispanic males. Teenagers of all ages were grouped together in ungraded classes, and SEM/LD (socially and emotionally maladjusted and learning disabled) and regular education students were placed together as well. In many cases, academic and behavioral approaches were individualized.

Typical City School adolescents disliked authority figures and mistrusted most adults. They were aggressively outspoken, defiant, and argumentative. On the other hand, some students started school cautiously, quietly surveying everything and everyone. Occasionally, a student was friendly. City School had a reputation for handling the "bad" kids, and few teenagers wanted this type of "sentence." Yet, in time, most students learned to love the school and regard the teachers as a second family, and in some cases, their only family.

The City

Longview had a population of approximately 170,000, including a large minority population and varied ethnic groups. Over the years, it had become one of the poorest cities in the nation. Once a thriving industrial town, its unemployment rate had grown to 15 percent as the factories closed down and moved to the suburbs. The only remaining financial boost to the city was a major university with its many employees and students. Other than that, the city, like so many others, had become a ready marketplace for drug dealers who, unfortunately, were the role models for many students at City School. They had the "fly" (good) outfits, BMW cars, gold jewelry, and "juice" (power) with the girls.

The School

To combat that influence, City School provided a six-hour safety net. Students were not permitted to wear gold jewelry or to carry headsets, boom boxes, beepers or wads of cash.

Located in one of the less kempt parts of town, City School had a men's shelter on one side and housing projects on the other. Supplies were short, and funding close to nonexistent. Started only four years ago, City School had had to prove its worth to the superintendent and the Board of Education.

The school had small classes, with an eight to one student-teacher ratio. Students received both counseling and academic help for ten months a year. For some, the breakfast and lunch served at school were their only meals. And for most, it was the one place they heard friendly and reassuring comments, such as "How are you?" "What's happening?" "Let's talk," "Take it easy," and "It'll be all right."

The students had five major subjects, shop, and a modified physical education program at a local club. A normal day went from 8:00 A.M. until 2:00

P.M., with a half hour for lunch. Academic subjects were held before noon, and shop, recreation, and enrichment (art, music, group games, cooking) were offered in the afternoon.

Since City School's primary purpose was to improve behavior, the entire program was built around a behavior modification system. Students had to earn daily and weekly points based on appropriate behavior and academic work in each class. There were 200 possible points a week. If students achieved over 160, they could go to "Friday reward" (a movie, bowling, skating, or recreational game). If students misbehaved, they were sent to "time out" to discuss the problem with a trained counselor or social worker. They could also refer themselves to time out before a problem occurred.

Each day, teachers ran a guided group intervention with their homerooms to discuss the students' daily experiences, both positive and negative. The purpose was to help students recognize their inappropriate behavioral patterns, learn to work through a conflict in an appropriate manner, and think of alternatives to acting out verbally or physically.

In a majority of cases, students needed to be at City School for at least a year. Some of them chose to continue there until graduation because they felt protected and nurtured. Others returned to their regular high schools. But for an unfortunate 25 percent, the streets had more appeal. Stealing cars and drug dealing offered more excitement and immediate rewards. Chronically absent, these students were dropped from the rolls and removed from the school system once they turned sixteen.

Monique Edwards

"Keep your hands off me, lady, and get out of my face," snapped Monique.

"Good grief," thought Ann. "What have I inherited? This girl is twice my size, and she means business. How am I ever going to reach her?"

Monique Edwards, age fifteen, had earned her way into City School through violent behavior. Looking like a "Wanted by the FBI" poster at the post office, she was huge and had a scar across her face. She didn't smile, and her only comments were nasty remarks and grunts. She looked well worn for her young years. Although she was of average academic ability and had no pronounced learning problems, former teachers spoke only negatively about her. Now, Ann was assigned to Monique as her liaison teacher for the rest of the year. Ann felt like she had met her Waterloo—Monique's goal in life seemed to be suspension or expulsion.

The Teacher: Ann Sorkin

Ann Sorkin loved being part of the staff at City School because of the knowledgeable veterans, a few exciting rookies, and an excellent support staff.

She was now in her third year at the school. After years of teaching health at a university, running her own business in marketing, and authoring two textbooks, she missed teaching children. Ann knew she needed to grow again and wanted the challenge of working with at-risk adolescents. She took the job because she could design her own health curriculum emphasizing substance abuse, nutrition, mental health, and problem solving, with a little marketing thrown in to liven up the class.

Ann identified with her hopeful, idealistic colleagues who treated their work like a mission. She learned from them, developing new strategies. For example, she learned not to take students' behavior or problems personally, and she developed better listening skills.

Ann decorated her room like a home, with a braided rug in the center of the floor, plants hanging from windows, brightly colored posters on the walls, and chairs in a circle. She made it into a safe place where kids could be comfortable. They learned to trust Ann, and she liked that. There was mutual respect.

Although Ann had earned the trust of many difficult students, she wondered whether she would be able to develop a relationship with Monique. There were few details in Monique's file about her personal life but volumes on her attitude, violent behavior, and poor peer and teacher relationships at other schools (she had been to three different schools in three years).

Reading her files was like reading about Dr. Jekyll and Mr. Hyde. Some female teachers found her cooperative and bright; male teachers generally wrote negative comments. "Aha!" thought Ann. "I wonder if there's a connection somewhere. At least being female is in my favor." A basic bond between Monique and Ann or another adult was likely to be the foundation for Monique's positive development. As Monique's liaison teacher, Ann hoped to be the change agent that Monique so desperately needed.

Initial Efforts

For weeks, no one could approach Monique. She was defiant, unruly, and frequently absent. Even her peers shied away, which was unusual, as most of the students became friends rather quickly. Ann knew that meeting Monique head-on in conflict would only aggravate the problems and add fuel to an already inflamed situation. Trying to reason with her was useless. Asking Monique to do errands or be a leader was a waste of time; such requests gave Monique too much power, and she was a master of manipulation.

In the beginning, Ann tried to ignore Monique when she was nasty and respond only when she behaved appropriately. When Monique cursed, baited, or harassed her, Ann followed a wise mentor's advice: "Keep doing what you were doing before you were interrupted." She would simply and firmly state, "Unacceptable behavior isn't an option," an assertion that few students continued to challenge. She also used favorite sayings like "Watch my lips,"

"Read my mind," "What part of 'no' don't you understand?" "I'm the mother, that's why," and "Excuuuuse me!" The lines were simple, direct, humorous, and generally effective, except with Monique.

Linda

Fortunately, two years ago, Ann had taught a student named Linda who turned out to be Monique's "home girl" (friend). At that time, Linda had been sent to City School from a drug rehabilitation center and was placed purposely in Ann's homeroom because Ann had extensive experience with recovering substance abusers and had volunteered weekly at a local drug rehabilitation center. Ann and Linda hit it off immediately and stayed in close contact even after Linda graduated.

During one of Linda's recent visits to her former school, Ann had mentioned her concerns about Monique, hoping Linda might know Monique from their neighborhood. Luckily Linda did, and Ann asked for a favor. "Would you please talk to Monique—ask her to 'chill out' (calm down) and trust me?" Ann had run out of ideas and resources; this was her last resort.

The following week, Monique came to school. She approached Ann after class and gruffly commented, "You know my home girl, Linda." Ann knew that a connection finally had been made; there was a light at the end of the tunnel.

Ann's and Monique's Relationship Develops

As the months passed, Monique started to joke around and occasionally even smile. Every once in a while, she put her arm around Ann's shoulder, and Ann could now return the gesture.

When Ann had first come to City School, she had no idea about the unspoken boundaries between teacher and student. For instance, one *never* touched a student or asked personal questions unless the overture was first initiated by a student. It might take weeks or months before a teacher was permitted these privileges.

One strategy for developing rapport with students was to take them away from school on miniwalks to the grocery store, a convenience store, the local bakery, an art gallery, the library, and museums. Once the students could handle small trips, they learned to travel on the bus for more distant field trips. Ann had a twofold purpose in mind: first, to see and get to know a different side of students' personalities away from school, and second, to help them develop acceptable social skills. In a different environment, many students would open up, just a little.

On these trips, Monique became more relaxed and would talk excitedly about friends at home. She had even shared a bag of potato chips with Ann on a recent excursion in May. What appeared to be so simple, like sharing food, was indeed a major breakthrough after six months.

Shortly after the chip-sharing episode, Monique came to school and tossed a pen set on Ann's desk. "Got this from my uncle. Take it. If you take the cover off, it makes a stand," said Monique. Ann had to suppress her joy because she didn't want to "stick Monique out" (embarrass her). At City School, it was the little things that counted because they could lead to bigger successes.

The Dilemma—The End of May

Ann's class was starting a unit on substance abuse that included decision-making and problem-solving skills. That day, there were only three students in her third period class. Half the staff and students were home sick with a virus.

She read the students a story dealing with a college freshman who was failing. The girl was scared to tell her parents about her poor grades because good grades were so important to them. Instead she wrote them a lengthy letter, fabricating a tale about getting caught in a fire, going to the hospital for treatment, meeting the man who rescued her from the fire, having intercourse with him, and consequently, becoming pregnant. At the conclusion of the letter, the freshman told her parents that all this was actually a lie, but she was really getting a *D* in History and an *F* in Biology. She hoped her parents would put her low grades in the proper perspective in light of possible worse problems.

The class listened intently. They were surprised by the twist at the end of the letter. When Ann asked for feedback, the responses ranged from "It's not right to do that to her mom" to "Why would she do that?" The students got into a lively dialogue about the risks of telling the truth and the consequences of lying. They felt trust was the major factor in how much one divulges.

Then, from the side of the room, Monique quietly said, "I told the truth, and my mother called me a liar."

Ann casually asked, "About what?"

Monique dropped her head and looked down. She was barely audible. "That my stepfather came to me in the night. My mother says I'm making it up, and I'd better not say nothing, or she'll get rid of me. I slashed her tires and smashed her windshield. I messed up in school real bad."

Ann felt her stomach churn. Swallowing hard, she asked Monique, "Is that why you're here?"

"Yes," said Monique. "I hate them!"

The room became so still that Ann could hear her heart beating. Monique's eyes were full of rage and despair.

Ann's mind was racing as she thought, "Now what? How can I meet my legal responsibility to report this apparent abuse without breaking the trust I worked so hard to establish with Monique? No textbook ever prepared me for this."

Advance Study Questions

1. What is the nature of Ann Sorkin's dilemma?

2. What are some underlying issues in this case?

3. What steps did Ms. Sorkin take to develop a trusting relationship with Monique?

4. If you were Ms. Sorkin, what would you do now?

Additional Readings

Dryfoos, J. (1990). *Adolescents at risk: Prevalence and prevention.* New York: Oxford University Press.

Esbensen, F. A., & Huizanga, D. (1991). Juvenile victimization and delinquency. *Youth and Society, 23*(2), 202-28.

Kempe, R. S., & Kempe, C. H. (1984). *The common secret: Sexual abuse of children and adolescents.* New York: W. H. Freeman.

Maag, J. W., & Howell, K. W. (1991). Serving troubled youth in a troubled society. *Exceptional Children. 58*(1), 74-76.

Morgan, D., & Jenson, W. (1988). *Teaching behaviorally disordered students: Preferred practices.* Columbus, OH: Merrill Publishing.

Sandberg, D. N. (1987). *Chronic acting-out students and child abuse: A handbook for intervention.* Lexington, MA: Lexington Books.

Shea, T. M., & Bauer, A. M. (1987). Secondary school students with behavior disorders. In *Teaching children and youth with behavior disorders* (pp. 327-352). Englewood Cliffs, NJ: Prentice-Hall.

Thompson, V. (1987). Washoe High School: An alternative system for dropouts. In R. B. Rutherford, C. M. Nelson, & S. R. Forness, (Eds.). *Severe behavior disorders of children and youth* (pp. 186-195). Boston: Little, Brown.

CASE 19

The Reluctant Freshman

Robert Piazza and Linda Pica

CHARACTERS

Student: Jodi Fuller
Jodi's parents: Mr. and Mrs. Fuller
Resource teacher: Richard Hernandez
History teacher: Mr. Higgins

Part A

A Late Summer Day

It was a scorching late August day. Mr. Richard Hernandez, a high school learning disability resource teacher, enjoyed the cool air-conditioned supermarket as he waited patiently for the deli clerk to finish slicing his cold meat order. Walking toward him were Mr. and Mrs. Fuller, parents of an incoming freshman named Jodi. Jodi was scheduled to be in Mr. Hernandez's resource room for one period a day for the upcoming year. Since they lived in the same town, Mr. Hernandez and the Fullers had met a number of times through involvement in community and church activities. After exchanging the usual pleasantries, Mrs. Fuller lingered to talk with Mr. Hernandez as Mr. Fuller navigated his cart toward the frozen food aisle.

"Actually, Mr. Hernandez, I'm glad I met you today. I'm really worried about Jodi going to the high school. So's she. You know, they held her Planning and Placement Team (PPT) meeting early in the spring, and I felt somebody from the high school should have been there. I don't think she's going to make it." A look of serious concern was etched on Mrs. Fuller's face.

Mrs. Fuller continued, explaining that although Jodi's reading and math scores had increased dramatically over the past few years, this improvement did not seem to be translating to better grades. She indicated that the past two years had been a tremendous struggle for Jodi and the rest of the family.

Sensing that the conversation would be too lengthy and inappropriate for the delicatessen counter, Mr. Hernandez offered to call Mrs. Fuller the next day.

The Child

On the way home from the supermarket, Mr. Hernandez stopped at the high school to pick up Jodi's confidential school folder. That evening he perused her records.

Jodi was referred for academic services when she was in the second grade. At that time, she was reading at a preprimer level and also struggling in other subjects. She began seeing the learning disability resource teacher one hour a day. For the next three years, she received remedial instruction in this program. A triennial review in the fifth grade found that Jodi was then achieving at a fourth grade level in all academic subjects. Her teachers reported that Jodi "works very hard, but has difficulty with following directions and with concepts, names, places, and so on," "never completes classwork on time, homework often late or incomplete," "seems distractible, socializes too much, but a great kid," "is pleasant and cooperative, but often seems lost," and "wants to succeed very badly, at times very frustrated." At the review, the PPT felt that Jodi should continue receiving remedial assistance at the middle school for her learning disabilities. Throughout her three-year middle school career, Jodi attended the resource program for one period a day (46 minutes). Basic remedial instruction in reading and math formed the bulk of this program.

A complete diagnostic assessment was performed in the spring of the previous year (eighth grade). Jodi's full-scale IQ placed her within the average range of intelligence. However, her verbal skills were found significantly lower than her performance skills. Other testing by the speech and language clinician confirmed a language-processing deficit. Norm-referenced testing of academic skills revealed the following:

Peabody Individual Achievement Test

- *Reading Recognition:* 9.2 grade equivalency score
- *Reading Comprehension:* 6.9 grade equivalency score
- *Spelling:* 7.9 grade equivalency score
- *Math:* 8.3 grade equivalency score
- *General Information:* 7.0 grade equivalency score

Data on Jodi's writing skills were limited, only indicating that she required assistance in organization of material and proofreading. The eighth grade resource teacher had also noted that although Jodi's word recognition skills were strong, a weakness was apparent in reading, especially in the areas of vocabulary and inference skills.

The schedule for Jodi's freshman year included remedial math, physical education, low-track levels of English, history, science, and health, and resource services for one period a day. Three major goals were listed on Jodi's Individualized Educational Program (IEP):

1. To improve reading comprehension skills.
2. To improve writing skills.
3. To increase vocabulary skills.

The School System

Amberville was a midsize town struggling with the economic realities of the current recessionary period in the northeastern section of the United States. Vocal taxpayer groups had been defeating education budgets over the last several years. Coupled with reduced funding from the state government, this town had cut programs and staff to legally mandated limits.

Special education services were currently in the process of being redefined. Many of the changes being proposed and enacted were philosophically supported by the Regular Education Initiative (REI). Advocates of this initiative wanted more exceptional children to receive their education within regular education classrooms. Not all programs and schools within the system were fully committed to the collaborative model suggested by the REI, however. This had led to considerable problems when students moved from one school in the system to another.

Amberville had three K–5 elementary schools, one middle school (grades 6–8), and one high school. In the middle school program, students were grouped in classes with others of differing abilities. A rotating daily schedule was used. Students with learning disabilities were limited to direct services in a resource program that pulled them out of one of their regular classes.

In contrast, the high school offered homogeneously grouped academic courses in a fixed schedule, eight-period day. Students with learning disabilities were not pulled out of regular content classes. Instead, they received instruction in the resource room when other students were in a study hall or an elective class.

Middle school special education teachers did not consult with regular classroom teachers to help them develop strategies to modify their curriculum for students with special needs. Their focus was on working directly with identified special education students. However, high school special education teachers did have time within their schedules for consultation and collaboration with regular education teachers, although there was no clearly defined model for these activities.

The Next Day—The Phone Call

On the phone the next day, Mrs. Fuller expressed her concerns:

> Those courses my daughter took last year were much too hard. She couldn't even understand her books, let alone some of the words her teachers were

> using. When she read, she just read words; there was no understanding of what was on the page. She didn't know what half the words meant. She has a hard time remembering things, and when her teachers were lecturing, she said she didn't know what to write down in her notebook. That notebook was a complete mess. There were more doodles in it than anything else.

Mr. Hernandez asked what went on in the resource room. Mrs. Fuller replied that the resource teacher spent most of her time reteaching what Jodi was supposed to learn in her mainstream classes. "Most of her teachers were nice people, but they certainly didn't know what to do with a learning disabled child."

Jodi's mother continued to express her apprehension about the future high school experience. She felt the stress of having a full load of classes and more teachers to contend with would put her daughter on a roller coaster ride all year. She revealed that Jodi already thought she was dumb and had poor self-esteem and confidence. "Mr. Hernandez, I don't want to see her so down on herself. I don't want another year like last year."

Mr. Hernandez offered words of genuine concern about Jodi's past school experiences. He suggested that they meet the second week of school to discuss Jodi's program. Mrs. Fuller agreed.

As he hung up the phone, Mr. Hernandez wondered how much Mrs. Fuller's anxiety was affecting Jodi. But, also, he knew things needed to change and felt a good starting place would be Jodi's IEP. He sat down at his desk in his study at home and outlined an assessment plan for Jodi during the first week of school.

Advance Study Questions

1. What problem(s) does Mr. Hernandez encounter in this case? When did all these problems actually begin?

2. What underlying dilemmas does the resource teacher face?

3. Describe the nature of Jodi's learning problems.

4. How should Mr. Hernandez assess Jodi? What type of diagnostic instruments should be used?

CHARACTERS

Teacher: Louise Feldman
Student: Jennifer
Jennifer's boyfriend: George
Social worker: Mrs. Perez

Part A

Mrs. Feldman's teen parenting class was just beginning. As she was rifling through her papers, collecting handouts to distribute on effective discipline techniques with toddlers, Jennifer slowly approached her. For the past two months, Jennifer, a ninth grader, had been hanging out in her class, and Mrs. Feldman had been wondering why.

Though not a teen parent herself, Jennifer listened intently to others' stories of balancing school and motherhood, worries about the future, and child-rearing concerns. But this time, she did not stay for class. When Mrs. Feldman looked up and warmly greeted her, Jennifer nodded and handed her teacher a letter. "Wait to read this after school, and don't tell anybody," Jennifer said with an ominous tone of voice.

The School and City

Martin Van Buren High School was located in Crampton, a city of approximately 140,000. Originally known for its tool and die trade and its garment industries, the city's manufacturing base had eroded, and there was a high rate of unemployment. In the past twenty years, the city had an increase in minority groups, particularly African-American and Hispanic.

The poverty of many of the city's residents was in stark contrast to the wealth of the residents in the surrounding "Gold Coast" suburban towns. Thirty percent of Crampton's families lived below the poverty level. While some suburbs might spend as much as $10,400 per year per pupil on schooling, Crampton spent only $6,500. State government initiatives and court cases had reduced this unequal funding of schools but had not eliminated it.

Still, the city's schools worked hard to create a sanctuary for their students amid the harsh urban ills that plagued the city: homelessness, AIDS, teen pregnancy, drug addiction, gang wars, and violent deaths. A comprehensive high school, Van Buren High had about 1,200 students, approximately one-third African-American, one-third Hispanic, and one-third Caucasian. The students' families were from a range of income levels, and the curricular offerings were designed to meet the varying needs of the students. There were remedial courses to improve the skills of the poorer students, and special counseling and peer tutoring programs to encourage and motivate them. The most able students took advanced placement courses or courses at one of the universities in the city. Extended day programs in gospel singing, tennis, chess, computers, and math attracted all students to learning and provided wholesome after-school experiences.

There also was a school-based health clinic run by a local community health clinic. Staffed by pediatricians, nurse practitioners, and a social worker, it was open every morning and offered students health services like routine checkups, nutrition information, inoculations, and pregnancy testing. The clinic could give birth control advice but not contraceptives. Counseling was available for depression and other mental health problems. Last year, one-third to one-half of the students had used the clinic's services.

Despite its efforts, the school struggled with a serious attendance problem. Each day, about 150 students were absent, many of them unofficial dropouts. The city's overall annual dropout rate was 15 percent.

The Teacher and the Class

Louise Feldman had not taken the typical path to becoming a high school teacher. She had studied nursing as an undergraduate and, after graduation, worked part-time in a community health clinic. Her family had lived in both east and west coast university towns while her husband was pursuing his doctorate. She focused primarily on raising their three children when they were young.

Then she took a part-time position as a researcher in the psychology department of one of Crampton's universities. Her project compared the academic standing of teenage parents before they had become pregnant with their academic performance after they delivered their babies. Nineteen percent of the babies in the city were born to teenage mothers, and there were several programs which targeted teen parents.

Louise's research took her into the schools, and she came to know the director of the Ernestine Johnson School, a public school specifically for pregnant teenagers. She also became friendly with the teachers of the parenting programs at Van Buren and the city's other high schools. The usual pattern was that a pregnant teenager would leave Van Buren to continue her education at the Ernestine Johnson School. Then, after her baby was born, she would return to Van Buren to complete high school. The parenting program at Van Buren would provide follow-up support.

When an opening occurred in Van Buren's program, Louise applied and was offered the position. She had started working part-time on her teaching certificate a few years before and had just become certified. Although she was an excellent researcher, Louise liked working directly with people even more, and she grabbed the opportunity. Now, at age fifty, she had been working at this job for ten years and loved it. About five years ago, she had begun a graduate program in social work and was completing this part-time. Her principal had once said, "You've got to be a damn social worker in this job," and Louise agreed.

Louise's class was clearly a haven for kids. Louise was a roundish woman, about 5 feet 6 inches tall, whose soft, reassuring voice coaxed students to participate in discussions. The students were seated in a circle, to allow for close communication. The room was richly decorated. There was a calendar of exemplary black women and a poster challenging students to recognize that "Education is a journey not a destination." There were photographs of past and present students and their babies. A poster of a sixteen-year-old teenager and his baby was titled, "Teen Parenthood. Think Before You Act." Another poster featured a teen mother saying, "I didn't know I had AIDS . . . . not until my baby was born with it."

In the parenting class, Louise had two goals. One was to provide her teen parents with the skills and knowledge they needed to be good parents. She taught them principles of child development such as why babies cry, how babies develop language, and how to encourage a toddler's growing independence.

Her other goal was to provide nurturance and emotional support to the teen mothers themselves so that they would develop the motivation and perserverance to stay in school despite the many demands on them. She explained:

> These kids are on an emotional roller coaster. They have to contend with the shock and anger over the pregnancy as well as confusion. In my class, the girls have formed a support group. When one feels down, the others and I will encourage her not to give up.
>
> They're dealing with the pressure to grow up immediately and take on adult responsibilities. Ironically, in some ways, city kids are too adult. For whatever reasons, their parents may not provide the basic care, guidance, and role models that their children need. There are too many kids who end up parenting themselves, so they've lost the ability to be children. While I don't believe there is any one typical teen parent or any single cause for teen pregnancy, one of the underlying reasons may be this deprivation of parenting. Teen parents hope to make a better family than the one they're in.

In educating her students and others, Louise energetically tried to counter the image that teen mothers are losers who drop out of school and go on welfare. In a recent school newspaper article on her program, she explained, "My students work hard and take pride in the fact that they stay in school. I call them working parents—their job is to be in school."

Louise had a reputation for going out of her way for kids. She was known to give students who had trouble getting to school on time a wake-up call in the morning. Because of transportation problems her kids faced and lack of experience in negotiating the system, she had picked kids up on the Saturday mornings when the SATs (college entrance exams) were administered and driven them to the test site at the private school several miles and a world away from most of their homes.

Louise had the regular load of five courses to teach—two teen parenting classes, one ninth grade study skills class, one peer leadership class, and one tenth grade violence prevention class. Although most teachers were assigned a collateral assignment, such as hall or cafeteria duty, she was not. She assumed it was because her principal knew she used every available minute to counsel students. Still, there was never enough time. Kids were drawn to Louise like a magnet. They would come to visit between classes or instead of going to lunch.

Jennifer

When Jennifer was a thirteen-year-old freshman, she was assigned to Louise's required study skills class. The students ranged from students with learning disabilities and those who were slower learners to those who would be the top students in the class. Louise worked to make this motley crew into a cohesive group. Through relaxed discussions, she tried to develop camaraderie and trust among the students so that they would open up and share their ideas and feelings.

After class, students would stick around and chat with each other, and Jennifer began to make friends. Pretty and sociable, with good academic skills, she made intelligent contributions to class discussions. She chose equally capable students as friends.

Jennifer came from a middle-class family. Her father was a police officer. Her mother had attended business school and worked as an accountant at a local university. The youngest of four children, Jennifer had two older sisters and a brother. The older children were all successful students, and she seemed to be following in their footsteps. She had loved elementary and junior high school. Now, her favorite subjects were English and history.

Jennifer soon started to attend Louise's teen parenting class, as well as the study skills class. After her lunch, she sat in on the class, mostly listening. Louise hoped that she was just seeking sex education and information about child rearing.

After Jennifer had attended for six weeks, the other students became suspicious. They took her aside and challenged her, asking if she were pregnant. Jennifer claimed that she was not. When they told Louise, she asked, "Why do you think she's pregnant?" and they responded, "Because we know what her boyfriend is like." They considered him a spoiled, rich kid who had transferred to Van Buren High after attending a fancy private school. He had a horse and was into cars and clothes. They saw him as just the kind of smooth-talking, flashy kid who could talk a naive thirteen-year-old into having sex.

They knew about the concept of denial from the parenting class and suspected that Jennifer was denying the fact of the pregnancy to herself. The course started with a discussion of pregnancy and delivery. Louise encouraged open exchange by asking, "When did you find out you were pregnant? How did you feel? Who did you share this information with? Who helped you with the delivery? What were the most positive and negative aspects of the experience?"

Rather quickly, many students admitted that they didn't acknowledge they were pregnant until late in the pregnancy. "I didn't tell anybody until I was six months," one student commented. Louise probed the answer with a question like, "How did your mother or father react?"

Louise would explain that when people are having trouble facing or dealing with something, they often deny it and refuse to acknowledge the problem. She hoped to help her students to be more conscious of their conflicts, so that they would have greater control over their behavior. Perhaps this awareness would help to prevent the pattern of teens having several unwanted pregnancies. "I want them to consciously choose when to have a second child," she often said.

Louise noticed that Jennifer was becoming more and more attached to her. She'd find a way to stop by to see Louise every day. In her journal required for the study skills class, Jennifer had begun to write to Louise as if she were a friend. Most students' journal entries were brief, a few lines often describing some positive experience, or some stress such as turmoil at home and distress with family. Jennifer's entries became longer, and although there were few specific details, she described feeling upset in a general way.

Then, she started complaining that she felt sick. She talked about food a lot and whether she was gaining or losing weight. Although she was obviously upset, she never explained why. Louise wondered if she had anorexia, an eating disorder in which people diet excessively and sometimes even stop eating. Since loose, baggy clothes were in fashion, there was no way to tell if Jennifer had been losing—or gaining—weight.

The Letter—January

When Jennifer abruptly handed her the letter, Louise had been surprised by her sudden entrance and departure from her teen parenting class. Usually, Jennifer stayed around for awhile and chatted with her teacher and the other students. And she was worried about Jennifer's terse warning, "Wait to read this after school, and don't tell anybody." She sensed that whatever was in the letter was too important to delay until later. Knowing that she would see Jennifer next period in her study skills class, she tore open the envelope and began to read:

> *Dear Mrs. Feldman:*
>
> *You're the only friend I can really talk to and share this with. I can't tell anyone else. I found out I'm pregnant, and I don't know what to do. I'm really scared. Life just doesn't seem worth living anymore. Ending my life seems like the only way out of this, but please don't tell anyone else. I trust you.*
>
> *Love, Jennifer*

Advance Study Questions

1. What is Mrs. Feldman's dilemma?
2. What are some underlying issues in this case?
3. How did this situation develop?
4. If you were Mrs. Feldman, what action(s), if any, would you take?

CASE 21

The Case of Competition

Linda Powell

CHARACTERS

Teacher: Chelsea Hart
Principal: Mr. Bryne
Student: Kevin Sims

Part A

The Principal's Request

It had been the longest opening week of school Mrs. Hart could remember. Her head was filled with a list of things to do: books to unpack, stamp, and distribute; meetings to attend; mounds of paperwork and mail to sort through, not to mention about sixty new students to get to know. As she headed into the office, the principal, Mr. Bryne, appeared in his doorway.

"Mrs. Hart—you're just the person I wanted to see."

He walked out into the hallway slowly and leaned back against the wall. His expression was serious, and he paused, as if collecting his thoughts, before speaking again. Looking down at the floor, he said he had a request.

"Kevin Sims wants to be in your class."

Chelsea Hart stared at Mr. Bryne in disbelief. "Does he understand what that means? He must be prepared to work, and he must realize that I won't tolerate disruption."

Mr. Bryne explained that Kevin Sims had sought him out that day to ask for a transfer into her third period Ancient Civilizations class. He said that Kevin had been very serious in the meeting. Kevin failed every subject last year and was repeating history with Mr. McHenry. Kevin insisted that he and Mr. McHenry had a personality conflict, and he wanted to start off the year with someone new. He had heard Mrs. Hart was a good teacher, tough maybe, but she would make him work. Although Kevin was repeating his freshman year, he had convinced Mr. Bryne that he really wanted to learn and that he was ready to work hard. Mr. Bryne hastened to add that Mrs. Hart need not give him an answer until the next day.

Kevin Sims

Driving home that afternoon, Mrs. Hart went over and over in her mind the conversation with Mr. Bryne. Although *he* may have been convinced of Kevin's "seriousness" and desire to "work hard," she found it difficult to relate those words to Kevin Sims. Memories of last year did little to ease her mind. A regular in the after-school detention program she supervised, Kevin was inevitably late and loud. The students' job was to clean the school during detention; Kevin was quite vocal about his opposition to any form of physical labor. While complaining about work he never did, he would grab a broom from another student and taunt the others with his new weapon, or throw a wet sponge at another.

Although Mrs. Hart didn't have Kevin in class last year, faculty meetings were full of discussion about him. He angered and frustrated teachers. Not only did he fail every class, but Kevin disrupted classes in a way that wore teachers down. One teacher allowed him to sleep in her class just so she could teach the rest of her students. Another teacher gave him a pass to leave class every day for the last two weeks of the year so the teacher could review for the final exam with the rest of the class.

Teachers who called Kevin's parents got little or no support. They had referred Kevin to the school Planning and Placement Team (PPT), but he was never assessed.

Mr. Bryne decided to meet with the Sims over the summer, present them with Kevin's report card, and urge them to enroll their son in a school that could better meet his needs. At the first meeting of this school year, when Mr. Bryne announced that Kevin's parents had accepted the proposal to transfer their son, there was an immediate loud cheer by teachers who had worked with Kevin. Mrs. Hart remembered her conflicted feelings; she felt guilty that teachers she worked with and respected behaved this way, yet she was relieved that she would not have to worry about having Kevin in class.

Those feelings did not last long, since three days later, Kevin and his parents were back at school. The other school had less to offer than they imagined and, as disastrous as last year had been, they wanted to give Mrs. Hart's school one more year. Kevin was readmitted to the school, and he reentered many of the same classes he had the previous year.

The School

Soundview High School (SHS) was an inner-city public arts and humanities magnet school. It was housed in an old, former grammar school on one of the busiest streets in Soundview, a midsized New England city.

The school, established in 1975, was one of five high schools (three large comprehensive schools and two smaller "schools of choice") in the city. SHS had an enrollment of about 260 students, of whom 95 percent were African-American, 4 percent Hispanic, and 1 percent Caucasian from primarily lower economic backgrounds. There were approximately 200 females and 60 males in the school. Enrollment was open to all high school students in the city, with the school population determined by a lottery. Most students performed at an average or lower level; many were not highly motivated.

Two-thirds of the staff were Caucasian, and most teachers had been teaching for more than fifteen years. For half a day each week, SHS had the services of a social worker and a school psychologist. Together with the full-time guidance counselor, the school nurse (who was assigned one day per week), and the special education teacher, they made up the Planning and Placement Team (PPT). The team made all decisions about special education or related services for students. The guidance counselor helped students plan their programs and make college choices. The social worker counseled students in crisis. More recently, SHS had added a parenting teacher to the staff to help a growing number of teenage girls who were already mothers or who were currently pregnant.

There was a social development course that taught students social skills. It included units on conflict resolution strategies, AIDS prevention, and drug education. Students were also referred to community programs for help with problems like drug addiction.

While SHS offered a solid four-year academic program, its small, supportive environment (a fifteen to one student/teacher ratio) aimed to encourage and strengthen self-confidence in students. Through participation in arts programming—visual arts, dance, creative writing, music, and drama—students were encouraged to explore new ways to see and express themselves. Three years ago, teachers had worked together to develop courses that shared common themes and identified common goals.

The school had recently formed a partnership with a large area bank. The bank provided financial and personal support to the school for needs the city could not meet, such as transportation and admission tickets to local and statewide cultural exhibits and performances.

The Teacher and Class

This was Chelsea Hart's twentieth year teaching high school in Soundview. For the first ten years, she taught history at one of the large comprehensive high schools. When a small, new "school of choice" opened ten years ago, Mrs. Hart applied for the history position and was chosen by the staff committee. She had been frustrated by her inability to get to know students in the big school and welcomed the opportunity to work with students in a small, friendly environment.

Mrs. Hart had a traditional background, earning her bachelor of science and master's degrees in education from the local state university. For many years, she had been a coordinator and fellow in a prestigious Teachers' Institute run by a private university. At the institute, she identified and researched topics for the courses she taught and wrote new curriculum units, connecting literary and artistic traditions to the historical framework of her courses.

Awarded a Fulbright grant, Mrs. Hart spent a summer studying in East Asia. Along with other travels, this experience enabled her to bring some of the world to her students. Her love of travel and strong belief that students should be actively involved in their education led her to incorporate frequent visits to the many local museums, galleries, exhibits and performances into her lessons. She took great pride in her students who were chosen as student ambassadors to the Soviet Union, China, Africa, and Nicaragua.

Of equal importance was her insistence that students strengthen reading and writing skills. Since most of her students were not strong readers, they usually spent two periods each week reading and discussing ideas in class.

The Ancient Civilizations course Mrs. Hart taught was the heart of the freshman humanities curriculum at Soundview. In this course, students traced the artistic, literary, and technological roots of western civilization by studying developments made by humans from the prehistoric period through the time of the ancient civilizations. In addition, the English, art, creative writing, and history teachers closely collaborated so that students were encouraged to see connections between the four courses. The humanities courses invited students to examine the theme of "self-discovery" and to relate the developments made by the "family of man" to their own lives.

The Class

The third period Ancient Civilizations class met five days a week back to back with the English class. Occasionally, the double period was used for a trip, movie, or other combined activity for English and history. The class was made up of twenty-one, mostly freshmen, students. Attendance was poor, with an average of four or five students absent daily. Mrs. Hart used a variety of teaching strategies, including large and small group discussions, writing assignments, hands-on projects, and films, as well as field trips.

Back to the Decision

As Mrs. Hart was driving home, she mulled over Mr. Bryne's request that she take Kevin into her Ancient Civilizations class. She wondered if she really had a choice. In spite of Kevin's reputation, Mrs. Hart had another, much more nagging concern. Last year had been the toughest in all the nineteen years she had been teaching.

The drug trade, and crimes connected with it, were having devastating effects on the school. There were so few boys in school to begin with, and many had been lost throughout the year. Students and staff went to five funerals last year for young men who had attended her school previously or who were known by many students at the school. Those not killed violently in the streets were in other "institutions."

Mrs. Hart remembered with agony that Friday last year when she lost two of only four boys in one class because each was jailed. Still others were in and out of drug treatment programs. Some of the boys' families sent them to other states because they feared for their safety. Nothing in her teaching experience or life had prepared her for those feelings of loss and failure last year.

Mrs. Hart pulled into her driveway, parked her car in the garage, and sat for a moment. She thought about her teaching these past nineteen years and about her determination to make this year a better one. As she closed the garage door, her decision was made.

"Okay, I'll do it, but he's gonna know what I expect of him." She would work to prevent Kevin Sims from becoming another student who dropped out of school—lost to violence, drugs, or other crimes.

Three Days Later (Kevin's First Day)

Just as the bell rang, Kevin Sims appeared in the classroom doorway. The other students had come in already, and all eyes turned toward the door. He continued to stand there.

"I'm not late. The bell just rung," he announced. "Where am I gonna sit?" he asked as he surveyed the room for familiar faces. Mrs. Hart pointed out a table at which two boys and a girl were seated, and she walked over to explain to Kevin what the class was working on.

Students had just finished a short unit on the prehistoric period. Now, they were working in small groups, pretending to be Cro-Magnon artists and re-creating images they had seen either in a slide show on the Lascaux cave paintings or from their textbook or other resource materials. The shades in the room were down, the lights out to create the atmosphere of the cave. Students were busy tearing edges of the brown paper bags they were using as the walls, and some were collecting containers of the four colors of paint they were going to use. Some were already beginning to sketch; others were still discussing plans for their projects.

Kevin sat down comfortably at his table and began talking with the boys. They all knew each other. "How come you doin' art? I thought this was history," Kevin began. Antonio explained that Mrs. Hart told them they would be doing art projects all year related to the historical periods they were studying and that it would be part of their grade. The other boy, Willie, was beginning to sketch a bull, and he and Monique, the third student at the table, continued to work as Kevin asked more questions.

Mrs. Hart headed toward her desk on the other side of the room to pick up the course description and classroom standards she had placed there for Kevin. As she did, she checked other tables to see if students had the materials they needed. Students were enthusiastic about the opportunity to re-create the world's first known masterpieces, although somewhat skeptical about their ability as artists. The noise level reflected their excitement.

With all groups working well, Mrs. Hart decided to use a few minutes of class time to sit with Kevin and go over her plans, goals, and standards for the year. As she approached his table, sheets in hand, she could see that all eyes at the table were focused on something Kevin had in his hand. His back was to Mrs. Hart, and as he turned toward her, she could see a huge wad of twenty dollar bills. She had come face to face with her "competition." The streets offered the possibility of immediate, big rewards that schools could not match.

Her heart sank. First she felt sick, then angry. "Oh great!" she thought. "He hasn't been in my class more than five minutes, and already he's presenting his first challenge."

Mrs. Hart stared at Kevin in disbelief. Just after detention yesterday afternoon, she had seen him in front of school flashing a similar wad of money and had spoken to him then. Hadn't he listened to her advice about the danger he could bring himself and others by displaying such a roll of cash?

Advance Study Questions

1. What problem(s) does Mrs. Hart face?

2. What are some underlying issues in this situation?

3. What conditions led to this situation?

4. What should Mrs. Hart do? How should she address the problem of the wad of money? What specific classroom strategies should she use to meet Kevin's educational needs?

CASE 22

Acceptance or Achievement

Linda Powell and Judith B. Buzzell

CHARACTERS

Teacher: Toni Robinson
Students: Celena Sledd
Karen
Yolanda
Therease
Celena's sister: Carmen

Part A

December Crisis

As Toni Robinson questioned her student, Celena Sledd, she watched Celena's eyes fill with tears. "But why were you late to class? And what about your homework? You always do your homework. Celena, what's wrong? You just weren't yourself today in class."

Suddenly, Celena began crying uncontrollably. Unleashing a torrent of feelings, she screamed:

> "I HATE this school! I HATE the kids here! I HATE my family! This school is boring. Middle school was much more fun and interesting. Here the kids don't want to learn. They say they won't be my friends if I don't let them copy my homework. Even when I do let them, they talk about me behind my back. I don't have any friends here. And things are even worse at home. My mother lost her job and wants to move to Arkansas with her boyfriend, but all they do is fight. I can't stand it! I think I'm going crazy." Covering her face with her hands, she continued sobbing.

Mrs. Robinson stood there motionless for some time, trying to think of what she could say. In ten minutes, her next class would come in.

The City and School

Marion was a city of approximately 150,000. Located in the northeast corridor, it suffered from many of the problems that older cities face. In the last few years, there had been a marked increase in gang and drug-related violence and crimes. The city had lost its manufacturing base and had a high unemployment rate, particularly among young adults. The universities and hospitals in the city were the main employers. Although there were a few integrated middle-class neighborhoods, many of the neighborhoods housed primarily minority families living at or below the poverty level.

Lyceum High School was an arts and humanities magnet school, drawing students from throughout the city. Of its three hundred students, about 90 percent were African-American, 5 percent were Hispanic, and 5 percent Caucasian. Recently, in an effort to achieve a better racial balance in the school, the superintendent and school board decided to open Lyceum's doors to children from surrounding districts who were interested in studying the arts. Students sometimes joked about Lyceum being an "all-girls" high school, because there were 220 girls and 80 boys. As was the case in all the city's schools, most of the students were from lower middle-class families or families receiving assistance from Aid to Families with Dependent Children (AFDC), a federal welfare program.

Lyceum's staff included eighteen full-time teachers, five part-time arts teachers, one part-time independent study teacher, one administrator, and one guidance counselor. For half a day each week, Lyceum also had the services of a social worker and a school psychologist. A school nurse was available one day per week. The staff met once a week for regular faculty meetings and committee meetings.

Most of the teachers had more than fifteen years of experience. Over half of the staff had participated in the Teachers' Institute at a local, prestigious university, developing curriculum for the courses taught at Lyceum. Mrs. Robinson had been very involved in this institute over the years. Although she was a twenty-year veteran, she was always looking for ways to improve her teaching. A dedicated teacher, she spent many hours preparing lessons and grading papers. Getting more than five hours of sleep a night seemed like a luxury to her. She was the mother of two young children, and her husband was a social worker.

The school actively involved students in making their education personally meaningful. Through the arts classes—visual arts, dance, creative writing, world music, and theater—students were encouraged to explore new ways to see and express themselves. Also, many of the courses were interdisciplinary and asked students to apply knowledge learned in one class to others. For example, arts classes often addressed themes studied in the literature classes. Teachers encouraged students to participate in local theatrical productions and to attend academic and artistic summer programs.

The Class

Mrs. Robinson's sophomore World History class met every day for forty-eight minutes just before lunch. The year began with the study of the fall of the Roman Empire and ended with the Age of Discovery (in the fifteenth century). Although the main focus was traditional European medieval history, cultural close-ups on Asian and Hispanic groups as well as a month-long unit on African history provided a multicultural perspective.

Mrs. Robinson gave homework three or four nights a week and offered a variety of activities in class: homework discussions, group work, debates, essay writing, role playing, and more. Three or four times a year, students also worked on related art projects such as creating their own coat of arms. A favorite annual event was the trip to see the medieval collection at the Metropolitan Museum of Art in New York City.

The class had twenty-three students, with seventeen girls and six boys. Since Lyceum did not homogeneously track history classes, students had a range of reading levels and abilities. One or two students were considered high achieving, three or four were remedial students, and the other seventeen or eighteen were at or near grade level.

Most students were not very motivated. About a fifth of the class was absent every day, and those four or five students who had not been in class the previous day (or days) had, of course, little idea of what was going on in class. On any given day, about 75 percent handed in their homework.

It often took Mrs. Robinson ten minutes to get the students settled so the class could begin. And once it began, keeping their attention was a challenge. She could hardly get through a sentence because of frequent interruptions—requests for lavatory passes, comments about who had done what the night before, or questions about the homework. Because of the many disruptions, students often missed her instructions and then asked that they be repeated several times.

During the class, students got out of their seats without permission, wandering to the wastebasket, the hall, or to the windows. They chatted with other students along the way. Reminding them that they were not allowed to walk around the room, Mrs. Robinson usually assigned two or three detentions each day. Each marking period, about half of the class received warnings of failure.

Celena Sledd: First Impressions

Mrs. Robinson thought about her first impressions of Celena earlier this year. While other students chatted with each other before class, Celena sat quietly alone at a table in the back of the room. Although there was a high rate of absenteeism in the school, she was never absent.

In September, Celena's written work had been consistently outstanding.

Her homework assignments were well written and thorough. Furthermore, they showed a level of thinking that was rare in the school. While most other students simply restated the ideas and information in the text, Celena's work showed insightful analysis. She compared ideas and drew generalizations; she developed apt analogies. Her grades on tests were always the highest in the class. She had received straight As in middle school.

She was also talented artistically. Her drawings were intricate and unconventional. She liked to make political cartoons that showed a sophisticated awareness of the problems of the day and a keen sense of humor.

Celena's attention to detail was reflected in her physical appearance. Although she experimented with different hair styles each day, each hair was always in place, framing her pretty face. Her skin looked freshly scrubbed. Although she didn't have many clothes, they were always clean, pressed, and stylish.

In class discussion, Celena never volunteered to speak. When called upon, she answered minimally, in a soft voice, even though she had written lengthy responses to the exact same questions for homework. When she did speak, her classmates quieted themselves to listen. Having been with her in classes in middle school, they looked to her to give the right answers when no one else could. However, their reactions did little to encourage Celena. They murmured and mumbled, as if to say, "Not her again." When tests were returned, Celena hurriedly turned over her paper to hide her high scores.

During art projects, students noticed her detailed drawings and commented, "Look at that, I bet she's the only one who's gonna get an A. Why does Mrs. Robinson expect us to do that kind of work? We're not like her." Mrs. Robinson's reprimands couldn't stem these comments.

During group work, Celena sat back quietly, allowing the other members of the group to determine the direction of the work. Many of these group projects were art projects. She worked best with the other "shy" girl in the class. Although the two hardly spoke, they generally produced an elaborate product. Celena was not only technically proficient in art; she had an unusual eye and color sense that added a personal, highly creative dimension to her work.

Celena lived with her mother (a single parent), a younger brother, and an older sister, who attended Lyceum. Her mother was Hispanic, and her father was African-American. Her sister, Carmen, was a poor student who had been held back one year. She was frequently absent, coming to school about three days out of five each week. When Carmen came to school, she liked to sleep in class, telling teachers, "I'm really tired. I don't feel well." When she completed even half of an assignment, she expected full credit. A beautiful girl, she was outgoing and very popular with both boys and girls. Celena and Carmen did not get along well.

October/November

Mrs. Robinson valued parental support and, in mid-October, she began calling students' homes to tell parents how their child was doing and to encourage them to attend the parent-teacher open house. Sometimes she suggested to parents that their child stay after school to get extra help from her or a tutor.

Although most parents appreciated this overture, the students clearly didn't. They complained to each other about the calls, commenting, "Who does she think she is? Now I have to bring my homework sheet home every night."

Although Mrs. Robinson's talk with Mrs. Sledd had been positive, the next day Celena mumbled about "getting a call, too," slammed her books down on the table, and left them closed. This was not her usual behavior.

Two other girls in the class continued to complain about the calls, so Mrs. Robinson decided to move one of them, Therease, to another table. The only other available seat was next to Celena. To Mrs. Robinson's surprise, the shy student moved over and welcomed her new table mate.

Therease was a low-achieving student. She occasionally did her homework and would begin a project with some enthusiasm, but because of frequent absences, she generally didn't complete her work. She missed approximately 40 days of school each year. But if she was in school, she made her presence felt. Protesting vociferously when demands were made on her, she complained, "I'm not taking this test. I haven't been here. You don't care about my problems. All you care about is this work." She was in and out of trouble and got suspended two or three times each year, generally for talking back to a teacher and refusing to comply with a teacher's requests. She was not a favorite of the teachers, but her forceful personality appealed to her peers. She had many friends.

Over the next few weeks, Celena's behavior changed. She began talking more during class to Therease and smirked and grumbled when Mrs. Robinson motioned to her to be quiet. Even more troubling was the fact that the work that Therease handed in was now a duplicate of Celena's. When Mrs. Robinson asked about this "coincidence," the girls responded that they worked together on the assignments. While Therease's grades were becoming higher, Celena's were going lower. And when Celena's papers were returned to her, she no longer turned them over.

December Distress

During the first week of December, students worked on a coat-of-arms project. Using a variety of art materials, each student created a coat of arms using three or four symbols to represent aspects of their family. They explained the symbols on the back. There was a less structured atmosphere, and students moved freely about the room, examining classmates' creations.

During this week, Mrs. Robinson noticed Celena's new relationship with her classmates. On Monday, as Celena worked, the other students came over to check out her sketches. The next day, she began to visit others, offer opinions, and even help with the design and drawing of symbols. By Wednesday, when she brought in her own art supplies (gold paint and gold and silver markers), she was the center of attention. When the projects were completed, all the shields reflected Celena's imagination, through choice of symbols or materials used.

Other teachers began to notice Celena's stronger social interactions, observing her with new friends in their classes, the hallways, and the lunchroom. But there were other changes that concerned the teachers. For example, Celena stopped carrying her book bag and came to some classes without books or notebooks.

On the Thursday before the Christmas break, Celena and Therease came to Mrs. Robinson's class five minutes late and without a pass. On the verge of tears, Celena plunked herself down alone at a new table and stared forward. When Mrs. Robinson told the girls to see her after class, Celena responded by slamming her notebook closed.

Hoping that Celena would settle down, Mrs. Robinson started to discuss the homework. After she organized the class into groups, she approached Celena, whose head was resting on the table. "Celena, may I see your homework?" asked Mrs. Robinson softly. "I don't have it," replied Celena, raising her head without looking at her teacher. "Where is it?" Mrs. Robinson gently prodded. "I lost it," answered Celena with a strained voice.

Just then, Mrs. Robinson was distracted by a shouting match on the other side of the room. The bell rang, and Celena quietly slipped out of the room. Mrs. Robinson spoke briefly to Therease, got her lunch, and went to find Celena.

Celena was just coming out of the office door. "Celena, I'm glad I found you. Can we talk? Why didn't you see me after class?" asked Mrs. Robinson.

Celena's eyes filled with tears and she shouted, "I HATE this school! I HATE the kids here! They say they won't be my friends if I don't let them copy my homework. Even when I do let them, they talk about me behind my back. I just want to do my work and make something of myself."

Toni Robinson's mind raced as she listened, in the hallway, to the distraught young woman. She had ten minutes left for lunch before her next class began and realized that that would never be enough time to talk this out. And there wasn't even an empty room in the building to hold a private conversation. Furthermore, Mrs. Robinson was in charge of the after-school detention, so Celena would have to stay until 3:00 P.M. to talk to her. Most students left on the dot at 2:37 to go home or to jobs. And there were only two minutes between classes.

There was never time to talk! Mrs. Robinson's stomach began to churn as she thought about what to do or say right now.

Advance Study Questions

1. What problem(s) does Mrs. Robinson face?
2. What are some underlying issues in this situation?
3. How did this situation develop?
4. If you were Mrs. Robinson, what would you say to Celena or do?

SECTION B

This section contains Part B of each of the following cases:

CASE 1

I Don't Believe This Is Happening

Robert Piazza

Part B

Amanda was beginning work on her Master's Degree in Special Education at the state university fifty miles away. Her first class, "Introduction to Special Education," had just finished discussing the law and the legal rights of exceptional children. She informed Harriet that public schools received federal and state funding for the education of handicapped children, including preschool children. The school system actually had to engage in active "child find" procedures to identify children with special needs before they reached school age. Rather than brainstorming what they could do to help Joey, Amanda suggested that they get the Grandfield school system involved immediately. Harriet nodded in agreement and replied, "I never thought I would feel like this, but I hope Grandfield has a class for him. I really would rather he not be at our school any longer. I don't know if he belongs here."

The next day when Linda dropped Joey off, Harriet asked her if she could inform the public school system of Joey's difficulties and request that their experts evaluate him. Linda quickly agreed that this was a proper step. Harriet sighed with relief. Joey was possibly one step closer to being gone.

Let's Consult

The Grandfield Special Services Department was comprised of eleven special education staff members, two school psychologists, three speech and language clinicians, a social worker, and a full-time administrator. Mrs. Murphy, one of the school psychologists who was primarily responsible for working with parents, teachers, and students when substance abuse problems arose, was quickly assigned by her administrator to this case.

Within one week after the Grandfield school system had received the call from Harriet Cooper, Mrs. Murphy had scheduled two morning observations of Joey at the preschool. Harriet and the Cummings were quite impressed with the efficiency of the school system. Mrs. Murphy spent five hours watching Joey during those two days. She felt quite confident that she had enough information to offer valuable suggestions to both the preschool and Joey's parents at a meeting that was scheduled the following Tuesday afternoon.

Tuesday's Meeting

Amanda had agreed to cover Harriet's group of children that afternoon so that she could meet with Joey's parents and Mrs. Murphy. Everyone arrived promptly at 12:30, and the group adjourned to a small room, adjacent to the classrooms, that also doubled as a planning room for the professional staff. Harriet reminded Steve and Linda that Mrs. Murphy had spent two lengthy sessions observing Joey the previous week at Busy Beaver. She indicated that she thought that his behavior during both of those times was quite typical. He was attentive at times; he was withdrawn at times; he showed his aggressive tendencies toward his peers on at least two occasions during unstructured play activities. Harriet then suggested that Mrs. Murphy share her findings.

Mrs. Murphy began by asking the Cummingses to discuss Joey's early developmental history and behavior. Linda summarized the problems they had noticed since they adopted him, and then she and Harriet described the difficulties Joey had been having adjusting to the school environment. Mrs. Murphy noted that what they had described was quite consistent with what the research was revealing about drug-exposed children:

> Our field has been finding that these children may experience deficits that might impair their later ability to learn and adapt to school. These problems include, but are not limited to, a heightened response to stimuli, hyperactivity, speech and language delays, separation and attachment difficulties, poor play and organization skills, problems shifting from one activity to another, motor awkwardness, outbursts of aggressive behavior intermingled with withdrawal tendencies, and social deficiencies. These children have a wide range of disabilities, from very mild to extremely severe deficiencies. I think, and I hope, that Joey's problems are more to the mild end of the spectrum. Before any formal testing is performed, I would like to suggest that the following strategies be employed within the preschool setting and at home to see if improvement occurs.

Mrs. Murphy said that the strategies she was offering were selected from guidelines issued by the National Association for the Education of Young Children for individuals working with drug-exposed children. She then handed Linda, Steve, and Harriet separate copies of her formal list of recommendations. They were as follows:

1. Provide as much emotional reassurance as possible.
2. Reduce classroom interruptions as much as possible.

3. Establish classroom routines with a minimum number of interruptions.

4. Recognize and consistently praise Joey for all his positive accomplishments.

5. Give Joey toys and areas within the classroom that are his alone.

6. Provide time when Joey has to model interactive play, and also time when he must share things with the children and adults around him.

7. Provide opportunities for physical contact and positive interactions like smiling at him during the day.

8. Respond to Joey's needs in a predictable and regular manner.

9. Provide daily opportunities for independent-living activities like feeding, dressing, washing, and toileting, with some degree of tolerance for messiness and dawdling.

10. Purposefully acknowledge the needs, wants, and fears of Joey as a way of fostering communication. Also model appropriate ways he can express these needs, wants, and fears.

11. Try to ignore inconsequential verbal behavior.

12. Give Joey motor activities that emphasize rhythm, balance, and coordination. Use songs, games, and play to achieve this.

13. Provide a variety of tactile and small motor activities.

Mrs. Murphy also indicated that it was necessary to establish formal and consistent communication between the home and school: "You must tell each other when successes have been achieved or regressions were observed. This will facilitate growth in Joey's overall functioning."

Harriet Cooper was a bit bewildered and overwhelmed. She was really expecting that Joey was going to be removed from Busy Beaver for a preschool special education placement within the public schools. She expressed these feelings openly to Mrs. Murphy: "I feel I'm already doing almost everything you're suggesting. I don't know if I can do any more for him." The school psychologist replied that a special class placement would not be consistent with Grandfield's policy of providing services in the least restrictive environment. She felt that her suggestions should be implemented fully and that Joey's progress should be monitored for one month. Mrs. Murphy did concede that a formal speech and language assessment was needed and told Harriet and the Cummings that a specialist in this area would schedule an evaluation in the next few days.

Mr. and Mrs. Cummings sat in silence. They were really not bothered by the fact that Joey would be remaining at Busy Beaver.

Additional Readings

Bennett, B., Lewis, K., & Schmeder, N. (1989). The case of infants menaced by cocaine abuse. *Infants and Young Children, 4,* 32–35.

Greer, J. W. (1990). The drug babies. *Exceptional Children, 56,* 382–384.

Krauss, M. W. (1990). New precedent in family policy: Individualized family service plan. *Exceptional Children, 56,* 388–394.

Los Angeles Unified School District. (1985). *D.A.R.E. curriculum manual.*

Rist, M. C. (1990). The shadow children. *The American School Board Journal, 177,* 19–24.

Schutter, L., & Brinker, R. (1992). Conjuring a new category of disability from prenatal cocaine exposure: Are the infants unique biological or caretaking casualties? *Topics in Early Childhood Special Education, 11,* 84–111.

CASE 2

A Case of Prejudice?

Judith B. Buzzell

Part B

The Conference

"I think the biggest mistake is to assume that racially charged statements by children are a sign of bias as we know it in the adult community," said Mrs. Phillips. "Can you think of any other experiences Daniel has had that might influence his feelings about race?" she asked.

Mrs. Rieser described their neighborhood and Daniel's relationships with Jeffrey and Dwight. The Riesers also were friendly with another black family. The two neighbors amicably shared tools or household supplies and helped each other. These seemed like positive influences to her. However, there had been the experiences of the toy thefts. Since she had implied that the thieves were poor children (and Daniel could see that most of the poor children near the neighborhood were black), she wondered if she inadvertently had made the association in Daniel's mind among poor children, black children, and bad actions.

"That's possible," commented Mrs. Phillips. "But I would assume that some of this is coming from outside of the family, even with a four-year-old. You think your children are never out of your sight, but the culture does have an influence. We're living in an interesting time. Fortunately, we're not in the time of Amos 'n Andy and other questionable stereotypes, yet there are vestiges that should be considered. Look at current books and TV. It's only recently that blacks have been featured on TV ads or that picture books or school readers portray children of many races."

"You mean I don't have to feel like I've necessarily caused these feelings in Daniel?" Mrs. Rieser asked, obviously relieved.

Mrs. Phillips nodded. She calmly began to describe other possible influences on Daniel's attitudes.

"Four is supposedly the age when the majority of children notice differences in skin color. Then, once children notice the differences, they believe that a whole range of changes is possible. Boys think that they can turn into girls, white children think they can become black, and I've known deaf children who believe that they'll be able to hear when they grow up."

"So do you think he may wonder whether his skin color will change?" Mrs. Rieser asked.

"Yes," said Mrs. Phillips. She continued:

> "Help to clarify his thinking by giving him information. Start with concrete facts but not too many. Storybooks are useful for this purpose. You might get a few books that have pictures of children of different races and use them as a springboard to talk about ways in which we're all similar and ways in which we're different. Try to do this in a relaxed way, so that Daniel feels free to ask questions. You see, this is also the age when children start to develop some understanding of sex and reproduction. You can defuse the racial issue by pointing out other genetic factors. You might say to Daniel, 'Now you're old enough to know that it takes a father and a mother to make a baby and they each contribute part.' Then you could ask him if he knows which part each parent contributes and talk about the sperm and the egg, saying, 'We each look like our father and mother in different ways. You have curly hair like Daddy and blue eyes like Mommy. Mommy and Daddy have white skin and you do, too. Our skin color and eye color don't change.' "

Mrs. Phillips explained how confusing the world might look to a four-year-old:

> "Adoption, cross-racial adoption, and mixed marriages or unions may further complicate the issue. Our school has a child, Stephanie, from a mixed marriage. Maybe Daniel saw Stephanie at one time with her white mother and at another time with her black father. To say nothing of the fact that color names are not accurate. We call tan people 'white' and brown people 'black.' "

"Actually, school is the new experience we haven't yet factored in," Mrs. Phillips mused. She added:

> "At school, we have black and white dolls, black and white people in puzzles, black and white 'people' accessories for the block area, and many picture books with stories that include black children. Even that's not enough because there aren't enough black children at the school. How do you think Daniel feels about the children at school who are not white?"

Although at home Daniel rarely mentioned the two Asian children, he recently had told his mother, "Stephanie's wild. She doesn't pay attention during stories."

"Do you think he perceives her as black?" asked Mrs. Phillips. "Maybe this reflects his divided feelings about being wild. Part of him wants to be wild, so he likes it in Stephanie; yet, he also observes that she behaves inappropriately at times, and he doesn't think that's so great. The issue may be behavior rather than race. We need to make clear to Daniel that Stephanie isn't bad, but that at times we wish we could change her behavior by helping her to remember the rules."

Although Mrs. Rieser was beginning to feel reassured that Daniel's comments were not necessarily a sign of prejudice, she still wondered what she should say or do if he again said, "I don't like blacks."

Mrs. Phillips suggested that Mrs. Rieser initiate some casual conversations with Daniel over a period of time in which she points out positive experiences that he has had with his black friends or other neighbors, after those concrete experiences have occurred.

"Then, if Daniel says, 'I don't like blacks' again, we need to look closely at the statement to see exactly why he said it. If Daniel seems to be biased, his prejudice should be addressed. But often children hold contradictory beliefs. To help him clarify his thinking, you might say, 'I notice that you sometimes say you don't like blacks, but I'm not sure why you say that because I know you like Jeffrey and Dwight and they're black.' I would also relate his statements to what we believe in 'our family.' Values are probably learned indirectly rather than directly, but we shouldn't hesitate to state them directly. You might say, 'I'm surprised to hear you say that because in our family we know and like people who are black and people who are white.' "

As the conference ended, the two women made plans to share their future observations of Daniel's behavior.

Afterward, Mrs. Phillips began to reflect on the situation. What should the center's role be? Was any action needed at all? Perhaps this was just an overwrought parent. Yet, Daniel *had* said several times, "I don't like blacks."

CASE 3

Lofty Aims

Judith B. Buzzell

Part B

The Following June: Preparations for the Fall

The staff at the Early Learning Center were eagerly awaiting the arrival of Sarah, her mother, and Sarah's physical therapist. Sarah would be attending the center in the fall, and both Denise and Mrs. Schultz felt that the therapist could provide helpful information to make the center safer for Sarah. After touring the center, the physical therapist made the following suggestions:

1. Use carpeting with nonskid backing in front of doors and sinks.

2. Put bright tape on the doorsills to make Sarah more aware of when she has to go up and down.

3. Build wider footstools to place at each sink so they can't be tipped and are wide enough for Sarah to plant both feet firmly on them. She doesn't have the balance to manage teetering on the edge, as many preschoolers can.

4. Place bars on either side of the toilet.

Denise was grateful for these suggestions. She certainly wanted to reduce the risk of Sarah getting hurt, and the accommodations were minor and could be handled within her tight budget. Sarah's public school system would be providing five hours of consultation to the center. A special educator had called and said she'd stop in sometime, so there would be more help coming.

The staff supported Denise's decision to accept Sarah, and they wanted to make this the best possible experience for everyone. Still, they had their worries: How much would Sarah be able to do without help? How would the other children react to her? How would Sarah handle that?

Lisa, who had little experience with people with disabilities, didn't want to treat Sarah inappropriately. She wanted to have a good mind-set and not make Sarah uncomfortable. A "feeling sorry" attitude would not be right. Although Dr. and Mrs. Schultz had given the staff a good basic understanding of spina bifida, she wanted to know more.

Since she was working on her master's degree in education, Lisa decided to do an independent study that summer on working with children with spina bifida. She immersed herself in the literature about the condition. She wanted to be able to handle anything that came up.

As part of the study, she made two dolls and an accompanying book to use with Sarah and the other children in the fall. They were large, cuddly cloth dolls, purposely made unisex so that any child could identify with them. One of the dolls had leg braces and held crutches. These were attached with Velcro and could be taken on and off. The other doll wore glasses. The book had a simple text describing the two doll "friends" visiting the Early Learning Center. There were photographs on each page showing the dolls playing with clay, building with blocks, and perched on swings. In the text, the dolls explained why they needed their crutches and eyeglasses. Lisa planned to use the dolls and book to help the children begin to understand and feel comfortable with the special needs that many of us have in varying degrees.

The teachers prepared in other ways. They made a wall hanging of pictures of children of different genders, races, and ethnic groups. About half of the children had special needs. They made sure they had books dealing with disabilities, such as *Grandma's Wheelchair*, on the bookshelves.

These materials could provide a springboard for discussion, so that the children could air their questions freely, without feeling that the subject of disabilities was taboo. The teachers considered how they would handle questions that might arise. They didn't want to force the issue but wanted to address any questions comfortably, honestly, and appropriately for preschoolers.

September/October: How Much Attention and Help to Give?

Sarah had been sitting in the reading corner since she'd come to school about forty-five minutes ago. She leafed through several books, telling herself the stories and occasionally showing a picture to the girl next to her. She began to look listless and uninterested in reading, yet made no motions to leave the reading area. When Lisa came over, Sarah asked, "Lisa, will you help me up?" "I think you can do it yourself," encouraged the teacher. "No, please help me," begged Sarah. Lisa handed Sarah her lofties (crutches), saying, "You can do it." Sarah continued to plead for help. When Lisa propped her gently from behind, Sarah finally lifted herself up.

Lisa felt torn during this interaction. She knew that there were times when Sarah was tired and genuinely needed help. Her parents had mentioned that she was less capable physically when she was tired. Yet, it was important to encourage her to be independent and to grow in her ability to do things for herself. It was often not clear which response was the appropriate one.

During Sarah's first months, she required—or requested—a lot of teacher attention. Sometimes, the staff worried that there wasn't enough time left over for the other kids. Yet, Sarah seemed to need this one-to-one attention for psychological and perhaps physical reasons.

Dr. Schultz had emphasized how important it was for Sarah's brace to fit correctly and had taught each teacher individually how to adjust it. Sarah's foot stiffened periodically, and then the brace no longer fit and was painful. If Sarah asked a teacher to adjust the brace, it was important to see if her foot had slipped. "I always stop to do it," Lisa told Denise. "But sometimes I find out another teacher has adjusted the brace only ten minutes earlier, which is frustrating. And sometimes Sarah asks right in the middle of a very busy time, like cleanup. At that time I need to oversee all the children and make sure kids are focused on putting away materials—not tossing them around. And there's Sarah, right in the middle, asking to have her brace adjusted. Maybe she's scared of being knocked down in the hubbub and wants some reassurance."

The teachers estimated that sometimes Sarah was asking to have her braces adjusted up to ten times a day. Was this an opportunity to manipulate the teachers to get their attention, was there genuine physical discomfort, or was there some other reason?

Sarah liked to talk with teachers and always wanted a lap. At circle time, she would broach sitting on a lap with each teacher, until she was seated on one. When Lisa arrived in the morning, Sarah immediately asked to be read a story.

Each day, Jean chose one child to help her prepare the snack food. Sarah had helped several times and loved doing it. One day, another child asked to help first. When Sarah noticed this, tears welled in her eyes, and she protested angrily, "Jean, I want to help with snack. I always help with snack."

The staff often speculated as to why Sarah gravitated to adults. Perhaps it was because she was used to so much contact with doctors and nurses. Maybe her disability made it hard for her to keep up with the children's active play. Her parents reported that her older brother was very adult-oriented too. Perhaps this had nothing to do with Sarah's spina bifida?

The teachers felt trapped between a rock and a hard place. On the one hand, they felt that it was important for Sarah, like other children, to learn to share adults' attention. On the other hand, they were always aware that she was dealing with some tough odds.

But this was not a simple case of teachers feeling sorry for a child with a disability—far from it. Despite Sarah's demands, they enjoyed and admired her. She had a quick intelligence and was highly verbal. She seemed aware of everything that was going on around her. And for the most part, she had a sunny, outgoing, can-do attitude. At one nap time, Jean was impressed to see Sarah on her cot, struggling to learn how to tie her shoe. She worked and worked on making a bow, showing unusual persistence for such a young child. In fact, it was, in part, the constant tension between Sarah's desire to do for herself and her desire to be cared for that made it hard for the teachers to figure out what to do.

Safety Concerns

From the beginning, the teachers had been worried about Sarah's safety. Because of the many art activities and water play, as well as splashing at the sink during hand-washing, there was often some water on the preschool floors. One of the problems with the lofties was that if Sarah hit a wet spot, they could slip out from under her and she would fall. Acutely aware of this, the teachers compulsively sponged up any drops.

Sarah had fallen a few times—mostly slides, landing on her knees and not on her head. But one day, outdoors, she fell flat over, directly onto her face. She injured her two front teeth, which would need to be prematurely removed because of nerve damage. The teachers rushed to help the bloodied child. Naturally, Sarah was very upset, crying, "Are my teeth going to be okay?" as she was comforted and washed off.

Yet, Sarah continuously challenged herself physically. Some of the physical feats she wanted to try made the teachers' hair stand on end. She insisted on climbing on the jungle gym outdoors and had gone right to the top. But, because her foot could slip at any point, safety required two teachers hovering near her.

Jean described one such experience to Denise. Denise happened to have been watching through the window. "My heart was in my throat," said Denise. "Yes," said Jean. "But I felt that I had to let her do it. She has to try her wings, like any child—perhaps even more than other children. Yet, I knew we also had to have enough teachers there to make sure she was safe."

Sarah's slowness also raised safety concerns. As happened in her introductory visit to the center, she took forever when it was time to go outside. She was the last child every step of the way: washing up for snack, eating snack, bathrooming, getting her coat on, and going out. Because one teacher had to focus on helping Sarah through these stages, only two teachers were outside, responsible for an active group of twenty-six preschoolers. No one was comfortable with this situation. They all felt under pressure; they felt it was important to be patient with Sarah, but they wanted to speed her up to adequately cover the other children.

After several discussions, the teachers decided to do some things for Sarah that they didn't do for the other children in the interest of quickening her pace. They brought her a wet towel to wash her hands before snack and lunch and brought her lunchbox to the table. Then, she didn't have to go to the sink to wash or to her cubby to pick up her lunchbox. Sometimes, they carried her to the bathroom—especially when she might soil herself (she was more prone to accidents than the other children).

Sarah's Relationships with Other Children

Although Sarah loved to interact with the teachers, she didn't want to have much to do with the kids. One day, the group was outside, and Sarah had been following Lisa around like a shadow, badgering her with questions to keep her engaged. Because one of the key goals of a preschool experience is socialization, Lisa tried to help Sarah connect with some of the other children.

"Who could you play with?" Lisa asked Sarah. "Maybe Becky," responded Sarah, and she went off to ask Becky to play. She soon returned, reporting to Lisa that Becky had refused. After Sarah made trips to two other children, Lisa said, "I'll go over, and we'll ask together." They approached a girl with short hair who was alone on the climber. Lisa said, "Sarah is looking for someone to play with. Would you like to play with her?" The girl said, "Sure." At that point, Sarah retorted, "No. I don't want to play with her. I don't want to play with a girl who looks like a boy."

Lisa felt that Sarah was making an excuse. In fact, she suspected, that in this instance, Sarah had never asked the other children to play. The children at the center were fascinated by Sarah and wanted to be with her and be her "helper." The teachers had never seen the other children make fun of Sarah or tease her.

Many times, Sarah had rejected children's overtures. They often wanted to try out her lofties, but she bristled and refused to let them. There were times when she had left her crutches behind and moved to another area by holding onto furniture or crawling along the floor. Then, when she needed her crutches again, she'd call to a teacher to get them. The children vied with each other to get the crutches, but she would say "No" firmly and insist that a teacher do it. Lisa wasn't sure whether Sarah was so dependent upon the crutches that she wouldn't allow others to touch them, or whether this response was a way to maintain contact with teachers.

Group Discussions

The children often played with the dolls Lisa made, taking the braces and crutches on and off. Teachers read the accompanying book several times a day at their request. Children asked, "What kinds of things can the doll do? Can she do this? Can she do that? Can this happen to me?" The teachers tried to respond simply and honestly to their questions and their expressed fears.

During discussions, the children might ask about Sarah, "What's wrong? What happened? Will she get better?" The teachers suggested that they ask Sarah directly because they didn't feel it was their right to answer all of the questions. Generally, Sarah was responsive. She'd clearly and forthrightly respond, "I was born this way. My legs weren't strong enough to hold me. That's why I use my crutches." If a child asked, "Will they get better?" she'd respond, "I don't know—maybe."

If Sarah didn't feel like responding to the questions, the teachers would tell the children, "Now's not a good time to talk with Sarah about it. Maybe another time." They felt it was important to respect Sarah's right to privacy. They were impressed by the matter-of-fact, positive attitude she had toward her disability.

The Conference: Late October

As for any conference with parents, Denise and Jean had prepared carefully. They felt they had an open, comfortable relationship with the Schultzes, and they weren't apprehensive. Sarah's parents and Jean chatted convivially about the weather, while Denise brought tea and coffee for everyone.

The teachers started the conference by describing a typical day for Sarah, including her interests and activities. They shared how much they enjoyed her curiosity and lively contributions to group discussions and admired her determination to master physical skills. In painting an honest picture of what life was like for Sarah at the school, they also discussed their accommodations to help her, such as bringing her a wet towel and her lunchbox to get her outside sooner and trying to facilitate more positive relationships with other children. They described her requests for frequent teacher attention by asking to sit on a lap or to have her brace adjusted. They assured the Schultzes that they were careful about her physical safety; when she was on the jungle gym, they had two teachers watching her.

Throughout the conference, Dr. and Mrs. Schultz had asked questions and shared aspects of Sarah's home life. At the end of the meeting, they expressed appreciation for the teachers' work with Sarah. Then Mrs. Schultz blurted out some questions which Denise and Jean did not expect. "Is Sarah too much of a burden for you? Do you ever resent her?" Tears welled in both parents' eyes. As the teachers struggled for a response, Mrs. Schultz asked, "Do you think this is the right program for her?"

CASE 4

Two Steps Forward, One Step Back

Robert Piazza

Part B

Establishing a Complete Program

The meeting between Cheryl Stone and Judy Bradley occurred the following day as scheduled. They both agreed that the mainstreaming of a child who is blind in a kindergarten class was more complex than they anticipated. To help Phillip's placement be more successful and his participation flow more naturally, Cheryl and Judy agreed that the following should happen:

1. Cheryl and Judy would conduct an informal discussion with the class about children with disabilities. A mini-unit about the five senses was thought to be a good way to get the children thinking and discussing similarities and differences among people.

2. Joan Rizzo, the consultant from the State Department of Education assigned to Phillip, would be asked to speak to the class about visual impairments and blindness. Miss Rizzo, who was blind herself, would also meet on a monthly basis with Cheryl. In the past, she had only consulted with Judy Bradley and Phillip's movement coach.

3. While it was recognized that Judy's primary responsibilities were to Phillip, she would try to become more of a classroom aide, helping other students as well as Phillip with classroom activities. She would attempt to wean herself away from Phillip whenever possible. Judy would also demonstrate to Cheryl the various special teaching apparatus used with Phillip, such as the Braille dial and labeler, and his special books. This training would allow Cheryl to be aware of all special adjustments made in Phillip's program.

4. Since social interactions between Phillip and his classmates were not occurring spontaneously, Cheryl would make a special effort to encourage communication during structured daily activities. Judy and Cheryl hoped that positive verbal interactions would then happen naturally between Phillip and the other children during independent activities and snack time.

The Next Few Months

Joan Rizzo, Phillip's consultant from the State Department of Education, taught the unit on disabilities to Cheryl's class. She spent forty-five minutes a week over five consecutive weeks showing videos, filmstrips, and discussing the problems associated with physical, hearing, visual, and other health-related impairments.

Cheryl and Judy also implemented their other plans. Slowly, Phillip became a complete and fully integrated member of his kindergarten class. He established close friendships with at least five children in the class (Karen was one of them), and he attended three birthday parties before Thanksgiving.

In class, Phillip wanted to be involved in all activities. One day when his classmates were being given an eye-screening test by the school nurse, Phillip demanded that his eyes be tested too.

He would go anywhere in the school with Judy except the gymnasium. "I don't know why, but that place scares me," he exclaimed to Judy.

Phillip tried not to draw attention to himself. His largest source of embarrassment occurred when he would sneeze and occasionally one of his prosthetic eyes would pop out of its socket. When this happened, he usually cursed under his breath, headed for the nurse's office, and put it back himself, without any assistance.

Cheryl and Judy both agreed that Phillip's inclusion in the kindergarten class was a complete success. "I have really learned a lot about what good teaching is. I don't know why other children with handicaps haven't been in my classes before. With the support I've gotten from you and others, this year has been a great one," Cheryl admitted to Judy as they watched Phillip get in his van to return home one day.

Shortly after that, however, a major setback arose. Phillip was absent from school for a few days with what everyone thought was a late winter cold. It was more than that. The following week Phillip entered the hospital for exploratory testing because of a jaundiced condition. Hepatitis was ruled out, but his condition was worsening. Finally, Phillip's doctors removed his gallbladder. When little improvement was observed, a pancreatic bypass was performed. Although Phillip's doctors told his parents on more than one occasion that he might not survive all the surgical intrusions, his health began to stabilize. He remained in the hospital for seven weeks under heavy medication and received intravenous feeding most of that time.

Phillip's classmates wrote him numerous get well cards, but it wasn't until late April that he felt well enough to have them read to him. Judy brought a bundle of cards to the hospital one day. When she began to read some of them to Phillip, he interrupted her. "Don't bother reading those cards to me. I'm not interested in them."

"Why, Phillip?" asked Judy in surprise.

"I don't know. Just come over here," he said. Judy moved over to the corner of his bed and received the strongest hug of her life.

On May 12, Phillip returned to school. His classmates planned a "Welcome Back" party for him. What should have been a happy occasion, though, was muted by the children's reaction to Phillip's physical appearance. He had lost seventeen pounds over the last two months and now weighed only thirty-two pounds. Mrs. Stone had warned the class that Phillip had lost weight and did not look the same, but apparently the children were still not prepared for his sickly appearance. "Are you okay, Phillip?" and "You gonna be in the hospital again, Phillip?" were two of the comments Phillip faced. On that day, most of the children did not talk to him at all, and he talked to no one.

Phillip's fine-motor skills had deteriorated greatly over the last few months. He had also lost his line-to-line tracking skills in his Braille books and nearly all his memory of Braille. Worse yet, Phillip had become selectively mute. The only person he would communicate with was Judy. When Judy asked him one time to talk to Cheryl or the other children, he whispered in her ear, "Don't ask me to do that. I don't want to talk to them. I don't even want to be here. Nobody likes me." Judy was reluctant to push Phillip too hard on this issue.

What's To Be Done Now?

Phillip's annual review was scheduled for June 15. Cheryl thought about what she was going to say at this meeting. After a great start in her class, Phillip had actually regressed so much that he was not developmentally any further advanced than he was in September. His physical, educational, and, now, his emotional needs were overwhelming. Because of his age, he couldn't spend another year in kindergarten. But could he go on to a regular first grade class? If he did, what kind of support would he need? She hoped somebody had some answers to these questions.

Additional Readings

Ammer, J. J. (1984). The mechanics of mainstreaming: Considering the regular educators' perspective. *Remedial and Special Education, 5*, 15-20.

Center, Y., & Ward, J. (1987). Teachers' attitudes towards the integration of disabled children into regular schools. *Exceptional Child, 34*, 41-56.

Curry, S. A., & Hatlen, P. H. (1988). Meeting the unique needs of visually impaired pupils through appropriate placement. *Journal of Visual Impairment and Blindness, 82*, 417-424.

Erwin, E. J. (1991). Guidelines for integrating young children with visual impairments in general educational settings. *Journal of Visual Impairment and Blindness, 85*, 253-260.

Hill, J. L. (1990). Mainstreaming visually impaired children: The need for modifications. *Journal of Visual Impairment and Blindness, 84*, 354-360.

CASE 5

A Matter of Perspective

Judith B. Buzzell

Part B

Weighing Options: The Planning and Placement Team Meeting

A week later, on Friday afternoon, the PPT was held. Peter's parents, Mrs. Jacobs, Ms. Winthrop, and the principal, Dr. Cleary, were present.

After a few pleasantries, Dr. Cleary asked Mrs. Jacobs to describe Peter's performance in her class. Mrs. Jacobs explained that Peter's skills were inconsistent. He did very well in certain areas like counting and identifying numbers, shapes, and colors. "But if I ask him a simple question, like 'Who lives in your house?', he doesn't respond, or just says, 'No, thank you.' Sometimes I wonder if he's trying to amuse the other kids!"

Mrs. Jacobs described Peter's social interactions, his difficulty sharing, and his distress when other children touched toys he was using. She explained that there were several times during the course of the day when she had to devote herself entirely to Peter and gave some of the examples she had told Ms. Winthrop earlier. "He's a nice boy, but I just can't give enough attention to him, and it's not fair either to him or to the other children in the class."

Mr. and Mrs. Powers were stunned. They had had a conference with Mrs. Jacobs in late October, and she had informed them that Peter had some difficulties, but they had no idea that it would come to this. Now Mrs. Jacobs was asking to have him transferred. Furthermore, while they struggled at home with Peter's temper tantrums and need for routine, they felt that his peer relationships had improved. They pointed out that he played well with his neighborhood friends. He rode bikes with them, and, even though he was the youngest, he kept up. He was in a Saturday morning swimming program at the Y and was doing fine.

Mrs. Jacobs said that she was happy to hear of these successes but that Peter was not managing as well in the more directed, more demanding school situation. She believed that his needs would be better served in Ms. Winthrop's class, which was smaller and where he could get more one-to-one attention to help develop his skills. Ms. Winthrop had only seven children and a full-time aide.

By this time, Mr. and Mrs. Powers were visibly distressed. Mr. Powers's first reaction was an emphatic, "He needs to be in a regular kindergarten class!" To which, Mrs. Powers quickly added, "Peter can count to 200 and he can do 500-piece puzzles. He's been doing that since he was 3½. And he knows his alphabet better than most children." The point they kept coming back to was that Peter had benefitted from a self-contained special needs class for two years, but he was now learning a great deal from his classmates in the regular class and he should continue to be with them.

This response didn't surprise Ms. Winthrop. She knew that Mrs. Powers spent a great deal of time drilling Peter so that he would know basic academic skills. And she remembered the time Mrs. Powers had commented to her, "We're not going to walk around telling people that our son has PDD." Sometimes Ms. Winthrop wondered whether they had even accepted that themselves. Mrs. Powers had said several times that Peter just had a speech and language disability.

At this point, Dr. Cleary turned to Ms. Winthrop and asked, "What about the possibility of placing Peter in Mrs. Esposito's kindergarten class, since she has a special education background?" Ms. Winthrop paused. This was the question that she had been waiting for. She reminded Dr. Cleary that Mrs. Esposito already had three children with special needs mainstreamed in her class. She also said that, since Peter had such difficulty with change, a switch in teachers and classmates at midyear probably would be very upsetting to him. She wanted to be helpful and offered to suggest some modifications to help Peter in his current class.

Mrs. Jacobs's face reddened, but she said nothing.

Dr. Cleary responded, "Since Mrs. Esposito is already working with several children with special needs as well as with the other students, it's unlikely that Peter will get the extra attention he needs in her class. Also, it doesn't seem fair to ask her to take on another child with special needs. Let's try to work with the situation as it is. I'd like the team to come up with some recommendations for modifications in Peter's program."

"Dr. Cleary," Mrs. Powers interrupted, "we'd like to make some comments to help you understand Peter better." She emphasized that if Peter didn't appear to hear a direction, repeat it again and make sure he was listening. Also, he was fearful of being wrong and needed to be reassured that it was okay to make mistakes. For example, he didn't want to take the training wheels off his bike until he was absolutely certain that he could balance without them. "He's really a good boy and loves to be in kindergarten. He just wants to be like the other children. We want you to keep us informed and let us know if there's anything we can work on at home," she said pointedly.

Dr. Cleary thanked the Powers for their comments and assured them that the lines of communication would be kept open. Then he turned to Ms. Winthrop, "Do you have any suggestions that might help?"

Ms. Winthrop began by emphasizing that Peter was not trying to amuse, irritate, or upset either Mrs. Jacobs or the other students. Because of his PDD, he was egocentric and had a very hard time reading the reactions of other people to his words and actions.

Then she shared several ideas. Because Peter had difficulty understanding oral directions, it would be helpful to give him written directions with some picture cues. Multistep directions were particularly hard for him. Instead of asking him to go get glue, scissors, and crayons and then to sit down and start his art project, Mrs. Jacobs could write the directions with picture cues and number the steps. Numbering could be used to help organize him at other times, too. If he had several papers to do, these could be numbered, so he would know which to work on first.

Because of Peter's difficulty with communication, he needed a predictable environment. If changes in his routine were necessary, there were ways to alleviate his anxiety. Mrs. Jacobs could make a small chart of the normal day's schedule for Peter, using movable pictures symbolizing puzzle time, snack time, work time, gym, recess, etc. When the regular schedule was going to be changed, the pictures could be switched around, and there might be a special symbol, such as a lightning bolt, to alert Peter to the change and give him a chance to prepare himself. Then he'd have a graphic message to reinforce the verbal warning of the change.

Ms. Winthrop suggested that it was inappropriate to ask Peter comprehension questions at story time, given his level of understanding of oral language. It was as if we heard a story in a foreign language and then were asked, "Now tell me what you just heard." Peter's attention and comprehension might be improved if he, with other children, could become involved in acting out the stories. Visual aids, such as telling the story with puppets or felt-board characters, also would help. Acknowledging the extra work involved, Ms. Winthrop suggested using such activities with stories once a week. Then, Mrs. Jacobs would begin to build up a stock of props which could be used over again.

By this time, Mrs. Jacobs was fuming. She had asked for Peter to be transferred so she could begin to meet the needs of the other children in the class. Now, she was being told to do even more for Peter. This was typical of specialists–they thought of help in terms of what else the teachers could do in the class, not what they could do to assist.

"I need help. I don't need advice!" Mrs. Jacobs said with exasperation. "I really don't have time to make all these visual aids!"

Mr. and Mrs. Powers stiffened. Although they were upset, they had hoped that Dr. Cleary's decision and Ms. Winthrop's suggestions would begin to solve the problem. Now they weren't so sure. Casting a reassuring sidelong glance at the Powers, Dr. Cleary hastened to reassure Mrs. Jacobs that Ms. Winthrop would provide ongoing support to her. Mrs. Jacobs looked doubtful but said that she was glad to hear that. Ms. Winthrop averted her eyes and looked downward to hide her astonishment. She would attempt to honor Dr. Cleary's suggestion but wondered how she could do it and still fulfill her commitment to her own class.

CASE 6

The New Child in My Class

Tracie-Lynn Zakas and Robert Piazza

Part B

The Longest Day Continues

After lunch, Terry had a long discussion with her class about leaving other children's property alone. She wasn't surprised that James was still defiant and argumentative. He insisted that Leslie needed to learn to share. He continued to verbally abuse Leslie and his teacher, so Terry left the room in charge of her aide and made a call to James's mother. When James realized what his teacher was doing, he became silent and sulked.

Terry was almost embarrassed that she had to resort to a phone call home on the first day a child was in her class. She felt, however, that she couldn't allow things to get out of control with James. She also wanted to know the type of support she would get from home.

When Mrs. Krosek arrived, she received a quick explanation of the lunchroom incident. She was very apologetic for James's behavior and informed him that he had lost his Nintendo privileges for the evening. Sobbing, James looked at Mrs. Simpson and said, "I hate you." Mrs. Krosek told James to be nice.

James's mother left, only to return unannounced twenty minutes later with potato chips for all the children in the class, including James. Terry Simpson was rapidly realizing why James behaved the way he did. She wondered if this was an example of the type of discipline James received at home. Another conference with Mrs. Krosek for the next day was scheduled.

Day Two

The second day with James had its ups and downs, but Terry Simpson felt it was a huge improvement over his first day in her class. She sensed that he viewed her differently. The other children in her class were intimidated by him, however. His outlandish behavior on Monday had both frightened and mystified them. Terry encouraged the other pupils to play with him during recess, but they seemed to be put off by his aggressiveness and do-it-my-way attitude. On the playground after lunch, Terry observed James alone sitting on the steps of the slide with his chin resting in the palms of his hands.

Although James's behavior was more subdued, he was very resistant to written work on this day. He didn't finish any of his ditto work. When Terry's aide prodded him to complete his math assignment, he asked her to leave him alone because he didn't want to do anymore.

At 2:45, all the children boarded the yellow van to go home. James's mother arrived for the conference promptly at 3:00. The first words out of Mrs. Krosek's mouth were, "Thanks for how you handled the situation yesterday. I think that's the first time my son has ever been put in his place. Since we are going to be working so closely together, please call me Vicky." Terry smiled at Vicky. Things appeared to be moving in a positive direction.

Vicky made Terry Simpson privy to many of the factors that might be influencing James's behavior. First, and foremost, was her attitude toward her child. She admitted that she and every other member of her family had catered to all of James's whims as a toddler and as a young child. "We all realize that MD is fatal. We're not blind to that. Probably for that reason, we've always treated him like he could do no wrong," Vicky sobbed. "It's now that I realize that we've done more harm than good."

Vicky also told Terry that during her pregnancy she smoked cigarettes and marijuana heavily and drank alcohol. Although her doctor had assured her that this could not have brought on James's disease, it still weighed heavily on her mind. Vicky indicated that she still feared that James's problems were directly related to her negligence.

Terry sympathetically clasped Vicky's hand. "They never taught me about this in college. What should I say to her now?" Terry thought to herself.

The Plan

In addition to James's physical difficulties, Terry saw him as a child with an attention disorder. She knew drugs such as Ritalin were often prescribed for such problems. Before suggesting to Mrs. Krosek that an evaluation for an attention deficit be performed by a pediatrician, Terry wanted to implement a behavior management plan.

Mrs. Krosek and Terry Simpson discussed changes that needed to be implemented both at school and at home. They agreed that all the adults in James's life should start treating him like a six-year-old rather than as an equal. Since he needed to accept responsibility for his actions at school, a behavior modification system was outlined that awarded points to him at half-hour intervals. Precise records were to be kept of the points James earned. Mrs. Simpson would sign these point sheets and send them home daily. Mrs. Krosek would provide appropriate rewards to James on Friday if he reached the agreed-upon point thresholds. Points could also be earned at home. Many of the privileges James enjoyed such as late-night television on weekends, weekly trips to the ice cream parlor, and Nintendo playing would now have to be earned. Terry knew this wasn't an ideal or perfect system; however, she felt it was a move in the right direction. James needed to become part of the group in class rather than the focal point. The hope was that improved behavior would also help him form relationships and friendships within his peer group.

And the Days Roll On . . .

The behavior management system did not have an immediate impact on James's self-control. Although Terry noted some improvement, James continued to assume a self-centered role in the classroom. The most disruptive of his behaviors was hitting other children when Terry's back was turned. This behavior led Terry to move his desk next to hers. Right away, James began to finish his written assignments. Also he became less aggressive, and the other children seemed more receptive to friendly interactions during social times in the classroom.

Within a month and a half, James's seat was moved back to the group during work times, he had made three friends in the class, and he was no longer seeking constant attention. His mother was very cooperative and consistently implemented the behavior management system at home. She informed Terry that the nightmares James was having at the beginning of the year had ceased, and he really seemed excited about attending school.

Then Came March

One morning Terry received a call from Vicky saying that James would not be in school that day, since he was feeling ill. No big deal, Terry thought. But what a big deal it turned out to be.

That afternoon Vicky phoned again stating that James had strep throat and scarlet fever, and would be out of school for at least two weeks. The next morning she came to school to pick up a bundle of homework assignments Terry had prepared for James. Vicky thanked her and expressed how sorry she was if any other child was exposed. As she turned to go, she said over her shoulder, "By the way, I don't have to stick to the rules if James is sick, do I?" and she was gone before Terry could respond.

James Comes Back

Positive changes and progress in James's behavioral functioning were apparent in the few months preceding his illness. Upon his return to school, those achievements were obliterated. Even at his best, James was selfish and self-centered. Before these attributes seemed to stem from habit and innocence. Now Terry sensed a calculating cruelty in his behavior toward others. One incident stood out in her mind.

It was the Thursday before the long Easter weekend. James's mother had promised cupcakes, juice, and a special surprise for the class party that afternoon. All went well that morning, and the children were electric with anticipation. After lunch, Terry returned to her room to find Jill, another child in her class, missing. James gleefully informed her that Jill had been sent to the principal's office by a lunchroom aide for hitting him.

Terry left the classroom and returned thirty seconds later with the alleged culprit. Jill was teary and adamant that she had not hit James, that he was lying. Other children in Terry's class corroborated her report. Terry turned to James and demanded the truth. At first he cried and stuck to his story, but with further prodding, he admitted he had lied. Then, the expression in James's face changed, and he calmly said, "I just wanted to see what it would be like to get someone else in trouble. That was fun."

Just then Vicky came hopping into the class with pink pajamas, paper bunny ears, and a basket of goodies in tow. Terry was completely disarmed, but confronted the situation quickly. She took Vicky into the hall and told her what had just happened, and that James would not be allowed to participate in the party. Vicky began to cry. She told Terry that she too was seeing a deterioration in his behavior at home. She agreed to return to the strategies and guidelines that had been so successful over the prior months. She then straightened her ears, readjusted her tail, and threw a party for everyone except her son.

Additional Readings

Gable, R. A., Hendrickson, J. M., Young, C. C., & Shokoohi-Yekta, M. (1992). Preservice preparation and classroom practices of teachers of students with emotional/behavioral disorders. *Behavioral Disorders*, *17*, 126-135.

Hinshaw, S., & Melnick, S. (1992). Self-management therapies and attention deficit hyperactivity disorder–reinforced self-evaluation and anger control interventions. *Behavior Modification*, *16*, 253-273.

Landruin, T. (1992). Teachers as victims: An interactional analysis of the teacher's role in educating atypical learners. *Behavioral Disorders*, *17*, 135-144.

Lazarus, B. (1990). A cooperative home-school token economy. *Preventing School Failure*, *34*, 37-40.

Williams, B. F., Williams, R. L., & McLaughlin, T. F. (1991). Treatment of behavior disorders by parents in the home. *Journal of Developmental and Physical Disabilities*, *3*, 385-407.

CASE 7

A Different Kind of Student

Loretta L. Rubin

Part B

A New Method

" . . . This report just came for you, Mrs. Lomax. It's a report from a private educational consulting firm concerning one of your students, Sara Moyer. After Sara left kindergarten at a private school, Mr. and Mrs. Moyer commissioned this firm to evaluate Sara. As you know, they want to make sure that Sara has every advantage in overcoming the learning disability that they documented at her previous school. The firm has made several recommendations that may interest you." Mr. Dworski handed Sharon the thick report, which she placed in her bag to read more carefully at home.

That night Sharon read the suggestions for Sara Moyer. "Use manipulatives to teach all mathematical concepts." Yes, she was already doing that. "Sara has a perceptual difficulty in tracking left to right that may affect her ability to learn to read." Hmm . . . she hadn't been experiencing too many problems so far, but then again, Sara wasn't reading independently yet either. "We recommend that Sara be taught to read using the Orton-Gillingham method of instruction. Auditory, visual, and kinesthetic-motor integration is essential for her learning . . . " That was it! She would use the Slingerland adaptation of the Orton-Gillingham method to teach Sara and the few others who seemed to be having some difficulty learning. This might be what would work for Colleen! Sharon knew of a few suburban school districts that automatically used this approach with pupils showing early difficulties with the language arts.

Sharon had read about this method in which children learned to read using movement and touching, as well as sight and sound. The Slingerland method, outlined in Beth Slingerland's book *A Multi-Sensory Approach to Language Arts for Specific Language Disability Children: A Guide for Primary Teachers* (Educators Publishing Service, Cambridge, Massachusetts, 1971), is a classroom adaptation of the Orton Gillingham method of instructing children who have been identified as having the symptoms of specific language disabilities. Their difficulty in using both oral and written language is disproportionate to their general intelligence. Teachers instruct using a multimodel approach in which auditory, visual, and kinesthetic activities support learning to read and write. When students successfully learned how to read, they were able to join the other students in their grade who might have been taught using a more traditional approach.

Sharon Lomax was excited. She thought that perhaps she had found what she was looking for, but these children would not be in a separate class. How would they feel if they were not reading from the books used by their classmates? Not only had she read about this method but she had also piloted it at her former school by using a reading series that specifically outlined the techniques and provided suggestions for activities. However, she didn't feel confident enough to work with these children without that support. How could she get books and materials to teach this group?

Materials

The very next day, Sharon Lomax began to research available sources. First she called the Supervisor of Reading at Middle City and asked him for copies of a series she knew was based on the Slingerland method. He didn't have any copies but knew of another city school that also had piloted the series. Their reading consultant was willing to trade her copies (which they no longer used) for additional teacher's guides for the new language series. Since Sharon was a member of the committee that had received preview copies of these guides, she was able to make the trade. After school, Sharon delivered the guides and picked up the materials for the next day.

Implementation

The next Monday, Sharon Lomax formed a new reading group using the series she had obtained. Each letter was represented by the name of a character in the series. Each character had his or her own book that was accompanied by a tape with songs and oral directions for some of the activities in the book. The children began by learning letters one at a time. Both consonants and vowels were introduced so that words could be created quite soon.

As the children learned a letter, they also learned its corresponding sound. A key word was presented so that a complete association could be made. For example, if the children were shown a flashcard with the grapheme /*a*/, they would say, /*a*/(letter), *apple*,/*a*/ (sound). For the grapheme /*s*/, they would say /*s*/ (letter), *sun*,/*s*/ (sound). Sharon put all consonant sounds on white flash cards.

With their fingers, the children traced the sandpaper outlines of the letters that Sharon had made. They drew the letters on paper with wax crayons, tracing them over and over again until there was a thick wax letter ready to touch. The books provided practice in writing the letters on color-coded lines, so that capitals and lowercase letters would be sized correctly. Students had fun guessing the letters that partners had outlined on their backs and calling out the sounds for letters written in water on the blackboard.

For seatwork, they drew all the things that they could think of that began with that letter. Many had already been suggested by the individual books that accompanied the series. The tapes provided listening activities for specific exercises and allowed the students to listen repeatedly to the songs and stories. As the students progressed in the series, new characters were introduced and added to the circle of established "friends."

The students then learned to build words from left to right. They organized cards with these letters to form words on tables and in pocket charts. Arrows from left to right provided additional visual cues.

After each book was completed, special stories, projects, and activities summarized the letters learned so far. Linguistic readers were often used for oral reading, since they were phonetically controlled. The children enjoyed the rhyming nature of these stories.

At first, the group went slowly. They were still having difficulty remembering letter sounds. But as they progressed through the letters, the students began to meet with success. It seemed as if they were understanding how to "unlock the code" of reading.

Concerned that this didn't become a permanent "low" group, Sharon also mingled these children with groups reading in the basal series. Consequently, they were receiving twice as much instruction as the others. She used some of the same methods to teach the sight vocabulary on which the regular series was based.

It was evident that this was just what Sara needed. She blossomed, learning to read quickly and soon surpassing first grade level.

Colleen made slower, more deliberate progress. She painstakingly learned the letter sounds and connections. It was taking her longer than the other children to master them, but she was retaining what she learned.

Mrs. Lomax began to give weekly spelling tests to the first graders. The words were used to teach regular spelling patterns. In April, Colleen got her first 100 percent on a spelling test. She rejoiced as her mother and Sharon shed a few happy tears.

Results

At this point, Colleen had shown a definite improvement in reading. She had learned several sight words and knew how to blend letter sounds to decode new words. But her reading level was still quite a bit below the rest of her classmates. Even mixed with the other class, Colleen might always be the "lowest" if she moved on to second grade.

Sharon, with Mr. and Mrs. Murphy, determined that it would be in Colleen's best interest to have another year of first grade. She had some friends in the upcoming class and would have an academic head start on the curriculum. Mr. and Mrs. Murphy requested that Colleen be in Sharon's class again, but Sharon wasn't sure that it would be best for Colleen.

Sharon was torn. She had struggled to teach Colleen and was committed to the child and her progress. No time would be lost if Colleen continued in her class in the fall. But in order for her progress to be accurately assessed, shouldn't Colleen be able to demonstrate what she had learned with another teacher? Sharon Lomax wondered if she had developed more than a professional interest in Colleen. Perhaps she was overly involved with Colleen's progress. What should she do?

CASE 8

How Much Can You Expect?

Judith B. Buzzell

Part B

First Grade

Rebecca's class this year had twenty-five children. The children sat at tables in groups of six. There was a floor rug, which made the room well suited to a child with hearing impairments because the rug absorbed noise. At the beginning of the year, the bulletin boards had a few welcoming words to the children and some bright pictures but were essentially empty—waiting to display the children's work, which Rebecca felt should be the main emphasis in the classroom. Soon the walls would be filled with children's drawings and the children's first efforts at writing. The group was varied in its needs. As Rebecca commented, "It was not an easy class. There were a lot of challenges."

Rebecca realized that she needed more information about Lesley. Because she felt that "it's important to know what you don't know," she called Anne and arranged a home visit to learn more about Lesley's equipment. She learned how to put in Lesley's ear molds and got some background information about Lesley. She borrowed some literature on hearing impairments, and later she conferred with Lesley's kindergarten teacher. She now knew that Lesley could see best at eight to thirteen inches and that with the FM system, Lesley's hearing was at a moderate level of impairment.

Anne was delighted with Rebecca's overture and interest. "It makes a difference when a teacher is genuinely excited about working with your child," she shared. Rebecca believed in letting parents know how much she enjoyed teaching their children. But, in fact, while she was enthusiastic about the chance to work with Lesley, she was somewhat scared about what she didn't know. She wished she could receive training on how to best teach Lesley from the system's teacher of students with hearing impairments.

First Efforts

Rebecca gave Lesley a seat in the front of the class to give her the best possible chance of seeing. Because she wanted the other children to understand Lesley's hearing problem and feel comfortable with her equipment, she played a game. Two at a time, the children left the room and listened to Rebecca, through Lesley's receiver. She told them, through the microphone, to hop, walk, or jump back into the room. This taught them, firsthand, how the equipment worked. "I think that before we played the game, they thought I could read Lesley's mind and know her secrets. This showed that the equipment only helped her to hear."

Rebecca changed recess time to accommodate Lesley's speech therapy. The times coincided, and she didn't want Lesley to feel she was missing out on a "goody." Although she couldn't make much of an adjustment because of other classes' need to use the playground and the speech therapist's fixed schedule, she made sure that Lesley had at least ten minutes of recess. Lesley's relationships with peers were positive, and she enjoyed jumping rope, chasing, and running around with her group of girlfriends.

The Greatest Resource

At the May PPT meeting, the principal of the school had suggested to Anne and Stuart that they have Lesley identified by the Services for the Blind. Anne was hesitant because she didn't want Lesley to be labeled further, but she also saw that Lesley needed services for her visual impairment. If Lesley were identified by the Services for the Blind, then the school system could get monies to provide more services. In fact, it turned out to be beneficial to have Lesley identified and labeled as visually impaired. The Services for the Blind assigned a tutor, Maria, to work in the first grade classroom with Lesley for two hours every day.

Although not a certified teacher, Maria was an enormous resource. Lesley could not see well enough to work from the blackboard. She could not see the thin white chalk against the black background and could not read well from a distance. For the first month, until Maria arrived, Rebecca had to transcribe any seatwork from the blackboard using heavy black marker on white or yellow paper propped on a stand at Lesley's desk.

When Maria came, she took over this responsibility. Maria also ran off and enlarged dittos and workbook pages. They discovered that, for Lesley, the issue was not how large the letters were but whether there was adequate white space between them.

Maria also engaged in prereading activities with Lesley. Before Lesley met with her reading group, Maria helped Lesley become familiar with the vocabulary in a new reading selection by using flash cards and actually reading the new selection with her.

The Services for the Blind supplied materials as well, including thick, colored chalk which could be used for any blackboard instruction that Lesley did not have to copy. There were several types of magnifiers for Lesley to use, from small, handheld ones to a large one with a light. Rebecca had just one meeting with a teacher from the city's vision department to have these materials explained to her. In retrospect, she commented, "They just gave me a bunch of stuff, and I was supposed to see what worked." Luckily, although Maria's hours were limited and she was not highly trained, she and Rebecca managed to figure out how to use the equipment.

A Time of Adjustment

Still, Rebecca needed to modify her teaching style somewhat to meet Lesley's needs. Often, it was just as she was starting the day and several young children were asking for her attention, that Lesley would come up and ask for help in putting her ear molds in and adjusting the equipment.

There were other adjustments. Rebecca didn't feel that she had the mobility she was used to.

> My style is to get with the children and to move from place to place, not stand in the front of the room. But, now, if I wanted to show anything, I had to go back to the front of the class because Lesley was there and couldn't see at a distance.

Rebecca also had less flexibility to spontaneously change a lesson as she saw a need or opportunity. "I tend to overprepare lessons, but I also love the freedom to throw them away when that seems right," she commented. Now, this was harder to do, since Lesley needed materials prepared in advance. Maria would have copied materials already from the planned lesson for Lesley's seatwork that day.

Although, in retrospect, the tutor turned out to be a wonderful asset, Rebecca didn't know what to do with her at first. It was not like working with a student teacher where there were well-defined goals and prescribed experiences. Moreover, Maria was not a trained teacher. "I didn't know how to help Lesley, and I didn't know how to help Maria to help Lesley," Rebecca explained. And there had been no advance meeting with Maria or representatives from the school system's special education department to help clarify her role and responsibilities. Both Rebecca and Maria were winging it.

Lesley's Progress

In many ways, Lesley was a model student, a "teacher's dream." She was attentive and followed directions well. If Rebecca asked the children to take out their papers, Lesley did it first. Anne commented that Lesley liked school and went eagerly. She focused intently on her work, insisted on finishing it, and clearly wanted to succeed.

Lesley got along well with the other children and was readily accepted by them. She especially enjoyed a small group of girls and often played jump rope or dodgeball outdoors with them. Barbara, her best friend, was her constant companion.

Math

Lesley was very able in mathematics. She was placed in the top group. She used manipulatives easily, but, in many cases, she didn't need them. Both her computation and reasoning skills were excellent. Rebecca, for example, often gave the children oral problems, such as "I see six children on the playground. Two went away. How many are left?" Lesley could do these problems easily. Also, until the end of the year, she was able to work right out of the workbook. By the end of the year, when the problems were in smaller type, the pages needed to be enlarged for her.

Reading/Language Arts

Rebecca felt that Lesley's early language skills were comparable to the other children's. She had been read to a great deal, and her oral language development was good. Although Lesley had some problems with articulation, she spoke slowly and deliberately in order to ensure that she was clear.

Lesley was placed in the lower reading group, and Rebecca used a variety of strategies to help those children learn to read. The children used basal readers. These reading textbooks teach new skills in a hierarchy from simple to complex, present controlled vocabulary and sentence length, and gear content to the level of the students' understanding.

Rebecca reinforced learnings from the basal reader through a tactile/kinesthetic approach. The children used alphabet cards with tactile letters, so that they could feel as well as see the letter and then say the letter sound. They traced the letters using crayons and then copied them. They wrote letters on the blackboard with water.

Rebecca did activities to impress the consonant-vowel-consonant sequence in the children's minds. For example, she would work on short */a/* words. The children wrote on the blackboard as she dictated to them. "Write 'cat.' Now change that to 'fat.' Now change the word to 'fit.' " They had to listen carefully to be successful, and the experience reinforced their understanding of the pattern.

Lesley read the first basal reader perfectly. However, Rebecca couldn't really tell what she knew. Before coming to Rebecca's reading group, Lesley had preread the stories with Maria. Lesley had an amazing memory and might just be remembering the text, not actually reading it. (Anne was aware that Lesley often read last in the group, which also gave her an opportunity to listen well and memorize what the other children were reading.)

The first basal had only a few words on each page, and they were in large print. In subsequent books, there were more words, and the print was smaller.

In order to adapt the books for Lesley, Maria copied and enlarged every page. Then she cut out the text in the book and pasted the enlargements in its place. Thus, Lesley's books looked like everyone else's. Although the Services for the Blind supplied copies of the basal readers in large print, these were big, black, legal-sized texts with no pictures. Lesley did not want her books to look different from the others.

Lesley avoided using some of the other special equipment for her. The large magnifier, which had a big arm-extension, could not be used at her seat because it needed to be plugged in, and the only available plug was at the back of the room. Although Rebecca made a special place for Lesley to use it there, Lesley didn't use it. Rebecca felt that Lesley was fighting being different from the other children and being separated from them physically as well.

Rebecca began to see hints of problems in Lesley's reading. For example, certain letter sounds were harder for her to discriminate, such as */f/* and */th/* or */m/* and */n/* or */p/* and */b/*. When working with the reading group, Rebecca pronounced the sounds, holding Lesley's hand to her mouth so that she could actually feel what Rebecca was doing differently. She did this with the other children, too.

Lesley also had some writing problems, not with handwriting, but with spelling and sentence structure. In spelling, Lesley might misplace letters in a word, so that, for example, "pond" would be written as "npod" or "is" as "si." Often these were words used in the basal reader that she had seen over and over. When Rebecca asked her to reread the word and sound it out, Lesley knew that it was wrong. "But it was almost like she was seeing them jumbled," Rebecca commented. She hastened to add that this was different than the invented spelling that children do with unfamiliar words.

Lesley liked to write stories and wrote interesting ones. However, she often left out major words in the sentences, such as verbs.

Rebecca used drawing as a kind of prewriting experience for the children. She felt they were related, believing that "you need to see details before you can write about them." They needed to understand the importance of critical attributes—those elements about something which make it what it is. She also spent a lot of time discussing the children's drawings with them, talking about what was in the foreground and what was in the background, for example, or what was happening in the picture. Lesley's drawing skills were not good. There was very little detail in her drawings. Her people had vacant eyes. Rebecca talked with Lesley about possible details for her drawings because she assumed that Lesley couldn't see these in the world.

A Call for Help

It was now early November. No one had contacted Rebecca from the school system's special education department. When she asked to confer with a hearing specialist, she was referred to the teacher of students with hearing impairments. Although this woman was willing, she had a full load herself and wasn't able to make herself available.

Rebecca decided to call Dr. Corman, Lesley's audiologist at the university. Rebecca commented:

> My strength is being in tune with kids, and I knew what I was doing wasn't hitting Lesley. I just knew something was missing. I didn't want the whole year to go by without Lesley being successful.

When she expressed her concerns to Dr. Corman and described her strategies, Dr. Corman replied, "We don't really know for sure what the right approach should be. It sounds like what you're doing is appropriate."

The Home Front

As Rebecca was becoming apprehensive about Lesley's reading skills at school, Anne was seeing problems at home. Anne called it an "up and down" year. Lesley seemed to be mastering some words on one day, and then the next day, she couldn't recognize more than one of them again. Anne also saw backsliding on the weekends and during vacations. She wanted to attribute these problems to Lesley's sensory impairments, but they worried her.

Lesley knew her ABCs and the vowel sounds, but she didn't know all the consonant sounds. She also didn't comprehend that letters in their uppercase and lowercase forms were actually the same letters. Lesley didn't know how to approach a word to begin to decode it.

Lesley consistently rejected reading at home. Although Anne's other children, as beginning readers, had enjoyed reading books like *Hop on Pop*, Lesley refused to read them. When Lesley was younger, she had enjoyed having her parents teach her new skills. Now Lesley was in a new stage, Anne realized, and no longer accepted their instruction. She didn't want help from her brothers and sisters either.

The May PPT—At the End of First Grade

By the end of first grade, Rebecca was convinced that Lesley was still having reading problems. Lesley performed well on workbook pages and spelling tests. Her reading group was reading a low-level first grade reader. Lesley read aloud fine, but often seemed to use her exceptional memory to repeat what others had read. If she were given an unfamiliar picture book, she could not read it. She could not read independently. "This was a child who was functioning okay, but you could tell that nothing had come together," Rebecca noted.

Lesley was also having difficulty writing independently in the many creative writing activities assigned—this, too, was a clue to Rebecca. Although Lesley was willing and interested, Rebecca didn't see the progress she expected to see by the end of first grade in Lesley's writing.

Rebecca convinced Anne to advocate for her child and insist that she be assigned a reading tutor in second grade. Lesley was not eligible to get help from the resource room teacher since she was not identified as being either emotionally disturbed or learning disabled. At the PPT, it was agreed that Lesley would be tutored in reading the next year. Rebecca offered to tutor Lesley in reading during the summer to tide her over.

At the end of first grade, Lesley took a major stride toward independence. Rebecca taught her to put in her ear molds for the FM system herself. This freed Rebecca of the responsibility and added to Lesley's sense of competence. Anne felt that this was a great gift that Rebecca gave Lesley.

How Much Can You Expect?

When Lesley returned to school in the fall, the school system had replaced the reading and math specialists with three computers in each regular education classroom. The computers offered highly structured, carefully sequenced, programmed instruction in the areas of reading and math. It was determined that this would be cost-effective and all children would benefit, not just the low achievers. Every child was to use the computer a few days a week. If a child were having particular difficulty with reading or math, the child would be assigned extra time on the computer since a reading or math tutor would no longer be available.

Administrators in the central office made the decision to replace the math and reading specialists with the computers in mid-August. Teachers, returning to school in the fall, had not been informed that the purchase of the computers would mean the loss of the specialists.

Anne felt that this computer-assisted instruction was a waste of time for Lesley. The sounds on the computer were not clear and, therefore, were hard for Lesley to discriminate. Although the screen was magnified, it was still distorted. The room was noisy, which added to the confusion for Lesley.

The second grade teacher, a warm, kindly woman, felt that Lesley was reading well. When Anne expressed concern, the teacher commented, "You have to remember that Lesley is a handicapped child. How much can you expect?"

Anne was devastated by this response. On the one hand, she was upset that she may have been pushing her child too hard. On the other hand, she was distressed that the teacher did not share her vision of her child's ability and potential.

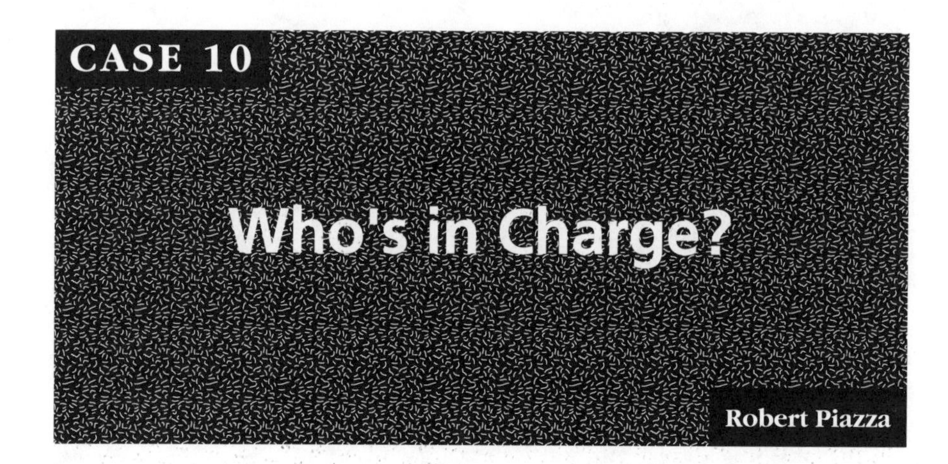

Part B

An October Observation

Dr. Lewis, in the back of Mrs. Kay's room, took notes while he observed Mark in his math class. Mark was working on a math ditto with word problems. "I don't know. I can't do this problem," Mark said dejectedly.

Mrs. Kay came over to Mark, looked at his blank page and said:

> Just read the directions again. They are very clear. Didn't you listen when I read them to the entire class? If you have questions, you should ask them before you begin your work. I've told you that time and time again. Why don't you bring that paper home for homework? Class, it's time for recess. Put away your work and line up.

A confused look came upon Mark's face. He looked as though he wanted to say something, but he remained quiet.

Late January

Mark's second grade teacher, Miss Dale, met with Mr. and Mrs. Jones to review his progress. She indicated that his progress had been quite limited and that he was still struggling to keep up with the work of the lower groups.

"Mark is not failing, but he does seem frustrated at the pace of instruction. I feel that he is a good candidate for a retention. As you know, he is not finishing his work, and he is becoming very inattentive. I've noticed a substantial regression in his behavior."

Mrs. Jones responded, "What? Why have you waited so long to tell me this? Weren't we supposed to have a PPT meeting last month? I was going to ask for a meeting after Dr. Lewis observed Mark in October, but you assured me that things were fine."

Further discussion continued. Miss Dale said she would talk with Mr. Capasso about having a PPT meeting as quickly as possible. A meeting was scheduled for the following Friday.

CASE 11

A Question of Ownership

Sally Francia and Robert Piazza

Part B

The Team Meeting

All members of the team arrived at the meeting at 3:00 P.M., aware of the problem because Sara had put a memo in their school mailboxes the previous afternoon. The team sat around Mr. Morrisey's conference table in the resource room. Lisa Weeks spoke first:

> As Sam's classroom teacher, and the one who has to give him his grades, I feel I have the right to judge the level of his performance. I feel the top reading group is reserved for serious students who need an accelerated pace. Sam's midterm test grades and his classroom performance do not place him in this category. Although he was doing adequately in this group until recently, I feel he's at a breaking point and can no longer excel at this pace. Sam's a sweetheart, but I don't want to see him overly frustrated. Also, remember he just turned nine. Other kids in my class are much younger. I think he was overplaced to begin with. All of you who work with him individually or in a small group may be overestimating his abilities. I see him in a class with twenty-four other children. I know best what he can do in this type of situation. Perhaps I should have sat down with this team first, but I don't do that with my other children. It was just a matter of routine. I didn't say Sam didn't belong in my class anymore. I just changed his reading group.

Sara thought that Lisa had made a number of valid points, but she reminded the group that Sam was initially placed in the top reading group for two main reasons: (1) he had covered the material in his preteaching lessons and was ready for a faster pace, and (2) the size of the group was smaller and made of students who were not disruptive, taking into account that Sam is easily distracted.

Lisa explained her concern about Sam's mastery of the lessons on prefixes and suffixes. Sara interjected that she saw this "deficiency" as somewhat predictable.

"These skills need to be taught differently to children with hearing impairments. It is confusing to them to be taught a few prefixes and then a few suffixes and then to jump back and be taught a few more prefixes." She continued, "I've been working the last several months on prefixes with him, but we've just recently begun to work on suffixes."

"How am I supposed to know all of that? And by the way, I thought you were supposed to be preteaching all of this material. Why did you wait so long to introduce suffixes?" Lisa questioned.

Sara didn't respond to this last question and was glad when Lou Morrisey broke the silence by requesting that the group discuss the midterm basal test results. He observed that Sam had scored 82 out of 90 and 85 out of 90 the previous two times he had taken the basal test. Lou added:

> I know Sam was given the test in a one-on-one setting and in a quiet environment the last two times, but when looking at some of Sam's incorrect responses, I noticed something else. He made four mistakes on the five items that required him to choose the correct syllabication of words such as *yellow*. For this word, he could have chosen *ye-llow*, *yel-low*, or *yell-ow*. Doesn't this type of test present a big problem for a child with a hearing impairment? He did very well on the reading comprehension section. Isn't this the most important thing?

Lori and Sara agreed with Lou that the syllabication subtest had a heavy hearing component and would be inappropriate for a student whose hearing was impaired.

Lori Nolan also commented that although Sam's group placement was important, it was not the main concern. She explained:

> We haven't been communicating the way we should be. Lisa, I can truly understand your need to control your own students' grouping and grading. I'm also amazed at how tolerant you have been with all of us coming in and out of your classroom. But decisions about curriculum needs for Sam must be made by this entire team, and you are part of this team. There are many issues to consider with Sam. Many at this table have been working with him for years, and you might say that we have a vested interest in his education. If you had brought your concerns to the team earlier, we may have suggested that Sara observe Sam to see if strategies could be implemented to improve the situation.

"Okay," Lisa said. "But give me some help. Even if I move Sam back to his original group, other problems still exist. How do I solve the problems of his losing his place when reading or becoming easily distracted? He really is slowing down the entire group. You're the experts. What should I do?"

CASE 12

Case of Inclusion

Deirdre Peterson and Robert Piazza

Part B

The Meeting With Mrs. Hill

Mrs. Sarah Hill was an attractive, energetic, and friendly teacher who was well regarded by her colleagues. Last June, she was excited to learn Lisa would be placed in her class. As a teacher with nine years of experience and a sixth-year diploma, she felt ready for the challenge. In September when Susan Johnson approached her about also placing John in her third grade class, she immediately replied, "Why not, Sue? This would be a great year to try it. I only have eighteen children assigned to me."

One afternoon in November, both teachers met to discuss Lisa's inability to make new friends in her third grade class. Susan began their conversation: "I wanted Lisa to be a true part of your third grade classroom; however, she tends to spend most of her day with me, the paraprofessional, or John. We need to include her more in the third grade curriculum. The problem is how to do it, still work on her ability level, and not frustrate her." She explained that Lisa had come home upset and told her parents she had no friends in her third grade class.

Sarah Hill looked puzzled. She thought Lisa was a true member of her class. To hear that she was unhappy was disturbing. "I feel I've included Lisa into my class. She attends the pledge daily, she hands me her milk money, and hangs up her bag and coat in the back. Lisa attends all the specials: gym, music, art, and library, and we included her with us for all auditorium performances like band . . . . What am I doing wrong?"

Susan replied, "You're doing just fine in including Lisa in your class. We just need to look at other ways to encourage Lisa to interact with her peers."

Sarah thought for some time and said, "Why didn't I think of this earlier? Lisa can join my Drama Club. We meet after school twice a week and will perform a play in a few months. The club just started meeting last week. In fact, a lot of Lisa's friends from last year participate in the club."

"That's a wonderful idea!" Susan responded excitedly. "Mrs. Wilson is constantly telling me cute stories about how Lisa likes to put on skits with her cousins for her aunts and uncles.

"I can," Susan continued, "speak to the cafeteria aides and have Lisa sit with friends from last year and from your class. And once a week, I can meet with Lisa and a couple of friends who seem interested in a computer rap club. We can meet in your class, have lunch, and play computer games."

Susan Johnson felt they were on the right track. However, she wanted Lisa to be included in lessons during the day.

"How can we adapt the curriculum so we can involve Lisa? If she is doing what her classmates are doing, then maybe she'll feel more accepted and truly be a full part of your third grade class. We can involve her more with her nondisabled peers rather than pulling her out of the class with John."

Both of Lisa's teachers thought they'd begin slowly, looking first at language arts activities where Lisa could be included. Sarah mapped out what would be covered during the next week in language arts.

> *Monday*—Introduce verbs in the present tense. The students will identify subjects as plural or singular, then choose the correct verb form for the sentences.
>
> *Tuesday*—Review Monday's homework assignment, and review concept of verbs in the present tense.
>
> *Wednesday*—Writing assignment: Students will pretend they have a new job. They will write a letter to a friend, describing the job and the people with whom they work. Students will be graded on whether they use the verbs in the correct present tense. Students must underline each verb they use.
>
> *Thursday*—Continue the writing assignment and assign a review of verbs in the present tense (numbers 4–28, page 112).
>
> *Friday*—Review Thursday's homework assignment. Quiz on verbs in the present tense.

Susan perused the schedule carefully. Finally she said to Sarah, "Okay, let's just take a look at Monday's assignment. Lisa can attend your lesson on verbs in the present tense. However, when it is time to do the assignment, she can work with Mrs. Carey and complete only half the work." Susan then reviewed Lisa's Individual Education Plan (IEP). One of Lisa's objectives was to identify verbs (action words) in a given sentence, 80 percent of the time.

"We can," Susan explained, "include Lisa into your lesson on verbs while working on her objective. Lisa, however, does not have to discriminate the correct verb form or whether the subject is plural or singular. Lisa can listen to the sentences and identify only the verbs given."

This plan sounded simple. It was decided to begin on Monday with the first assignment.

Monday's Assignment

Mrs. Carey sat with Lisa as Sarah Hill presented the lesson on verb tenses. Lisa did not participate in the discussion, but seemed to follow along. She was assigned items 9–15 on the accompanying assignment sheet, but refused to do them because she could not read the words in the third grade language book. "I can't read this. I don't want to do it," Lisa stated stubbornly to Mrs. Hill. She also resisted Mrs. Carey's attempts to help her.

Sarah Hill used the interschool telephone and called Susan to her room. Within three minutes Susan was there. "Lisa doesn't understand this stuff. I think we're making a huge mistake by including her in the language arts area. Maybe we're wrong about our plan," Sarah said.

Susan Johnson took a deep breath and replied dejectedly, "Maybe you're right—let me take a look at the assignments tonight and see what I can do to adapt them even more." The special education teacher left school that day with a heavy heart.

"This is too much to handle . . . . I'm afraid we're failing Lisa and ourselves," she thought.

CASE 13

A Child's Disability—A Teacher's Handicap?

Barbara Heinisch

Part B

Seeking Solutions

As the weeks progressed, Hallie was gradually accepted by the other students. Their interactions with her were initially based on curiosity. They had questions about her wheelchair and about how serious a handicap she had as a result of her CP. Once they understood Hallie's problems, they were eager to be her helper. Ann was actually grateful for their help. Although Hallie was fairly independent for most activities, she still needed a lot of support for physical tasks. There were many times when help was needed simply to pick up an object Hallie had dropped. The school nurse took on the job of helping Hallie with toileting. Larry was in the classroom frequently offering suggestions, but hadn't planned a program for working with Hallie yet.

Academically, Hallie certainly seemed to be on a level with her classmates. She was a bright child, with no evidence of the learning disabilities often seen in children with CP. She had a mature use of language, and spoke clearly using complex phrases, but she had yet to write them. Ann had determined that Hallie was reading on grade level. Hallie had lost some of her initial shyness and was beginning to contribute to class discussions. She was often the first child to raise her hand to answer a question.

The children had made a good adjustment to having a child with a physical difference in the classroom. Ann was enjoying the challenge of teaching Hallie, but she was spending an inordinate amount of time creating special worksheets for Hallie, on which she could choose answers instead of writing answers to open-ended questions. She had Hallie dictate compositions to her. Ann literally had no free time during her "free" periods.

At the end of a particularly hectic school day, Ann sank into her chair. Hallie's Planning and Placement Team (PPT) meeting was scheduled for the coming week, and she needed to prepare her report. Something had to be done! It just wasn't humanly possible for her to teach her class effectively and spend as much time as she was spending with this one child. She hoped they would somehow find the means to restore a classroom aide position.

The PPT—Early December

Ann looked around the table. This was the largest group she had ever seen at a PPT. Besides Mr. and Mrs. Berman, Larry Jones, and Ms. Copeland, there were a speech therapist and a physical therapist, both of whom had recently evaluated Hallie; the school social worker; the school psychologist; and the physical education teacher. The social worker, who was also the PPT coordinator, thanked everyone for coming and began by asking for reports from the therapy team.

The physical therapist was concerned with Hallie's ability to transfer herself from her wheelchair to other seating or to a toilet. Hallie needed a lot of assistance for transfers. The physical therapist suggested that a major goal would be for Hallie to improve her ability to transfer independently. She also suggested that the school acquire a piece of equipment called a "prone stander." This would give Hallie the opportunity to do some of her work in a supported standing position. The therapist noted how important it was for children who use wheelchairs to get out of them sometimes, pointing out that standing improves circulation, alleviating a problem for people who use wheelchairs. She also mentioned an additional benefit of having Hallie in a standing position—the fact that bearing weight strengthens the bones.

Larry's report was short and sweet. "Hallie has minimal use of her right hand. She is able to use it effectively to control her chair, but she has a limited range of motion with marked muscle weakness. In terms of ADL skills—oh, sorry," he said, noticing Mr. Berman's puzzled expression, "I mean, Activities of Daily Living skills. We've already discussed the issue of toileting independently. Hallie can feed herself if someone gets her lunch tray—she can't balance it and drive her wheelchair at the same time. Dressing is a problem. She needs help with her coat. The big challenge that I see, though, is the problem of Hallie's writing."

Ann spoke up. "It is really difficult for me to teach a child who can't write. As much as I would like to, I can't spend the amount of time I'd like to with Hallie. The other children would love the opportunity to help Hallie by writing for her, but they need to do their own work." Ann paused, and looked at the people gathered around the table. "Is it possible to get someone to assist me with this class?"

At first no one spoke. Then Mrs. Berman said, "There was an aide with Hallie in her other school. Can't one be assigned to her here?"

Ms. Copeland frowned: "There were some aide positions in the system, but they were eliminated with the last round of budget cuts."

Hallie's father cleared his throat. "What about a computer?" he suggested. "I've been reading about people with disabilities using computers for their writing. There was a newspaper article about a computer lab at the state university for people with disabilities."

"I saw that article, too!" Larry's face lit up. "I wondered what they could suggest for some of our students." He turned to Ms. Copeland, "Would the central office pay for an evaluation?"

She looked dubious. "I don't know," she said, "but it's worth a try. I'll make some calls. Meanwhile let's schedule Hallie for an evaluation by our district's computer coordinator and see what he thinks."

The other teachers finished with their recommendations. As the meeting was adjourned, Mr. Berman asked Larry what he thought about the use of computers for children as young as Hallie. Larry replied that he didn't know too much about computers, but he felt that they could be a good solution for some children.

The District Computer Coordinator's Evaluation

Ann sat at her desk, slumped over in defeat. It was the end of the day. The children had left, and Ann was catching up on her mail. In her hands she held the report from John Watson, the computer coordinator:

> This child is not a good candidate for computer use; her hands are too weak to press the keys effectively. A greater problem, however, is the fact that this child is basically a one-handed typist. Although she was able to type some words, her typing was exceedingly slow, and her coordination is such that she hits many unwanted keys. Also, she sometimes has trouble releasing keys, resulting in many key repeats. Perhaps when this child is a little older, she will have greater control over her hands. We teach keyboarding skills in the sixth grade. A child who begins typing before that may learn bad keyboarding habits which later have to be unlearned.

Ann felt frustrated and angry. She didn't understand how John could be so narrow-minded! Hallie couldn't wait until sixth grade to learn to type. She needed help for Hallie *now!* She knew the child had limitations. Surely there were some modifications that could help Hallie type successfully. Why didn't he suggest any?

The phone beeped. Ann had a phone call in the main office. It was Hallie's father. Mr. Berman had also received John's report, and he was angry. "I'm going to try to get Hallie an evaluation at the university's adaptive computer lab. I'm convinced that this guy Watson doesn't have a clue about what's out there to help kids like Hallie. We'll have to track down some solutions ourselves."

Ann told him she thought it was a good idea. She was becoming desperate for a solution to Hallie's problems. She was working harder than she had ever thought possible, and she never felt that she had done all she could for each child. There were some children in the class who needed more one-on-one time with her, and right now they weren't getting it. Hallie was taking up larger blocks of her time. It was fun to work with her. She was very bright, but she needed to be able to express her ideas independently. Mr. Berman told Ann he had set up another meeting with Ms. Copeland.

The Adaptive Computer Lab Evaluation

Hallie, her parents, and Larry Jones arrived at the computer lab early; they had been afraid of getting lost on the campus. Larry was chosen to go along for two reasons. The first was that he already had an interest in computers and was eager to find ways to make them accessible to his students. The second reason was that the staff of the lab had requested that an occupational therapist be present for the evaluation to help them resolve issues concerning seating or positioning.

The evaluator, Linda Hope, was expecting them. After talking briefly with Hallie and her parents, Linda suggested that they try some typing options for Hallie.

"By the way," Larry said, "I did some checking and found that there's a laptop computer in the system that we could use for Hallie. It was ordered two years ago for a child who then moved away."

"That's good to know," said Linda. "What kind of computer is it?" Larry said that he wasn't certain, but he thought it was IBM-compatible.

Linda turned toward Hallie, who had been looking around curiously at the computers. "Why don't we try some typing?" Linda said, placing a keyboard on the desk in front of her. "Can you type your name for me please?"

Hallie reached out her right hand and tentatively began to type her name. She did not capitalize the *H*. It took about a minute and a half to type her first name.

"Good for you!" said Linda. "How about your last name?"

While Hallie was typing, Linda spoke with Larry about positioning for typing. "If a laptop computer were mounted on Hallie's wheelchair, her arm could rest on the wheelchair tray and her hand would be stabilized. She would have more control."

Larry nodded in agreement.

Linda continued, "Is this a wheelchair she will be using for a while? The mounting would have to be custom-made by a rehabilitation engineer."

Mrs. Berman said, "Oh, yes. This is a new wheelchair, and it has room for her to grow into it. She should be in it for a while."

Larry asked if Linda had a rehabilitation engineer working in the computer lab. "No," she said, "but I can give you some names."

By now Hallie had completed her name and had continued typing. She had written, "hallie berrmaaan i likkle tto ty[peee."

"That's very good, Hallie." Linda pointed to the delete key. "See this key? If you press it, it will erase your mistakes. Try it!"

Hallie pressed the key and watched in fascination as her typing disappeared. "Awesome!" Hallie grinned.

Linda gave Hallie some more things to type. While Hallie was typing and experimenting with the delete key, Linda spoke to the other adults, all of whom had been uncharacteristically quiet as they watched Hallie type.

> These are the problems I see with Hallie's typing so far. She is a weak one-handed typist. There are some membrane keyboards which don't require as much pressure, but I think Hallie will do fine with a standard keyboard. If we use an IBM-compatible computer, we can use a software program called Access DOS to modify the way the keyboard works. This will allow Hallie to capitalize by pressing the shift key and then an *A*, for example, to get a capital *A*, instead of having to hold the two keys down at the same time. Hallie also has a problem getting off a key once she has hit it. This same program can delay the key repeat function to prevent unwanted multiple letters being typed. We could also use the program to delay the acceptance rate, so that Hallie would have to hold down each selected key for a preset number of seconds before the letter would appear on the screen. I'm not sure yet if she needs that, though.

Linda paused to check on Hallie, who was still typing happily. While Linda had been speaking, Larry had repositioned the keyboard. He was holding it balanced across the armrests of the wheelchair. Hallie was typing more accurately and faster in this position.

Mr. Berman cleared his throat. "How expensive is all this?" he asked.

"Access DOS is free," said Linda. "IBM provides it free to anyone who requests it."

Mr. Berman asked if it would work on all computers.

"No, only on IBM or IBM-compatible computers. But Macintosh computers come with all these access features built into them. Most Macintosh users probably don't even know they exist."

Larry asked if Access DOS could work in conjunction with other software programs.

"Oh, didn't I tell you?" smiled Linda. "It's completely transparent. You can use it with any software. We should try some other things. I'd like to try a word prediction program with Hallie." In response to the blank looks on their faces, she explained,

> Word prediction programs were created to speed typing by saving keystrokes for people for whom every keystroke is an effort. When you start a word by typing a letter, a list of word choices appears on the screen. Each word has a number or symbol before it. Typing that number or symbol results in the whole word being typed. Why don't I load up the Access DOS options along with a word prediction program for Hallie to try?

Hallie was looking tired; she needed a break. While she and her parents went out for a walk, Larry stayed and asked questions, making copious notes. He knew that the role of computer support person would fall to him. John

Watson, the district computer coordinator, was rarely in the school and had not felt that starting Hallie on a computer was a good idea at all. Larry knew that while Ann would be open to anything that might work for Hallie, she was not yet very comfortable with computers.

When they returned, Linda showed them the MindReader program. "Interestingly enough, this is one of the first word prediction programs. It was written originally for businesspeople who were poor typists. It is relatively inexpensive."

Hallie didn't even wait for instruction. She typed a *T*. A window appeared with a numbered list of words beginning with *T*.

"Look, Hallie," said Linda. "If you just type the number *2* you will get the word *this* on the screen."

"Oooh," breathed Hallie.

"See? You get the word *this* and a space after it." Turning to the others, she said, "This is how the program saves the person keystrokes."

"This is unbelievable!" Mrs. Berman exclaimed.

Linda told Hallie to keep typing and see what happened. She watched for a minute, noting how quickly Hallie caught on. The child was typing, watching the screen in fascination, and smiling as she pulled up whole words. Her parents were watching their child in wonder.

Linda continued:

> The newer word prediction programs predict not only by the first letter selected, but also by context. If you select the word *good*, for example, it might offer you the word *morning* next. If you don't want that word, you ignore it and keep typing. Some of these programs are wonderful tools for students with learning disabilities. Students with severe spelling problems or word-finding difficulties, for example, are finding these programs very helpful. Some of the more sophisticated programs work on the Macintosh. The PowerBooks are Macintosh laptops, but the built-in trackball, which replaces the mouse, is not usually successful for people with Hallie's type of CP—she has too much spasticity to control it easily. We're not even going to try it. It would be frustrating. Besides, if the school already has an IBM-compatible computer, we should look at solutions for IBMs. There are some new word prediction programs being developed for IBMs. There might be a better program for Hallie down the road, but for now I think the combination of MindReader with Access DOS would be good for her.

Linda assured the Bermans and Larry that she would send in a complete evaluation report, with information about the software they had seen and with the name of a rehabilitation engineer. She reminded them that they still had some serious issues to resolve:

> Who would teach Hallie typing skills? Would Larry be able to provide the type of computer support Hallie and Ann would need? How would Hallie's use of the computer be integrated into the classroom? Would the school allow Hallie

to take the computer home? If not, the Bermans might want to look into acquiring a computer for Hallie to use at home.

Linda suggested that another PPT meeting be scheduled to formulate a plan for Hallie's computer use. It needed to be made clear that Hallie was to be allowed to do all her written work on the computer, including the taking of tests, and that one should be available to her at all times. This would eliminate potential problems with future teachers who might not fully understand the potential tool that a computer would represent for Hallie.

CASE 14

The First Mistake

Robert Piazza and Judith B. Buzzell

Part B

Monday, Mid-January

During the afternoon math class, Ms. Berlein told Emily's group that they would be solving some word problems. The problems required the use of operations that the students were already proficient in performing—addition, subtraction, multiplication, and division. After carefully reading the problems to themselves, they were to reflect upon the words to see if they really understood what the printed material said. Ms. Berlein did not assume that the whole group could do these problems. She orally offered the following strategic hints:

> The problems on this page can be done best by thinking carefully about the information given in each problem. Try to search for key strategic words that will let you decide what operation you are to use. All four major operations will be found within this page, so you only have four choices.
>
> After you have analyzed the information, plan the way you think the problem should be done. Visualize the information. This should allow you to make an educated guess about which operation to use. Then, estimate what you think the correct answer should be. Write this estimate on another sheet of paper.
>
> Now you are ready to solve the problem. You may need to do the problem on a practice sheet before you do it in your workbook. It's a useful strategy, and it also prevents erasures and a messy workbook. After you have solved the problem, look at your answer and compare that answer with your estimated answer. They should be very close. If not, go back through the process I have just explained, and start your work all over again. Are there any questions?

No hands were raised. These were the problems:

1. On the way to the kite-flying tournament in Salem, John will pass four towns. Medford is between Scranton and Danbury. Salem is five miles from Scranton. Danbury is thirteen miles from Scranton. If John starts in Danbury, how far will he have to travel?

2. Tom and Frank were 32 yards apart. They threw frisbees toward each other. Tom threw his frisbee 12 yards. Frank threw his 6 yards. How many yards apart are the frisbees?

3. There were 24 children in the class. The teacher wanted to play a game with 4 children on each team. How many teams will there be?

4. Jan is four years old. When she is four times this age, she can apply for a driver's license. How old will she be when she can make this application?

5. There were 218 candies in a jar. In 6 weeks the Washburn twins ate 34 candies each. How many candies were left?

Emily only solved problems 3 and 4 correctly. Ms. Berlein was distraught. She felt that she had given adequate cues to help *all* the students be successful. Yet Emily was still stumbling. Emily had made the choice to stay with this group, and she had agreed to it, but she couldn't allow Emily to experience five months of failure. Her student seemed to grow more frustrated daily.

During the next few days, Ms. Berlein realized that she needed to reinforce Emily's foundational understanding. At seatwork activities, Emily belabored each problem, and her papers were covered with erasures. Since Emily hadn't fully mastered earlier skills, she was on shaky ground when new concepts were introduced. Over the weekend, Ms. Berlein took time to consider the problem more thoroughly.

CASE 15

Chen Yang

Judith B. Buzzell

Part B

A Tough Question

The student's question reverberated in Jim's ears. "Hey, what's the matter with him? Can't he talk?" In truth, Jim didn't know the answer, since there were no records on Chen. But Jim realized that he had to say something to satisfy this student's and others' curiosity—and perhaps to protect Chen from malice.

"I'm not really sure," responded Jim. "We're all going to have to take some time to get to know each other and appreciate each other during the course of this year." Not wishing to draw further attention to Chen, Jim quickly moved into an overview of the curriculum for the year.

Later in the day, one of the students told Jim that she didn't think that Chen understood much English. When the class was involved in math, Jim took Chen aside. As he talked to the boy, Chen first stared at Jim and then averted his eyes downward. "I wanted to show empathy toward him," Jim reflected. "I wanted to let him know that I realized how hard this might be for him and that I would try to help him." Yet, Jim felt that he wasn't able to communicate this understanding to Chen. He knew he needed to assess the level of Chen's ability in English. He also wondered how he was going to help Chen to feel comfortable in this very social group.

The Week Proceeds

On the second day of school, Jim brought a collection of books that spanned a variety of reading levels. While the other students were engaged in silent reading, he and Chen leafed through these books, reading from them. It seemed to Jim that Chen was at about the first or second grade reading level.

During the writing period, Jim told Chen to draw or to write in Chinese letters. He hoped that Chen would write, both as an opportunity for self-expression and as a release of tension he might be feeling. Afterward, Jim threw a football to Chen, and the boy seemed happy to be outside and play catch for a while.

On the Friday of the first week, there was a breakthrough. Outdoors, Jim glimpsed one of his students from last year, Ming Lo, a Chinese boy who was fluent in English. Ming Lo was now a fifth grader in another teacher's class. Jim realized that Ming Lo could help him. He grabbed Ming Lo's hand, and they walked over to Chen who was standing alone by a tree. With Ming Lo as his translator, Jim explained to Chen that he understood how difficult this adjustment must be and that he would try to help him to have a good year. Through Ming Lo, Chen responded that he was appreciative of Jim's efforts. He explained that he had arrived from China only last January. After spending his first few months in another school, he had just begun the new school year here at Washington Elementary School. He also shared that he was very comfortable with math, which gave Jim food for thought over the weekend.

On Monday, Jim set Chen up with a math game, Math Climbers, on the computer. In the game, math sentences move up the screen, and the object is to solve the problem each sentence poses before it reaches the top. Some of the sentences are complex, involving two functions, such as $20 - 12 \times 9 =$ ______. Chen focused intently on the game. Soon a buzz spread through the room as the students seated at the neighboring computers commented, "Ya gotta see this!" Chen was remarkably good at playing the game.

That same day, the students were conducting their first experiment as part of a science unit on the human body. The students first took their own pulses. They then ran in place for one minute and took their pulses again to determine how long it takes for the pulse to return to its resting place. Chen did not participate, although Jim's aide tried to show him what to do.

Jim suspected that Chen didn't understand the purpose of the activity, so the boy didn't participate. Yet, Jim had begun to question whether there might be more than simply a communication problem involved. Perhaps Chen didn't speak English because he couldn't. On the other hand, perhaps he was just shy or too inhibited to join in the activity.

Jim felt that Chen might be like his good friend from Mexico who spent six months every year in the United States. Jim knew that this friend appeared to know less English than he really did, and he chose not to speak English many times when he might have. Jim thought that his friend wanted to be perfect in all areas and wouldn't risk making a mistake in English, which led him to be inhibited about speaking English. Perhaps Chen felt the same way—he would only perform in areas where he knew he would be successful.

Jim's Strategies

Jim decided to build on Chen's obvious strength—his mathematical ability. This seemed to be a potential avenue for Chen both to experience academic mastery and to gain social acceptance. One day, the class was playing Math Trivial Pursuit. As they were dividing up into teams, several of the boys called out, "We want Chen!" Chen joined their team and was able to solve one of the problems that no one else could get. "While they may not be buddies, at least now," Jim thought, "the kids consider Chen very intelligent."

Another day, Jim gave the class a timed, multiplication test. They were to complete a grid of the multiplication table in three minutes. Chen finished his in two minutes—and the class applauded.

In a game of Force Out, students were to compete in pairs, using geometric and reasoning skills, to fill up a grid with Cuisenaire rods. The goal was to make your opponent fill in the last block. Jim was surprised that Chen lost to his particular opponent. Still, he felt that both Chen's math computational and critical thinking skills were more advanced than a typical fourth grader's. Chen also excelled at chess.

Jim tried to help Chen build relationships with the other students. There were times when he would hear other kids quietly ask one another, "I wonder what's going on with him?"

Jim would respond, "It must be so difficult for Chen to come to a completely different country, with different ways of doing things and a new language and without his friends. Imagine how you would feel if you were in a class in China."

Jim thought that the other students now felt concern for Chen because of the classroom climate which fostered caring for one another in general and also promoted an interest in problem solving. The naturally inquisitive students saw Chen's difficulties as a kind of problem that they were interested in solving.

One student, George, a hefty redhead who had been held back in school a year, showed special interest in Chen. He was very social and the quintessential class clown, able to break the class up into laughter with a single comment or funny face. Jim felt he had a sweet temperament. One day, George asked Chen to play football with him. Although Chen refused, George was not deterred. The next day, George offered to help Chen with a research project.

Jim also continued to try to communicate with Chen. Although he never formally took attendance before, he began to call the roll—just to provide an opportunity for Chen to talk by saying "Here." A few times a day, he would try to pat Chen on the back or rub his shoulder. Chen neither pulled away nor acknowledged Jim's overture.

Whenever possible, Chen wanted Jim to play football with him outdoors. Although Jim had asked George and his friends to teach Chen the game, Chen avoided playing with the other boys. Jim suspected that this was because the boys were very aggressive and already adept at the game.

English Language Acquisition

The ESL teacher was tutoring Chen for forty-five minutes on three mornings a week. Although Jim had not formally met with her, she caught him for a few minutes one day. She was confused by Chen's shyness. She thought that perhaps he was learning disabled because he seemed shyer than other children she had worked with.

Also, the reading teacher met twice a week with a group of four kids from Jim's class, including Chen. She reported to Jim that Chen was on about a first or second grade reading level. However, although he could decode at that level, it was not clear how much he understood. She had tried to test him individually, but the language barrier was so great that she couldn't assess his comprehension. She thought that he simply didn't have the vocabulary base he needed for meaningful comprehension.

She commented that she could barely hear Chen when he talked, although the other kids said this was the loudest they had ever heard him speak. She decided not to ask Chen to read aloud because she felt the situation was too intimidating.

Chen was showing some progress in the area of language in the classroom. Jim had been able to commandeer another computer for his classroom, an Apple, and scrounge up some reading and vocabulary programs that were at a lower level. Now, Chen could read simple books, such as those by Tomie Di Paola. On a recent spelling test, Chen wrote twelve out of twenty-five words and got them all correct. Jim was delighted.

However, Jim continued to be concerned about Chen's ability, or lack of ability, to comprehend the fourth grade curriculum. Most of the time, Chen seemed "out of it." Chen wrote very little. There were games played in class, such as Twenty Questions or a colonization simulation game, which Jim was sure Chen didn't understand.

"It seems like such a waste to see Chen sitting there with nothing to do," Jim commented.

Late October: No Miracles

By this time, the Jostens computer program (an IBM language and mathematics program) was set up in the classroom, and Jim was able to put Chen through the Basic Skills Inventory. Chen scored on the first grade level in language (including reading and language usage) and at the high third grade level in math. Jim had expected the math score to be higher, but some of the math problems assumed a knowledge of English.

The reading teacher had started to work with Chen individually once a week. Jim had not had formal meetings with either the reading or ESL teacher.

Jim now was putting Chen on the computer during times when he felt it would be more fruitful than the work of the rest of the class. He gave Chen a choice of either a math or language assignment. Chen consistently chose to do the language assignment. "He really does want to learn English," Jim observed.

Jim felt that Chen was warming up to his new situation. "The kids respect and really like him, and I'm looking forward to actually talking with him," he commented. Jim was asking Chen to do more and more, like passing out papers, and Chen was comprehending. But there were no miracles. Chen used almost no sentences—or even words. Mostly, he just shook or nodded his head to communicate.

Chen still always sat alone at lunch. One day, a few kids approached him and said, "We really want you to sit with us," and Chen joined them. The next day, he was sitting by himself again.

A Talk with Chen's Mother

In mid-October, on Parents' Night, Jim met Chen's mother. Although she could not speak English well, she shared some of the family's experiences. Chen's father, a visiting professor in economics at the local university, had been the first member of the family to come from Shanghai to the United States. She had come a year later, and Chen's younger, seven-year-old brother had come the next year. Six months later, Chen had come last. The family had a visa to stay here two more years. Mrs. Yang hoped to stay even longer as she was enjoying life here.

According to his mother, Chen really liked his American school with its informal atmosphere. In China, he was used to sitting for long periods, with arms folded in front of him and eyes focused straight ahead on the teacher. Mrs. Yang shared that Chen was an unusually shy child. He was reticent even among his classmates in China, in that familiar setting.

Mrs. Yang did express concerns about American education. She felt that the training in mathematics was not as rigorous here, and she was worried that Chen was not getting enough exercise. Chen had told her that Jim played football with him, and she was appreciative of that.

Jim remembered his earlier question of whether Chen simply couldn't communicate or was too inhibited or shy to communicate. Chen's mother had added another dimension to the communication problem. There was the issue of cultural differences. Jim envisioned Chen's classroom in Shanghai. He pictured students sitting in rows, like dutiful soldiers. The switch to his freewheeling classroom would certainly require a formidable adjustment! He never even considered the issue of cultural differences before . . . .

True Assessment

Joseph Amato and Robert Piazza

Part B

To Test or Not to Test

"Let's get started," said Sarah Howard, special education supervisor for the Bennington school system. "Let the minutes reflect the fact that the parents were invited to attend this PPT meeting but are not present. We'll continue with the PPT and send them a copy of the minutes. Mrs. Matthews, would you begin?"

Yuri's teacher told of his lack of progress and the frustration he was having trying to master the fourth grade curriculum. She indicated that since she had filled out the referral form, his grades in social studies and science had dropped to a failure level, and he was just barely passing spelling, reading, and language. Math was reported to be his only strength, where he maintained a solid B average. Mrs. Matthews concluded by stating that he needed more help than she could adequately give him and reiterated her plea for formal testing and a different placement.

Sarah Howard looked at Tony Jackson and said, "You observed Yuri in his classroom. What do you think?"

For the next ten minutes, Mr. Jackson reported on the problems he saw in the content area subjects. He informed the group that he made pre-referral suggestions to Mrs. Matthews that were to be implemented within her class. He asked if any of the strategies were useful.

Jane Matthews looked directly at Mr. Jackson and replied, "I really haven't tried any of them. I don't have the time. You can't expect regular classroom teachers to drop everything and work with children like this. I have many other good students who deserve better."

Mrs. Howard fumbled through her paperwork on Yuri while everyone waited for the verdict. She finally spoke:

> It appears that Yuri is having some severe difficulties in the fourth grade. Mrs. Matthews, we really need you to try our suggestions in the future, like you always have before. I could legally hold off on a decision until the appropriate

> strategies are implemented in your class. But that wouldn't be fair to Yuri. Let's sign him up for some testing and meet in a few weeks to discuss the results. I'll call the parents and ask for their permission.

Tony Jackson shrugged his shoulders and asked Mrs. Howard if he could see her after the meeting. She agreed to stay.

Help!

Mr. Jackson requested some help from Sarah Howard. He reminded her that he was a rather new teacher with not much experience testing children who did not have proficiency with the English language.

> If a child is dominant in Albanian, how am I supposed to test him with the tests I have? I mean, how much confidence would you have in the results I get? You know this isn't the only time this is going to happen, too. It seems like a lot of Albanians are starting to settle in Bennington. I think we are going to be facing this problem again and again. What should I do?

Mrs. Howard said that they should just deal with the problems one by one as they arise. For this situation, an interpreter would be provided for him and Mr. Bates. This interpreter, Mrs. Yanosh, was a sister-in-law of one of the guidance counselors at the middle school. Although she had no formal training in testing or education, she had been used several times before in the same capacity. "Besides, I doubt whether he's even going to qualify for special education, because of the bilingual problems associated with this case. Let's just get the testing done and see."

Mr. Jackson gathered his things, nodded, and smiled at Mrs. Howard's final comments.

Testing Time

"Hi, Yuri. My name is Mr. Jackson and we'll be spending some time together for the next couple of days. I'm going to give you some tests to see if there may be any way that I could help you with your classwork." Mr. Jackson looked at the woman seated next to him and said, "This is Mrs. Yanosh. She speaks Albanian, and she'll help with explaining anything that you don't understand, okay?"

Yuri nodded his head and smiled. Before testing commenced, Yuri and Mrs. Yanosh conversed for a few minutes in Albanian. The diagnostic battery of tests used by Mr. Jackson was no different from what he would use with any other child he tested to determine whether they were eligible for special education services.

During the testing, it struck Mr. Jackson as peculiar that some simple questions required Mrs. Yanosh to use so many words in Albanian to translate. For example, when he asked Yuri to give him a word that meant the opposite of "difficult" it took Mrs. Yanosh nearly thirty seconds to translate that simple question to Yuri. When Mr. Jackson later asked her what she had done in that instance, Mrs. Yanosh explained that sometimes there were no words in Albanian for what Mr. Jackson had said in English. She often needed to describe, sometimes in detail, what he had asked, in order to get a response from Yuri.

> When you say a word like "difficult" and you want Yuri to give the opposite, I tell him you want a word that is opposite of hard, something easy. Mr. Bates, he give Yuri a picture of a "strainer," and I tell Yuri you use it to take macaroni or noodles out of the pot after they are cooked. Yuri then told me, yes he knows now, and I tell Mr. Bates he knows the answer. I have to do that a lot. For both you and Mr. Bates. If I don't do this, Yuri tells me he is frustrated and gets mad at me.

"Does Mr. Bates know what you've done? How you have given Yuri some of the answers?"

"No," Mrs. Yanosh replied, shaking her head, almost in tears. "He didn't ask. I thought that was okay. Sorry!"

Time to Reflect

Tony Jackson returned to his resource room. On his desk he found a copy of Mr. Bates's psychological report on Yuri. An attached note said, "Hi, Tony. Please read this tonight. Have to go to another school this afternoon, so we'll have to discuss our findings tomorrow."

The resource teacher perused the report quickly. The Leiter International Scale of Intelligence placed Yuri within the average age of intellectual ability. His own testing revealed a two-year lag in all language arts subjects. What happens now he thought? Can these results be presented validly at any placement meeting? More important, how can a true assessment be accomplished for any child such as Yuri?

Additional Readings

Baca, L. M., & China, P. (1982). Coming to grips with cultural diversity. *Exceptional Education Quarterly, 2*, 33–45.

Deno, S. L. (1987). Curriculum-based measurement. *Teaching Exceptional Children, 20*, 41–42.

Figueroa, R. (1989). Psychological testing of linguistic minority students: Knowledge gaps and regulations. *Exceptional Children, 56*, 145–152.

Rueda, R. (1989). Defining mild disabilities with language-minority students. *Exceptional Children, 56*, 121–128.

CASE 17

The Performance

Denise LaPrade Rini

Part B

While preparing to leave her classroom, Christina noticed that Mrs. Ruby's office was still lit. She went down and peeked in. Mrs. Ruby was sitting at her desk, loaded with two stacks of files and papers. "Am I disturbing you?" Christina asked.

"Just trying to catch up on my testing and lessons so that I won't be totally swamped," Mrs. Ruby sighed.

"I know how busy you are, but I decided to take you up on your offer to help with my student, Matt Andrews." Now, Christina explained, in addition to her ongoing concern about this student, there was an immediate situation that required some type of intervention.

"If we arrange this on an informal basis, I might be able to help you out in the early mornings several times before the civics project," said Mrs. Ruby and outlined her plan for Christina.

She decided to meet in the morning with three of Christina's students, one at a time, so that each child might feel freer to express concerns as well as to concentrate on his own work. More important, Matt's speech would not become a focus for attention for the other students as he practiced.

At 8:30 the next morning, Mrs. Ruby went down to Christina's classroom to meet Matt and two of his classmates who also had city council roles for the project. Christina had explained to them that Mrs. Ruby was a communication expert for the school who could help children prepare for oral presentations. Since these children had expressed a desire to do extra practice for their roles, Christina thought they might like to try out before a small audience of one, who could also give them pointers on how to best present their parts. The children agreed.

Meeting with each child briefly, but separately, Mrs. Ruby asked each what he or she wished to practice most. When it was Matt's turn, he responded, "I'd like to be able to do my lines without getting so nervous that I'll get stuck and choke on my words."

"That must make you very uncomfortable and frustrated," Mrs. Ruby replied. "I have some suggestions that I hope will make talking easier for you."

Mrs. Ruby then told Matt that, for people who get stuck on their words, slowing things down and using a very gentle voice can really help. She demonstrated what she meant by using a slow, gentle voice, as she read a list of words in time to the beat of a metronome. She asked Matt to follow her example with the word list. Matt had brought along his civics project cue cards and tried reading them using the slower speech that Mrs. Ruby had showed him. "Try to remember the beat of the metronome when you speak," she reminded Matt. She suggested he practice at home as well as meet with her four additional mornings before the civics project.

Matt seemed to enjoy his private meetings with Mrs. Ruby. When he focused on speaking softly and slowly, his speech was markedly improved with fewer stutters and virtually no blocks. Mrs. Ruby agreed to see Matt the morning of the project for warm-up practice. "Good luck!" she waved to Matt as he headed down to class for the project.

Later that afternoon, after the children and buses had left, Mrs. Ruby went to Christina's classroom. She and Marc Davis were reviewing the tape from the civics' project. "How did it go?" Mrs. Ruby asked.

"Well, I think it was obvious that Matt's speech is not quite like everyone else's," Christina commented. "But the other kids were nervous, so the difference didn't seem as great, and Matt was definitely slowing down his speech and speaking softly as you had suggested to him. Some of his facial grimaces still occurred, but not as much as usual. All in all, Matt did a decent job, and the project went well. The kids really put a lot into the content of their speeches. I can't thank you enough for your help. I'll be discussing a referral for Matt for speech therapy when I meet with his parents next week."

The Parent Conference—January

During the school's open house in September, Christina had met Mr. and Mrs. Andrews briefly. Since the students were still new to her, Christina had nothing specific to convey, except that Matt was performing well on all his assignments and quizzes. The Andrews did not attend the November parent conference. Christina had attempted to schedule an individual conference with Mr. and Mrs. Andrews, but their working schedules, the holidays, and Christina's additional work at school with the civics project precluded a mutually agreeable meeting time. Now, in January, Christina urgently requested to meet with Matt's parents.

Mrs. Andrews came alone to the conference, since her husband was at work. She was a tall woman who appeared shy and a bit nervous about the meeting. Christina outlined her concerns about Matt, her attempts to assist him, and the experiences Matt was having in the classroom.

Christina explained that she had approached the speech pathologist who worked at Kennedy School and that Mrs. Ruby had been very supportive and helpful to Matt and her. Christina asked whether Mr. and Mrs. Andrews had appealed the school system's denial of speech therapy. Mrs. Andrews reluctantly admitted that she and her husband had not focused much on Matt's speech, since it had been that way since he was three, and they were accustomed to it. Furthermore, it never had been an issue for Matt—until he had come home in November upset about having been called "Porky Pig" by boys on the playground when he tried to join them for a game of kickball. Mrs. Andrews stated that physical education activities were not Matt's forte, and she believed that had separated him from the children.

As Christina and Mrs. Andrews exchanged this information, Christina realized in shock that Mrs. Andrews also stuttered. Her mind was flooded with questions as she struggled to maintain her composure. How should she approach the situation now? Would she be insulting Mrs. Andrews if she made an issue of Matt's speech? How much more could Matt's speech be expected to improve? Should she press the Andrews to pursue assessment and therapy for Matt? Who could be available to help her do something to break the cycle of social rejection in which Matt was caught?

CASE 19

The Reluctant Freshman

Robert Piazza and Linda Pica

Part B

The Second Week of School

Mrs. Fuller stopped at the high school's main office to ask directions to Mr. Hernandez's resource room. She meandered through a maze of corridors until she finally found room 161. Jodi and Mr. Hernandez were sitting in his room at a corner table. "I'm glad you're here, Mrs. Fuller. Jodi and I were just looking over some of the results of the testing I did last week," the teacher said.

"What?" sighed Mrs. Fuller, "I thought enough of those things were done already. Jodi gets really upset when she's being tested. Why didn't you tell me he was testing you?"

"No, Mom, these were different. It wasn't too bad. I think Mr. Hernandez knows what he's doing," Jodi interjected.

Mr. Hernandez smiled at Jodi's last comment and hoped she was right. He explained to Mrs. Fuller that he did an assessment that was completely informal in nature. Jodi was asked to read from books assigned in her content area subjects. He told Mrs. Fuller that he monitored Jodi's rate of reading and also did informal probes to determine her comprehension ability and vocabulary. "I did find that she reads very slowly. This may be one reason her comprehension is poor. I also made some discoveries about how she learns best, the types of tasks she handles well, and some techniques that may be useful for her."

Jodi's resource teacher suggested to Jodi's mother that a new PPT be convened to adjust her IEP and discuss reasonable modifications that could be implemented in her regular classes.

"That's fine with me. You're the expert," said Mrs. Fuller.

Jodi Fuller's name was put on the agenda for the next PPT meeting the following Tuesday afternoon. Since all of her teachers with the exception of her PE teacher were invited to attend this meeting, it was scheduled for 2:15, five minutes after the high school was dismissed for the day.

Tuesday's Meeting

Mr. Hernandez acted as chairperson of the PPT that day. As he glanced around the room, he noted that everyone was there except Mr. Higgins, Jodi's history teacher. "That's typical. It's 2:15. Higgins' record for missed PPT meetings remains intact," he cynically thought to himself.

The meeting proceeded smoothly. At Mr. Hernandez's suggestion the focus of Jodi's support program would shift from one of academic remediation to a learning strategy model. A strategy approach, it was hoped, would build independence and help Jodi learn efficiently in the mainstreamed setting. Mr. Hernandez outlined the study strategies he wanted Jodi to develop. They included notetaking, outlining, listening, time management, and test-taking skills. He would attempt to develop these skills in the resource room, within the context of what was being taught in the regular curriculum.

> It's crucial that Jodi begin to develop these skills during her freshman year, if high school is to be a successful experience for her. My job as the resource teacher will be to teach these strategies to her. But in the interim, some modifications in her program will be needed. All of you have to help me with these.

During the next thirty minutes, the PPT developed the following modifications that would be implemented in Jodi's regular classes:

1. Jodi would be allowed to tape-record material so that she could hear it repeated at a later time.

2. Jodi would be provided with written as well as oral directions for all assignments.

3. Jodi would be given preferential seating in all classes. Also, teachers would attempt to provide visual or gestural prompts when important information was being presented.

4. Jodi would be assigned peer helpers to assist her with notetaking.

5. Jodi would be allowed to use a highlighter in her textbooks.

6. Jodi and other class members would be given written outlines of daily lectures.

7. Jodi would not be penalized for spelling errors.

8. Jodi would be pretaught a list of difficult vocabulary words in future lessons by Mr. Hernandez.

9. Jodi would be given tests on an untimed basis in the resource room.

Much was accomplished in this relatively brief meeting, Mr. Hernandez thought to himself. Jodi's parents appeared to be cautiously optimistic and thanked him as they left. One hurdle was left. He had agreed to inform Mr.

Higgins of the modifications in Jodi's program. "The last piece of a puzzle is supposed to be the easiest one to fit. I don't know about this one," he mumbled to no one in particular.

What's Fair?

Forty-seven-year-old Ronald Higgins was acknowledged by the faculty of Amberville High School as a scholar. He was also known as a teacher who loathed teaching low-track courses. He set his standards high and expected his students to reach them, no matter what their ability levels were.

The morning after Jodi Fuller's PPT, Mr. Hernandez was sitting at his desk waiting for his first period students to arrive. He glanced up and saw Mr. Higgins in the doorway. "I guess you got my memo and the revisions of Jodi Fuller's IEP in your mailbox this morning," Hernandez said.

"I did. But don't expect those things to happen in my class. She seems like a nice kid, but she's going to sink or swim like the rest of them. It's not fair that her program gets modified like that and the other kids' programs don't. What am I supposed to tell them? Is Jodi that special?"

CASE 20

The Letter

Judith B. Buzzell

Part B

Jennifer's Story

In the section that follows, Jennifer, at age 17, reflected back on her experiences as a pregnant teenager during her sophomore year. She described these in her own words:

> I remember sitting in Mrs. Feldman's class, listening to students' teen parent stories. I knew I was pregnant, but I didn't want to believe it. I was in denial. That led to depression and brought me to the point where I wanted to kill myself. I felt there was no one there to help me.
>
> I was going to that class every day—even though I didn't admit to myself that I was pregnant, I wanted to get information. I think Mrs. Feldman sensed what was going on because she said, "You're tired a lot." I did sleep a lot.
>
> I was afraid to tell my family, even though we're close. I talked about most things with my sisters, but this wasn't something I wanted to discuss. My mother and I never talked openly about sex. I learned about menstruation from the school nurse. In seventh grade, I started my period in school. I went to the nurse and said, "Something's happening," and she helped me. Maybe my mother thought my sisters would tell me the facts of life, but they didn't.
>
> I had been going to the teen parenting class for about two months. I sensed I was pregnant because I had stopped having my period, and I was tired all the time and getting bigger. My mind kept racing with thoughts. I was worried about what my family and friends would think and how my boyfriend, George, would take it. I thought my family and friends would look down on me. I didn't want George to think that I'd tried to trap him. I think he sensed I was pregnant, but he didn't want to believe it either. He denied it, too.
>
> One morning, my mother walked in on me while I was getting dressed. She looked at me and said, "Oh, my God." Later, when I came home from school, my father asked me if I was pregnant, and I said I was. They took me to the doctor that afternoon; I was five months pregnant.
>
> My father was really hurt. He was more hurt than angry. He cried a lot. He said I had sisters I could talk to and a mother and father. But they never would talk to me about sex at all, so I kinda disagree with him when I think about it now.

My mom was hurt, too, but she also understood in a way that Dad didn't. See, she'd been a teen mom, too. She was seventeen when she had her first baby.

The next day at school, I gave Mrs. Feldman the letter. I was still so upset. I couldn't figure a way out of this. When I came back to her class for seventh period, she took me aside. She said we had to deal with this and get some help. I told her that I was depressed, that I was going through a lot of problems, and sometimes I felt like I wanted to commit suicide. She tried to reassure me. She said that we could work it out, and it was good that I shared my secret, that it can only get better if you tell. "This is a step that will make things better," she told me. I wasn't mad that she wanted to tell somebody. I guess deep down I was relieved.

Then she took me to the school social worker, Mrs. Perez. I let her read the letter. She called my parents while Mrs. Feldman and I were still in the office and explained the situation to them and said we needed to meet.

I told George that same day. I wanted him to know that I planned to go through with it and asked if he would help me. I never considered abortion or adoption. George was upset and scared, too, because before me, he'd always treated girls disrespectfully. He bad-mouthed them, and he had a bad temper. Even though he never treated me that way, he was afraid that if he had a daughter, men might treat her disrespectfully.

The next morning, we had the meeting with Mrs. Perez, Mrs. Feldman, my parents, and me. My father was very upset again—more than my mother. Of course, this isn't the first time they've reacted differently. He cried and said we should go for some counseling. They both said they felt sorry that they hadn't talked to me about sexual things. He wanted to call my boyfriend's parents. Mrs. Perez explained the program at Ernestine Johnson School, the school for pregnant teenagers, and my dad called and made the arrangements for me to go there.

Being a Teen Parent

Two days later, I transferred to the Ernestine Johnson School. I felt welcomed there because there were girls in the same situation and also supportive teachers. Plus, there was a nurse there to help.

I had a regular school day, except that I got out at 12:00 P.M., instead of 1:00 P.M. I had the same courses as I had at Van Buren. I did well with my courses and even made honors.

I went to school right up to the day my baby, her name is Sonia, was born on April 2. I had Sonia on the Friday before April vacation and came right back to school the Monday after the vacation. I finished the school year at Ernestine Johnson.

Going to school and being a teen parent is very hard. My sister watched Sonia until I got home from school, and then I had her. You have a lot of work. Not only do you have to worry about your school work, you have to worry about your responsibility, your child. The hard part was trying to get homework done at night and still take care of her. Both my mother and sister helped to take care of Sonia, but I worked out a schedule of trying to get all my homework done during my free period at school.

Working out my relationship with George has taken effort, too. I'm no longer with him, but we're still friends. He goes to college now, in the south, and sees Sonia when he comes home. He treats her okay, but he's still confused. He acts like a big kid around her. Instead of saying "no" when it's necessary, he lets her do what she wants. He's an only child, he's kiddish. He still relies on his parents.

Returning to Van Buren High School

I returned to Van Buren in the fall for my sophomore year. It felt scary because you worried about what people would say. I've always had many friends, and I'd stayed close to at least six girls. It turned out when I explained my pregnancy to my friends, nobody looked down. And when I came back to Van Buren, no one did either.

I was trying to adjust that year—getting the feel of friends and teachers and getting back into the routine. I kept a regular schedule. My grades were As, Bs, and Cs.

What helped with the adjustment was Mrs. Feldman's class. It was the best thing that ever happened to me because there were girls who had the same experiences and you could talk about everything—down to your child, down to yourself.

She helped me to understand my child better. She gave us tips on how children develop, what they'll go through. We discussed how to handle emergencies—like what to do if your child chokes.

When we talked about ourselves, we talked about how difficult it was to fit in school and parenting. We discussed what was hard at school and how our boyfriends were acting toward us and our child. I had a lot of support at home, but many girls didn't.

Besides Mrs. Feldman being a teacher, she was a friend. Someone you could talk to. Not only did she look out for us, she looked out for everyone. She was real supportive. If we had a problem with a teacher, she was there to help us think about how to solve it.

Now, when I think about it, I don't think I was really seriously considering killing myself. My main concern was how I was going to handle everything and how upset my father was. He still hasn't forgiven me. He hasn't adjusted.

CASE 21

The Case of Competition

Linda Powell

Part B

The Money

Kevin's first day in class was only a preview of coming attractions. It was rare for Mrs. Hart to get through a day without some form of confrontation with Kevin.

Mrs. Hart had decided to invite Kevin out into the hallway the day he had the handful of twenties. He denied having more than a single ten-dollar bill in his pocket, adding, "It's not against the law or any school rule to have money." Principal Bryne approached Mrs. Hart, asking if there was a problem. As he did, Kevin pulled his pockets inside out and added, "You wanna check my underwear?"

After Mrs. Hart explained about the money, Mr. Bryne asked to check Kevin's book bag and then asked each of the students sitting at Kevin's table what they had seen. As he questioned Willie in the hallway, Mrs. Hart noticed Kevin patting himself just below his waist. She passed this information on to Mr. Bryne, who then escorted Kevin to the office.

In the privacy of his office, Mr. Bryne was able to convince Kevin to reveal the wad of money. Kevin assured him that he was only holding the $560 for his brother, who was twenty-four years old. Mr. Bryne called Kevin's mother. Mrs. Sims knew nothing about the money, was quite upset, and said she would send Kevin's brother to school to pick up Kevin and the money. Kevin's brother arrived and took Kevin and the money home.

The next day Kevin's brother returned the money. Although Kevin's brother had covered for Kevin in a family meeting the night before, Kevin admitted it was actually his friend Antonio's money. Kevin's mother called Antonio's mother and accused Antonio of involving Kevin in his drug business. Later that morning, Principal Bryne had two sets of angry parents in his office. No one was willing to claim the money, and both Kevin and Antonio were back in class and both were angry with Mrs. Hart.

Changing Gears

The dynamics of the class changed that day. Mrs. Hart found that the same circular arrangement of tables which had been so conducive to encouraging most students to participate in discussions now enabled Kevin to command complete attention. He took longer each day to sit down when class began, and he came with no pen, book, or notebook. After borrowing paper and a pencil from other students, he would chat, write notes to others around him, and then read their responses out loud.

Mrs. Hart asked Kevin to stay after class on the third day to ask him how he thought the class was going and why he thought she had asked to see him. Kevin said he liked the class, but he needed help on the work. Mrs. Hart explained that he had to help himself by bringing his book, notebook, and pencil and that he had to pay attention. Kevin said it was hard because everyone was staring at him.

After school that day, Mrs. Hart rearranged the tables into the traditional rows. She hoped that it would take some pressure off Kevin. Then she spoke to the counselor to initiate the PPT process for Kevin.

Mrs. Hart began to write a daily log on Kevin's performance. During one week, Kevin was late three times, he had slept wearing his sunglasses during a film-strip one day, and, another day, although he had copied the questions from the board on his paper, he had not answered a single one after thirty minutes. Every day he asked for a bathroom pass.

Mrs. Hart tried talking to Kevin after class again, kept him for detention twice, and finally sat down to talk with him Friday afternoon. "Why are you picking on me?" he asked. Mrs. Hart explained she was just getting to know him. She decided to share her log with him. Kevin read one side of the sheet and asked why she was writing "all this stuff" about him. Why, he asked, didn't she write anything good? She turned the paper over, and he was pleased to read that "Kevin worked well on his group project." She asked him why he had done so well that day. He said he liked art better than reading and writing and that it was more fun to be able to talk while working.

Mrs. Hart decided to call Mrs. Sims to share her concerns about Kevin's inability to complete any writing assignments. Mrs. Sims said she had given up on Kevin; she was tired of giving him everything she could and getting nothing but trouble back. She wanted Mrs. Hart to ask the counselor to call her about referring Kevin to a group home. She wanted him out of the house.

The next week Mrs. Hart began to inquire among other teachers about Kevin's progress. She wanted to know if anyone was having success with Kevin. She discovered that Kevin had been removed from his Spanish class for the rest of the year and that he was kicked out of his math class for a week. In desperation, the math teacher had called home, only to be told that he might have better luck talking with Kevin's probation officer. Mrs. Hart was beginning to see a pattern emerge. Clearly, there were not many people left who were willing to work with Kevin Sims.

Again, Mrs. Hart approached the counselor about a Planning and Placement Team meeting. The PPT met only once a week, and many other students had been recommended for PPTs. They had not reached Kevin's name yet.

Although Kevin continued to be Kevin, Mrs. Hart was more determined than ever to find out what he could do most successfully. The few assignments he handed in were copied. For the next few days, Mrs. Hart decided to hold fewer teacher-directed discussions and, instead, to ask students to work in small groups, reading short passages, discussing questions, and writing in their own words responses which the group had discussed. Kevin had a hard time getting started and keeping focused, and he often irritated students in his group, but he was completing assignments for the first time. Kevin didn't wait for Mrs. Hart to collect his papers; as soon as he finished, he brought them to her. Kevin was finally beginning to work, and he felt good about it.

The PPT

After a few good days, Kevin had his worst day. He was late and slow getting seated. As he looked for his book and notebook in his book bag, he talked loudly to another student. Mrs. Hart asked Kevin to take his seat immediately. Kevin talked over Mrs. Hart's voice to Jamie. Mrs. Hart urged both boys to sit down immediately.

As Mrs. Hart began her lesson, Kevin kept calling out for her to repeat everything. Mrs. Hart reminded him to raise his hand and wait to be called on. While his hand was up, he talked to the girl next to him. As Mrs. Hart started to speak to Kevin, the girl shoved Kevin hard and shouted at him to stop bothering her. Through clenched teeth, Mrs. Hart told Kevin to move to the table in front of her and warned him that any further outbursts would result in his being sent out of class.

Then, as Mrs. Hart turned around to write on the board, she heard a loud scream. Kevin had put a lit cigarette lighter against the shoe of the girl next to him, leaving a black burn mark on her sneaker. "Kevin," screamed Mrs. Hart, "that's it. Get your notebook. We're going to the office."

As Mrs. Hart marched Kevin to the office, her only thought was to remove Kevin from her class. She felt defeated again, and this angered her even more. She filled out the disciplinary referral, knowing that Kevin would be suspended. She had hoped that this would be one boy that she would save.

At lunch, Mrs. Hart described the episode to some of the teachers. She also shared with them her recommendation for a PPT. One of the teachers commented, "A PPT on Kevin Sims. They'll never PPT him—then we'd have to live with him for another four years."

Mrs. Hart went to the guidance office after lunch to inquire about the PPT. "Kevin Sims?" repeated the social worker. "He's nearly at the top of our list. We'll be doing our preliminary meeting very soon."

Additional Readings

Brophy, J. (1987). Synthesis of research on strategies for motivating students to learn. *Education Leadership, 45*(2), 40–48.

Dryfoos, J. (1990). *Adolescents at risk: Prevalence and prevention.* New York: Oxford University Press.

Gibbs, J. T. (Ed.). (1988). *Young, black and male in America: An endangered species.* Dover, MA: Auburn House.

Hechinger, F. M. (1992). *Fateful choices: Healthy youth for the 21st century.* Carnegie Council on Adolescent Development. New York: Hill and Wang.

McPartland, J. M., & Slavin, R. E. (1990). *Increasing achievement of at-risk students at each grade level.* Washington, DC: U.S. Department of Education.

Morgan, D., & Jenson, W. (1988). *Teaching behaviorally disordered students: Preferred practices.* Columbus, OH: Merrill.

Ornstein, A. C., & Levine, D. (1989). Social class, race and school achievement: Problems and prospects. *Journal of Teacher Education, 40*(5), 17–23.

Wilson, W. J. (1987). *The truly disadvantaged.* Chicago: University of Chicago Press.

Wright, W. J. (1991). The endangered black male child. *Educational Leadership, 49*(4), 14–16.

CASE 22

Acceptance or Achievement

Linda Powell and Judith B. Buzzell

Part B

Peer Support

Mrs. Robinson knew there were two senior girls who ate lunch in her classroom to avoid the cafeteria hubbub. Still, she decided to take Celena there and try to calm her down in the ten minutes left in the lunch period. That might give her enough time to plan another meeting after school.

She put her arm around Celena's shoulders and asked her to come into her classroom. Sitting at one of the tables, she handed a box of tissues to her sobbing student. "You know, you don't *have* to give the other kids your papers. If they still talk about you, it doesn't sound like they're really your good friends. And how can they be good friends if they want you to do something wrong, like cheating?"

Celena nodded, "That's the problem. I don't really have any friends here. Even if they say they're my friends, they just use me! I let Therease borrow my homework, but then she passed it on to someone else. I never got it back—that's why I didn't have my homework today."

"What about in your other classes? Is there anyone there you work with who doesn't use you? Who do you sit with?" Mrs. Robinson asked.

"All different kids. Nobody special," said Celena.

At this point, the senior girls walked over and Mrs. Robinson introduced them to Celena. After apologizing for overhearing the conversation, Karen described how she had been ostracized and ridiculed as an underclassman because she took her studies seriously. Mrs. Robinson asked the girls how they—two very bright, hard-working students—had survived in a school where most kids didn't have the same drive.

Karen acknowledged that it was tough, but she had adjusted to being a "loner." Much of her determination and support came from her grandmother, a very independent person who was raising her. Karen was an enthusiastic photographer, and her long hours in the darkroom filled the time others spent in the busy social swirl.

Yolanda got support from her mother and her church—especially the youth choir in which she sang. She added that instead of letting kids copy her homework, she assisted them by showing them where they could find answers for themselves. Although this wasn't always appreciated, she felt that at least she had tried to help them without compromising her values.

Both agreed that they found little support from their fellow students because the few studious, high-achieving students were spread out among all the classes and grades. They urged Celena to get involved in after-school programs (such as history courses or language courses in Swahili, Chinese, or Arabic) and to apply to the summer programs for gifted students where she would meet like-minded peers. As the bell rang, Karen was inviting Celena to join them every day for lunch in Mrs. Robinson's classroom.

Mrs. Robinson sensed that Celena felt better, at least for the moment. But the challenge remained of how to help Celena find support and acceptance in her classroom and in the school at large.

One Month Later: The End of January

During the month since her outburst, Celena had seemed to become more of an outsider again. She did her homework thoroughly, but she sat alone and interacted minimally in class.

One day, Mrs. Robinson received an announcement requesting teachers to nominate students to be tested for the Independent Study Program (ISP). This program pulled high-achieving students out of class once a week to participate in a seminar on special topics, such as psychology or the Middle East, not usually covered in the regular classes. Top students from other schools came to Lyceum to participate in the program.

Mrs. Robinson selected a few students and then announced the program in class, asking students to give her their name if they were interested in taking the entrance test. After class, Celena broached her, specifically asking *not* to be listed. Mrs. Robinson suspected that she didn't want to be singled out as special and to be separated from others anymore. Yet, she felt that the program would be a positive experience for Celena; she had two weeks before the list had to be submitted to influence her.

Mrs. Robinson urged Celena to eat lunches in her classroom, where the two seniors always met. Mrs. Robinson stayed, too. Karen and Yolanda chatted with Celena about their interests—exhibits they'd gone to, books they'd read. They involved her in their philosophical debates about religion.

Mrs. Robinson sat with Celena a few days a week and gently inquired about her classes and her class projects, which Celena loved doing. Gradually, Celena began to open up. She asked her teacher, "Are we gonna work on any more projects in your class?" Mrs. Robinson seized the opportunity to point out that students worked on sophisticated topics and projects in ISP. She mentioned the names of a few students who were taking the test, trying to accustom Celena to the idea of being tested. Karen shared that, through ISP, she'd had the opportunity to use her photography and even take a photography course at a local university.

Two days before Mrs. Robinson had to hand in the list, she asked Celena if she'd be willing to be tested. "You'd meet more interesting kids, new kids, maybe more people with the same interests as yours," she entreated. "And the ISP teacher is nice, too." For the first time in a while, Celena smiled broadly, revealing her large, beautiful dimples.

The next day, as Celena entered class, she stopped by her teacher's desk. "Is that the list?" she asked Mrs. Robinson. Mrs. Robinson nodded, adding that there was room for more students. Celena just walked away. But at the end of class, she walked by the desk again. Without stopping, she gruffly said, "Okay, put my name on it." The implication was "And don't you tell anyone about this." Still, Mrs. Robinson felt this decision was a real breakthrough.

A Schoolwide Solution: To Track or Not to Track?

Celena's situation made Mrs. Robinson aware of the isolation that the high-achieving students, scattered throughout the school, experienced. At a faculty meeting, she raised the issue that there simply was not adequate support for these students. It was not enough to list twenty Honor Roll names on the bulletin board each semester. She felt that the faculty needed to think of ways that these students could be together more.

However, the school had worked hard to avoid tracking, the placing of students of apparent similar ability in the same groups or classes. The goal of tracking was to closely match the level of teaching to the students' needs in order to improve students' skills and understanding. Yet research indicated that tracking didn't always work that way. In lower tracks, students began to see themselves as the "dummies." Teachers emphasized drill and rote memorization, and some students complained that they were tired of doing the "sheets" (worksheets). In the higher tracks, students were exposed to a wider variety of instructional materials, and teachers were more likely to emphasize critical thinking skills. Rather than receiving the kind of remediation that would allow them to catch up, students in the lower tracks tended to fall further behind students in the higher tracks. Lower tracked students were rarely moved into the higher tracks.

The teachers didn't want to destroy what they'd worked hard to create—a heterogeneous setting for students. Furthermore, in a small school, it was even logistically hard to track. The school might have as few as five highly motivated students in a freshman class of fifty. It couldn't allocate the resources—a teacher, a classroom—for those five students alone.

Yet, if Celena was any example, the needs of these students were not being met. Indeed, some educators of the gifted argued that, in general, highly gifted students were not adequately challenged in heterogeneous classes. *They* were at-risk for school failure if their special abilities were not specifically addressed and nurtured. Bored by the humdrum of the regular classroom, they might fail to reach their potential and might even drop out of school.

The teachers were torn. They had basic objections to the stratification that tracking produced, but they were unsure how to support their most able students without tracking.

SECTION C

This section contains Part C of each of the following cases:

CASE 2

A Case of Prejudice?

Judith B. Buzzell

Part C

The Center's Role

Mrs. Phillips shared details of the conference with the teachers at the center, and together they discussed ways to deal with the situation. The staff felt that it was important to begin by observing Daniel. They saw Daniel as a highly verbal child who asked probing questions. He used materials inventively and particularly enjoyed block play. Sensitive and self-conscious, he could be timid with adults. Yet at times, he impulsively lashed out at children, screaming at them or hitting, often when he seemed threatened. He was very dependent upon Sally, his long-time friend who had started day care with him. The teachers wanted to get a better sense of his relationships with the other children. Was there something that he feared?

In addition to making observations, the teachers planned a series of activities and discussions to be carried out over several months. Many of these, such as a discussion about Martin Luther King, Jr., on his birthday, would have occurred normally in this school where there was already a high level of sensitivity to multicultural issues.

Several activities were designed to help children feel comfortable with physical similarities and differences, as well as to develop positive self-concepts and skills. An eye-color graph charted the number of children in the class having blue, brown, or hazel eyes. Children drew self-portraits in another small group activity. The teachers provided a large collection of crayons and encouraged children to color their self-portraits with a color approximating their own skin color. As the children worked, teachers commented on the many variations of skin color represented in the group. Books such as Paul Shower's *Your Skin and Mine* were read occasionally at story time, so children could see and talk about differences in skin color.

The teachers observed that Daniel appeared to be struggling with his own aggressiveness. He seemed to admire the rough-and-tumble boys, yet he was afraid to join their play. When they chased around the playground, he trailed behind at a safe distance.

Perhaps Daniel felt Stephanie was too aggressive. She *was* unpredictable—she could be moody one moment and boisterous the next. She might grab toys from other children, knock them over, or hit. Was it confusing to Daniel to see aggression in a girl? Did he feel the need to protect himself? How could the teachers help him to express his own aggression in an acceptable way, as well as to deal with his feelings about blacks?

In mid-September, the teachers noted an incident involving Stephanie. Daniel and another child were outdoors, intently twisting the tire swing round and round. When Stephanie barged into the play and tried to stop the swing, Daniel frantically pushed her down and screamed at her. A teacher restrained him and calmly reminded both children of the school rules.

In late November, Stephanie knocked down a block building which Daniel and another boy had made. Daniel looked sad but did not lash out.

Two days later, Stephanie bit a girl on the arm. Daniel and some other children were aware of the incident. At lunch, he commented, "Stephanie is the only one with black skin at this school."

During nap time, the teachers gathered informally in the center's kitchen, discussing Daniel's comment.

"He seems to be relating Stephanie's behavior to her race," said Emily, an experienced and dedicated teacher. "I'm beginning to wonder whether it's worse to have only one or two black children in the program than none at all," she added with a pained look on her face.

The other teachers were stunned. "What do you mean?" asked Sarah.

"Maybe, inadvertently, we're encouraging the development of prejudice in children," responded Emily. "If we have only one black child in the center and that child happens to have behavior problems, the other children may conclude that all black children misbehave. Unconsciously, they may think 'She's black, so she acts wild.'"

"But there are several white kids who also have difficulty with self-control, some far more than Stephanie," countered another teacher.

"Yes, but because we have twenty-two white children, we see a wide range of behaviors within that group," said Emily. "There are enough white children so stereotyping of whites is not likely to occur. In other words, a child is unlikely to think, 'She's white so she breaks the rules,' because there are other white children in the group who are showing different types of behavior such as accepting rules, reluctantly complying with rules, and rigidly following rules."

Sarah looked uneasy. "We've always talked about fostering better racial understanding by increasing the number of minority children in the program. Are you suggesting now that we not have any black children at all?"

Emily shrugged her shoulders. "I'm not sure. It seems like a Catch-22."

Feeling very uneasy, the teachers went to wake the napping children.

The next day, Mrs. Phillips remarked that Stephanie clearly had an effect on Daniel. On several days when Stephanie was high-pitched and disruptive, he was also. Once, soon after Christmas vacation, they each misbehaved (separately) and were given time-outs. Like a matched set, Stephanie sat in her cubby for a brief period while Daniel sat across the room on a bench, after having thrown ice at a teacher.

During a lunchtime discussion in March, Daniel mentioned Stephanie's skin color. Debbie, the teacher, asked him if he knew why her skin was black. He said that he didn't. Debbie explained that Stephanie's father was black. Later, he asked, "But I have one more question—how come a black baby came out of a white mom?"

Debbie responded, "Stephanie's mom is white, and her dad is black. Children get their looks from both of their parents." Daniel seemed content with her answer.

In June, as the year ended, the teachers shared with Mrs. Rieser that Daniel had grown more and more comfortable at school. He was calmer and seemed less self-protective. By September, when the new school year began, they noted that Daniel was much more tolerant when Stephanie invaded his space.

On Saturday nights now, Daniel had a Chinese-American baby-sitter whom he adored. He eagerly looked forward to their evenings together.

Additional Readings

Aboud, F. (1988). *Children and prejudice.* New York: Basil Blackwell.

Derman-Sparks, L. (1990). Understanding diversity: What young children want and need to know. *Pre-K Today, 5,* 44–50.

Derman-Sparks, L., & The A.B.C. Task Force. (1989). *Anti-bias curriculum: Tools for empowering young children.* Washington, DC: National Association for the Education of Young Children.

Goodman, M. E. (1964). *Race awareness in young children.* Cambridge, MA: Addison-Wesley; New York: Crowell-Collier.

Greenberg, P. (1989). Parents as partners in young children's development and education. *Young Children, 44*(4), 61–75.

Kendall, F. E. (1983). *Diversity in the classroom: A multicultural approach to the education of young children.* New York: Teachers College Press.

Milner, D. (1983). *Children and race.* London: Ward Lock Educational.

Phillips, C. B. (1988). Nurturing diversity for today's children and tomorrow's leaders. *Young Children, 43*(2), 42–47.

Ramsey, P. G. (1987). *Teaching and learning in a diverse world: Multicultural education for young children.* New York: Teachers College Press.

Wardle, F. (1987). Are you sensitive to interracial children's special identity needs? *Young Children, 42*(2), 53–59.

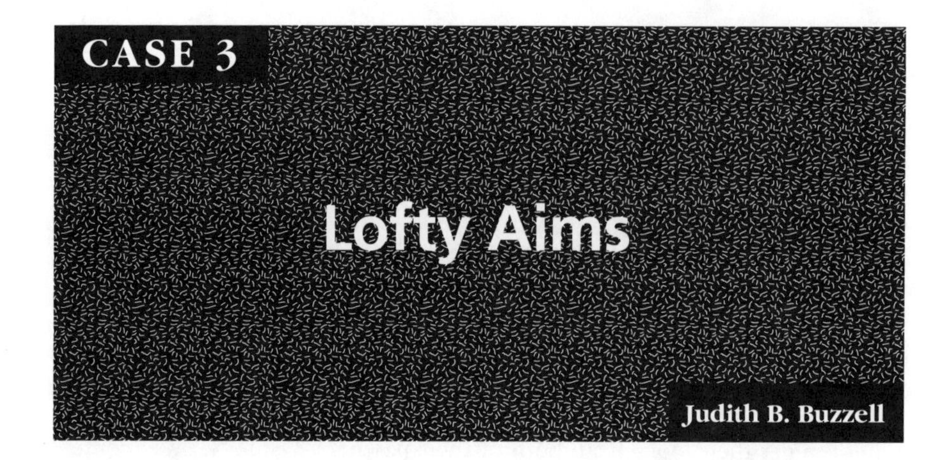

Part C

Since late November, Sarah had grown progressively more independent. Also, the teachers had come to know her better. Because they knew more clearly her abilities and limits, their decisions about safety and her needs in the classroom were less fraught with conflict.

In general, Sarah took less staff time. She was handling bathrooming completely by herself, and she could pull herself up with her lofties. She could move by using just one loftie, instead of two. Rather than asking to have her boot fixed repeatedly during a day, she was asking for adjustments just a few times. In general, Lisa noticed that once she started playing with children more, she asked less for help from adults.

Relationships with Other Children

Throughout the fall, the teachers had continued to try to promote Sarah's relationships with other children. Jean observed that when they initiated a structured activity with several children during free play time, such as acting out "Three Billy Goats Gruff," Sarah would always participate and often requested the same activity the next day. Sarah caught on to the games quickly and remembered them. Jean also thought that she wanted to do something that she *could* do and the other kids *would* do. This wasn't just an instance of wanting teacher attention.

In early November, Sarah started reaching out to other children. At nap time, Sarah would talk to the child on the cot next to her, and they laughed together. Jean speculated that this time fostered interaction because, in a sense, it was a controlled situation. The whole group was not around, no one could get rambunctious (with the risk of Sarah getting hurt), and the children were equally mobile—or immobile.

Shortly before Christmas, Sarah started playing with other children in the dramatic play area where there was a raised, wide bench. She would climb up on it, then sit or lie down, and pretend to be the baby in the family or the patient during doctor play. She didn't need her lofties when she was on the bench. Jean noticed that Sarah was really participating, laughing, enjoying herself. In later months, she insisted that she wanted the role of the doctor.

There were three older girls with whom Sarah tended to play most. These were nurturing, quiet, low-key children. She didn't seem to have a best friend. Many of her interactions with children revolved around them helping her. Noticing this, Lisa remarked to Denise, "She's still set apart in many ways. She's still a focus." However, now Sarah was accepting when the children dashed to get her lofties for her and didn't protest that a teacher get them. She allowed others to play with her crutches, which they adored. In fact, she barely seemed to notice if she was involved in an activity and a child picked them up and hobbled off.

By mid-January, Sarah was still spending a fair amount of time by herself. She had been initiating interactions more during the last few months, for example, by asking at the snack table, "Will you play with me outside?" But sometimes by the time she got outside, it was time for the children to come back in. The teachers' various shortcuts had helped to an extent, but Sarah still tended to be last.

Jean identified another problem when talking to Denise one day.

> One of the hardest things is when I see Sarah start to play with another child and then the play changes so fast that Sarah can't keep up with it. Outdoors, all of a sudden, everyone will run to the other end of the yard, leaving Sarah in the dust. I guess I could tell the kids that they have to wait for Sarah, but I'm concerned that they will resent my interference. It may lead to some kind of power struggle with me, and overstructuring isn't necessarily in *their* interests developmentally. Also, that would highlight Sarah's difference and make her more "special"—maybe then they would resent her as well as me. I haven't had any special education classes, but it seems like there must be ways to deal with this better.

"You know, the special education liaison from the public schools is obligated to give us five hours of consultation time. At the beginning of the year, she said she'd drop by, but she hasn't. Maybe I should give her a call," said Denise.

"It might be helpful," responded Jean. "On the other hand, we do have experience in accommodating kids' needs. All of them have special needs of some sort or another—Joannie manages better with more limits, and Mark plays best in a small group. But we do pretty much take for granted that most kids can get around."

Self-Awareness

More and more, Jean had heard Sarah asking, "Why do I have to have these lofties? Nobody else has them. Everybody else can walk without them."

Jean would respond, "Sometimes you wish that you didn't have to have your lofties. I can see why you'd be feeling that way." Then, Sarah's focus would shift, and she'd be engrossed in something else. Jean had seldom seen Sarah give up or be self-pitying.

Jean felt that it was good that Sarah could express those feelings, since probably one would feel a legitimate sense of loss. It seemed healthy, a sign of self-acceptance, for Sarah to be able to acknowledge this difference, yet not be undone by it. Although the difference shouldn't be blown out of proportion or become an excuse for not doing anything, Jean felt that it could be more detrimental for Sarah if she didn't even notice it.

As they were cleaning up at the end of a long day, Jean and Denise were reflecting on the changes they had observed in Sarah. Jean pensively commented:

> You know, for the most part, I feel fine about Sarah being here. It's certainly been valuable for the other children and for us. But, at times, I've wondered whether it's hard for Sarah to be the only one who's disabled. I suspect that there's a special burden or tension that comes with being the only one—like being the only black child in a group of white children. And I'm not sure whether this would have worked if we had a smaller class with fewer teachers. Many preschool classes have fifteen or sixteen kids with only two teachers. Would two teachers be enough to care for Sarah and fifteen other children? I really don't think so.

Denise didn't hesitate in responding. "It might have been a problem in the beginning of the year, but Sarah's progress has been so phenomenal that I think she'd be fine in that situation now."

Jean wasn't convinced.

Additional Readings

Bigge, J. L. (1990). *Teaching individuals with physical and multiple disabilities* (3rd ed.). Columbus, OH: Merrill.

Caldwell, T. H., & Sirvis, B. (1991). Students with special health conditions: An emerging population presents new challenges. *Preventing School Failure, 35*(3), 13–18.

Cole, K. N., Mills, P. E., Dale, P. S., & Jenkins, J. R. (1991). Effects of preschool integration for children with disabilities. *Exceptional Children, 58*(1), 36–45.

Derman-Sparks, L., & The A.B.C. Task Force (1989). *Anti-bias curriculum: Tools for empowering young children.* Washington, DC: National Association for the Education of Young Children.

Eggers, N. (1983). Influencing preschoolers' awareness and feelings regarding depicted physical disability. *Early Childhood Development and Care, 12*, 199–206.

Heitz, T. (1989). How do I help Jacob? *Young Children, 45*(1), 11–15.

Surr, J. (1992). Early childhood programs and the Americans with Disabilities Act (ADA). *Young Children, 47*(5), 18–21.

CASE 5

A Matter of Perspective

Judith B. Buzzell

Part C

The Teachers' Perspectives

Ms. Winthrop felt that the decision to keep Peter in Mrs. Jacobs's class was the best option. She was convinced that Peter was ready to be with his normal peers and was able to manage the situation with the right support. He needed the opportunity to know, learn from, and grow with them. Ms. Winthrop was eager to help Mrs. Jacobs when she could, but she knew realistically that her own work demands gave her little time to do so. She also was worried about Mrs. Jacobs's resistance to keeping Peter in her class.

Mrs. Jacobs felt that the principal had let the parents run the show and that her professional judgment about her limits and the needs of her class had not been respected. She had been willing to acknowledge that she had a problem working with Peter, and, somehow, this had boomeranged on her. The others obviously felt that she *was* the problem, not that she *had* a problem. She had been made to feel inadequate.

She thought that Dr. Cleary had made a poor choice, and she was angry about it. Since he hadn't taught in a classroom in twenty years, he no longer knew the realities of classroom life. She felt even more burdened than she did before the PPT and worried about how she could begin to make the many modifications that had been recommended. She resented Ms. Winthrop's suggestions. Ms. Winthrop didn't really understand her situation, since she had only seven children in her own class and was a relatively young, inexperienced teacher.

The Days Unfold

On Monday morning before school started, Ms. Winthrop stopped by Mrs. Jacobs's classroom to ask her what she could do to help. Mrs. Jacobs suggested that Ms. Winthrop develop the daily activity chart and told her that she'd contact Ms. Winthrop if she needed anything else.

The next day, Ms. Winthrop returned with the chart. Mrs. Jacobs used the chart regularly for a few days and then only occasionally. She found it cumbersome to carry around and resented taking the time to show it to Peter. At the special education teachers' bimonthly meeting with the kindergarten teachers, Ms. Winthrop realized that the chart wasn't being used. She was distressed and offered to make another chart that Peter could keep at home. This was a calendar having days with vacations and specials (such as gym or art) highlighted. Each day, Peter could check his calendar and know if there was going to be a change in his usual routine. Mrs. Jacobs had been conscientious in trying to follow the established routines.

Mrs. Jacobs tried some other modifications. She worked on giving Peter simple directions and always one step at a time. She also asked an especially caring, accepting child to be his partner at cleanup time to help him figure out what to do and stay focused on the task. She identified a few other children who were able to help, so they alternated helping Peter. She matched him with a partner in other situations when it seemed appropriate. This was an idea she had come up with, and it worked well to encourage the growth of Peter's social skills.

She never followed the suggestions for modifying the storybooks. She felt that one child's needs did not warrant the time and effort of making the materials and preparing the activities. If Peter became too distracting during the story time, she asked him to leave the circle and go to his seat. After doing so twice, Peter sat more quietly with the group. Mrs. Jacobs no longer asked him questions about the story.

Ms. Winthrop felt frustrated both that Mrs. Jacobs didn't implement more of her suggestions and that she didn't have time to be more actively involved in helping Peter. Still, she thought that it had been in Peter's best interests to remain in the kindergarten class where he could get to know and imitate his peers. She also felt it was important for the other children to get to know him.

Recommendations for Next Year?

Ms. Winthrop remained the special education liaison for Peter and was responsible for calling the PPT to plan Peter's program for the next year. When she spoke to Mrs. Jacobs to arrange the meeting, Mrs. Jacobs responded strongly, "If you think I'm going to recommend Peter for first grade, you're wrong. He's definitely not ready. I think it would be unfair to him to promote him in the regular education classes. And it would be unfair to the other children and the teacher."

Mrs. Jacobs was pleased that Peter had made strides in her regular kindergarten class in several academic areas. He could identify colors and color words. He could name numbers and identify the written words for numbers up to ten. He understood concepts of one-to-one correspondence, combining sets, patterning, and graphing (using Unifix cubes). He knew the alphabet. He could name the letters and match them to their appropriate sounds. He had an advanced sight-word vocabulary and could identify the beginning consonant sounds in many words.

However, she felt he still had many areas of weakness which would make it hard for him to manage in a regular first grade class. His interaction with the other students was limited. He played next to children rather than with them and didn't know how to initiate play with other children. His play was unimaginative. He tended to repeat scenarios in dramatic play rather than expanding on them or developing new ones. When he went to the housekeeping area, he always pretended he was having breakfast and tended to make toast over and over in the play toaster.

Mrs. Jacobs continued to be concerned about Peter's inability to follow multistep directions, and he still couldn't respond to comprehension questions about a story. She doubted he would understand enough to take tests, which began to be more common in first grade. This year, she had just overlooked the fact that Peter copied other children's test papers.

She also didn't think Peter would be able to handle the independent work required in first grade. Children had to work on their own for long periods at their desks while the teacher taught reading groups. Peter was still calling out whenever he finished even a small task.

Additionally, Mrs. Jacobs foresaw that Peter would need one-to-one tutoring in reading since he would learn best using a sight-word method. Phonetic rules would be too complex for him to comprehend. She felt that he had mastered some beginning letter sounds this year only because he could already read the words, but rules about blends and silent *e*, for example, would confound him.

"Overall, I can see that it was beneficial in some ways for Peter to remain in my kindergarten," summarized Mrs. Jacobs, "but in first grade there are many things he's just not going to be able to understand. And I don't want to pretend that he's ready for first grade. I feel I did all I could for Peter, but I really think he'll need more than a regular education class can offer from now on."

As Mrs. Jacobs talked, Ms. Winthrop felt her earlier conviction that Peter should go on with his peers to a regular first grade class begin to waver. How could she respond to Mrs. Jacobs's observations and recommendations? And what really was in Peter's best interest?

Additional Readings

Dunlop, G., & Plienis, A. J. (1991). The influence of task size on the unsupervised task performance of students with developmental disabilities. *Education and Treatment of Children, 14*(2), 85–95.

Ellenburg, F. C., & Lanier, N. J. (1984). Interacting effectively with parents. *Childhood Education, 60*, 315–318.

Gaylord-Ross, R. (Ed.). (1989). *Integration strategies for students with handicaps.* Baltimore: Brookes.

Healy, A., Keesee, P., & Smith, B. (1985). Parent-professional interactions. In *Early services for children with special needs: Transactions for family support.* Iowa City, IA: University of Iowa.

Raynes, M., Snell, M., & Sailor, W. (1991). A fresh look at categorical programs for children with special needs. *Phi Delta Kappan, 73*(4), 326–31.

Sailor, W., Anderson, J. L., Halvorsen, A. T., Doering, K., Filler, J., & Goetz, L. (1989). *The comprehensive local school: Regular education for all students with disabilities.* Baltimore: Brookes.

Sarason, S. B. (1971). *The culture of the school and the problem of change.* Boston: Allyn & Bacon.

Semmel, M. I., Abernathy, T. V., Butera, G., & Lesar, S. (1991). Teacher perceptions of the regular education initiative. *Exceptional Children, 58*(1), 9–24.

Zigler, E., & Hodapp, R. M. (1987). The developmental implications of integrating autistic children within the public schools. In Cohen, D. J., Donnellan, A. M., & Paul, R. (Eds.), *Handbook of autism and pervasive developmental disorders* (pp. 668–674). Silver Springs, MD: Winston & Sons.

CASE 7

A Different Kind of Student

Loretta L. Rubin

Part C

Follow-Up

Colleen spent her next year in first grade with a different teacher. By midyear her progress in reading began to lag, so her parents hired a tutor to help her. In subsequent years, Colleen "held her own" in each of her classes. With the assistance of Mrs. Jones, the resource teacher, Colleen maintained a position in the middle of the class.

Several years later, as Colleen prepared to leave the sixth grade at Parkview for junior high, the following statements were made about Colleen.

Mr. and Mrs. Murphy

We are pleased with Colleen's progress. She is working hard for her C average and is functioning at the middle of the class. She is on grade level in reading and language and, with help from Mrs. Jones, is able to keep up with the class in math. We understand that she will probably always need some special services and accommodations. But overall, we're pleased with her present level and the progress that she's made.

Mrs. Jones

I assist Colleen in math and with tests in all her subjects. If I work with her without a time restriction, she is slow and deliberate and can show what she knows. With these exceptions, I think she's performing well. She can keep up with her class and is reading on grade level. She is squarely in the middle of her class, and she keeps plugging, even when the work gets difficult.

Classroom Teacher—Sixth Grade

Colleen is doing okay, but you can see that there are problems there. Everything is so hard for her. The parents don't even want to discuss it. They are satisfied with her progress. They don't realize that she'd never be able to keep up if it weren't for Mrs. Jones. She has been wonderful working with

Colleen. She helps her in math so she won't fall behind and administers tests separately to Colleen. Otherwise, Colleen would mark just any answer. I feel that Mrs. Jones has a blind spot about Colleen, too. She doesn't recognize how difficult junior high will be for Colleen. I don't know how Colleen will manage without Mrs. Jones, and I am worried about her. How will she be able to keep up with the increased independent work at this higher level?

Additional Readings

Alexander, J. E., & Heathington, B. S. (1988). *Assessing and correcting classroom reading problems.* Glenview, IL: Scott, Foresman.

Anderson, R. C., Hiebert, E. H., Scott, J. A., & Wilkinson, I. A. G. (1985). *Becoming a nation of readers: The report of the Commission on Reading.* Washington, DC: National Academy of Education, National Institute of Education.

Carbo, M. (1987). Reading styles research: "What works" isn't always phonics. *Phi Delta Kappan, 68*(6), 431–435.

Schultz, T. (1989). Testing and retention of young children: Moving from controversy to reform. *Phi Delta Kappan, 71*(2), 125–129.

Slingerland, B. H. (1971). *A multisensory approach to language arts for specific language disability children: A guide for primary teachers.* Cambridge, MA: Educators Publishing Services.

Smith, M. L., & Shepard, L. A. (1987). What doesn't work: Explaining policies of retention in the early grades. *Phi Delta Kappan, 69*(2), 129–134.

Spiegel, D. L. (1990). Decoding and comprehension games and manipulatives (instructional resources). *Reading Teacher, 44*(3), 258–61.

Stratton, B. D., & Grindler, M. C. (1989). Assessing reading achievement: Look at what's available. *Reading Improvement, 26*(2), 156–159.

CASE 8

How Much Can You Expect?

Judith B. Buzzell

Part C

At the end of second grade, the Wights arranged for private tutoring for Lesley. Rebecca had recommended to them a highly experienced, knowledgeable older woman who had been a reading teacher before her retirement. In considering her own work with Lesley, Rebecca commented, "I don't feel that I solved the problem of teaching Lesley to read. The best thing that I did was to connect her with the reading teacher."

By the time Lesley was in fourth grade, she was reading on grade level.

Joan, her speech pathologist, reflected back on her four years of working with Lesley. Although she wished she had had more time to consult with Lesley's teachers over the years (her itinerant schedule required her to visit additional schools, so consultation time was limited), her work with Lesley was a pleasure.

> She has to be the best student I have ever worked with. She's magnificent. She's a dynamo. She's social, intelligent, witty, helpful, and curious. Even as a kindergartner, she'd come in and stay on task and try anything you asked her to do. She always had incredible oral language. She loves to write now, and I'm addressing her grammatical needs through her writing. As far as I'm concerned, Lesley's a regular student. She's not a handicapped student. I never thought of her as a child with hearing impairments in the mainstream, because her language was so strong.

Additional Readings

Bateman, B. D. (1963). Reading and psycholinguistic processes of partially seeing children. *Council for Exceptional Children Research Monograph* (Series A, No. 5).

Bose, J. (1991). Listen to me. *Exceptional Parent, 21*(4), 28–30.

Degler, L. S., & Risko, V. J. (1979). Teaching reading to mainstreamed sensory impaired children. *The Reading Teacher, 32*, 921–925.

Haladian, A., & Rose, S. (1991). An investigation of parents' attitudes and the communication skills of their deaf children. *American Annals of the Deaf, 136*(3), 273–77.

Jose, R. T., LaBossiere, S., & Small, M. (1988). A model for integrating low vision services into educational programs. *Education of the Visually Handicapped, 19*(4), 157–166.

Lieberman, L. M. (1985). Special education and regular education: A merger made in heaven? *Exceptional Children, 51*, 513–516.

Raynes, M., Snell, M., & Sailor, W. (1991). A fresh look at categorical programs for children with special needs. *Phi Delta Kappan, 73*(4), 326–31.

Wurzbach, L. (1988). Teaching reading to braille, print and aural readers. *Education of the Visually Handicapped, 19*(4), 167–184.

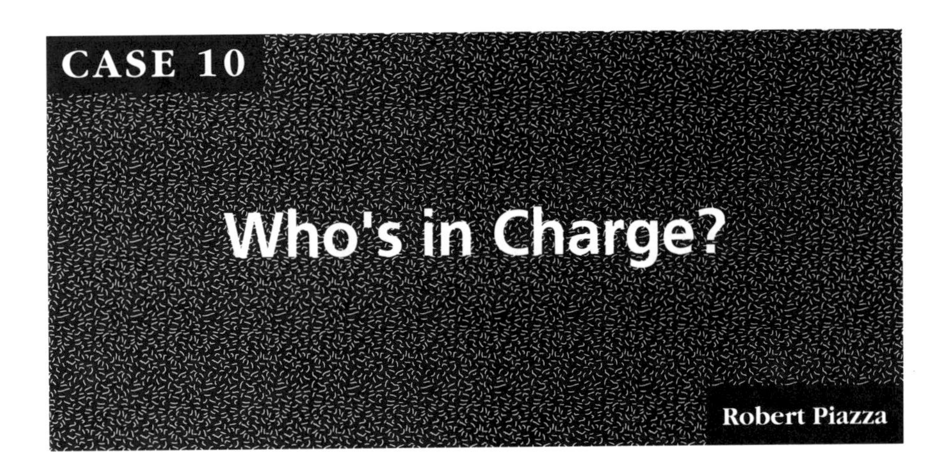

Part C

In Mark's Bedroom

"I hate it! I hate it! I'm not going anymore!" Mark bellowed.

It was 8:00 A.M. on a cold January morning, two days before the scheduled PPT. The new school bus was about to come to the neighborhood to pick up the children attending Thomson School. Mark's mother had sensed the frustration building in Mark over the last few weeks. All the extra remedial attention was taking its toll. Mark articulated in the best manner he could all that was troubling him.

> Mom, you don't understand. When I go to see Miss Schultz in school, I miss some other work. Then I have to do homework. I have to come in early from recess to go to that room where she makes me talk. I don't wanna go there. You and Daddy try to help me a whole lot, but I don't never get to go play tennis with him and Jeff no more. He takes Jeff to play every Tuesday and Wednesday before he goes to work, but I have to stay and read books and do math with you before the school bus comes here. I'm dumb, huh?

Mrs. Jones tried to reassure Mark that he wasn't dumb, but that he did have some learning problems that people were trying to help him with. Instead of making him take the bus, she drove Mark to school and told him that they would talk more when he got home that day. She reminded him that he had to get on the special bus going to the church for religious instruction after school. When Mrs. Jones returned home, she sat down and outlined the special services that Mark was receiving:

Mrs. Ellis (since September): Monday and Wednesday—1:00–1:30

Miss Schultz (since September): Monday, Tuesday, Thursday—10:00–10:30

Private language tutor (over the last year and a half): Saturday morning—11:00–12:30

Learning disability clinic (at local college; started last week): Monday and Wednesday—4:00–5:30

Staring at the list, Ann Jones started biting the polished nail of her left index finger. After several sighs, she walked slowly toward the phone . . . .

Additional Readings

Chalfant, J., Pysh, M., & Moultrie, R. (1979). Teacher assistance team: A model for within-building problem solving. *Learning Disabilities Quarterly, 2*, 83–96.

Connecticut State Guidelines for identifying children with learning disabilities. (1983). Connecticut State Board of Education. Hartford, CT

Friend, M. (1988). Putting consultation into context: Historical and contemporary perspectives. *Remedial and Special Education, 9*(6), 7–13.

Phillips, V., & McCullough, L. (1990). Consultation-based programming: Instituting the collaborative ethic in schools. *Exceptional Children, 56*(4), 291–301.

Pugach, M., & Johnson, L. (1989). Prereferral interventions: Progress, problems and challenges. *Exceptional Children, 56*(3), 217–226.

Will, M. (1986). *Educating students with learning problems: A shared responsibility.* Washington, DC: U.S. Department of Education, Office of Special Education and Rehabilitative Services.

CASE 11

A Question of Ownership

Sally Francia and Robert Piazza

Part C

Coming Together

After analyzing their main concerns, the team decided to take the following actions. Lori would inform the Gradys of the events of the last few days and of this day's meeting. Since this wasn't a PPT meeting, the Gradys had not been invited to attend. In fact, they had given prior approval to the team to meet spontaneously about Sam if it would improve his functioning. Sara was going to observe Sam's reading group to gather information about his difficulty following along in the book, his response to prefix-suffix lessons, and his general behavior within the class. Merle was asked to script the kinds of phrases Lisa used when delivering reading lessons. Lisa would keep a checklist of every time Sam was disruptive in the group, in order to get a sense of precipitating factors or patterns. Lou Morrisey agreed to review past reading tests and to consult with Mrs. Hayes, the school's reading consultant, about an appropriate reading placement for Sam.

The Observation

Sara North observed Sam from behind a bookcase, out of his view. Lisa had the reading group seated at a semicircular table facing the blackboard. The children had their books open to the story "The Farmer and His Strange Animals" and were taking turns reading the story aloud. Sara noticed that Sam was not using the table microphone and amplifier designed to pick up his groupmates' voices. Without this amplification, he had to look at each child's face to tell when they were reading and when they had stopped. As a result, he had to look away from his book several times in a session, causing him to lose his place. In addition, the bookstands purchased last year to facilitate speechreading were not being used by the children in Sam's group. As a result, Sam's comprehension of the story may have been affected. When Mrs. Weeks posed questions later in the story, she did not use visual prompts, such as facial gestures. She seemed to have a rather laid-back, understated teaching style, which in Sara's opinion lacked the necessary drama for Sam to gain information through his visual abilities.

Soon the children were engaged in a lesson on prefixes and suffixes. Lisa wrote the word *admission* on the board and asked a child to identify both the prefix and suffix in that word. When the child answered, she circled *ad* and drew a line under *sion.* When the next child correctly responded to the same request for the word *prevention,* Lisa drew a line under the prefix and circled the suffix in that word. Lisa sporadically alternated this procedure throughout the lesson. Sam seemed unsure of what was expected and had two poor trials before he was finally able to give a correct answer. Sam showed no signs of disruptive behavior, but he did get up twice to get tissues from the teacher's desk because his nose was runny.

Merle had time to observe and transcribe four lessons with Sam in Lisa Weeks's class. She noticed that Lisa used idiomatic phrases, such as "pass the buck," "give him a call," "by the seat of his pants," and "in one ear and out the other."

Friday's Meeting

The follow-up team meeting did not start off on a positive note. Lou Morrisey had in his hands a copy of the report card that would be going home with Sam next Tuesday. He began the meeting by asking, "Lisa, did you really give Sam a C in his reading for this grading period?" The rest of the team looked astonished. Although Sam's grade in reading had not been discussed in depth before, they thought there was an implicit understanding that Sam's performance would not be formally evaluated until after this day's meeting.

Lisa countered, "I believe if I'm Sam's teacher, I can grade him as I see fit. Unless this group's findings can convince me that this grade is unfair, the C stands. It's misleading to give him an A, or even a B, if he truly doesn't deserve it. He is not producing the same quality work as his peers in that top group."

The team agreed to put that argument aside for a while and discuss what they had discovered that week.

Sara North's report of her observations led to a discussion on the use of specialized equipment and its importance. Sara planned to use Sam's microphone with him in their afternoon sessions until he again felt comfortable with it. She offered to co-teach Sam's reading group with Lisa and provide hands-on experience with enhancing lessons by the use of visual aids. Lisa nodded when Sara described what she had seen during the prefix-suffix lesson. She agreed that her markings could have confused a child whose hearing was impaired such as Sam. "I'm glad you noticed this. I think these are the subtle, helpful hints I need," Lisa said.

Merle Evans shared the phrases and vocabulary Lisa had used during her lessons. Sara agreed to teach these terms to Sam, using speechreading and sign language to expedite the transfer of information.

Mr. Morrisey reported that Mrs. Hayes (the reading consultant) felt Sam had satisfied the criteria on the midterm test. Even though his score of 76 was not as high as that of his peers, it was still passing. She also noted that he had strong word recognition and comprehension scores. Mrs. Hayes confirmed what members of the team had noted before, that most of his errors occurred on tasks requiring inner-sound recognition.

Lisa Weeks presented her checklists of off-task behaviors. It appeared that Sam's disruptions occurred more frequently during oral and silent reading activities. They were less frequent when the children were involved in a skills activity or in board work. Lisa had included Sam's tissue breaks in her list of disruptions. The others explained that Sam had allergies, which may have been why he kept getting out of his seat.

For the next ten minutes, Lori and Sara reiterated that Sam was a sensory-impaired child who needed specific modifications to succeed in the mainstream. Lori indicated that although Lisa's commitment to fairness was commendable, it was unfair to require a hearing-impaired child to acquire information through his ears. Furthermore, she felt it was in violation of federal and state policies. Sara noted that tests for children such as Sam need to be taken in private in order to maximize concentration and to allow the deletion of inappropriate subtests. Both Lori and Sara felt that the decision on the assignment of grades should be made by the whole team, since they were all working with Sam. They emphasized, though, that Lisa was a member of the team and should certainly express her feelings.

Lisa appeared a bit agitated but expressed herself in a very controlled manner:

> Fine, I'll change his grade to an A. And I'll keep him in the top group. Grades are meaningless anyway. I understand Sam's needs are different, and I'll conform to what we discussed here today. But just as Sam's needs are different, so is his performance. I hope his parents are aware of this. Sam is being mainstreamed in my class with a lot of extra help and many modifications, but I hope we are preparing him to be mainstreamed in life, where there will be fewer modifications and less extra assistance. I have to leave now. My social studies class is starting in five minutes. I'll see you next week.

The rest of the team sat for a few moments after Lisa left. Finally, Sara broke the silence by sighing, "This job isn't an easy one."

The Plan in Action—Two Weeks Later

Sam sat upright in his chair. His reading book was affixed to a small bookstand, as were his groupmates' books. He could easily see their mouths and faces from this perspective. The microphone was still not being used because Sam refused to experiment with it. However, Merle Evans unobtrusively encouraged all the children to turn toward Sam as they spoke. Lisa Weeks had taped a few key words to the blackboard, which she pointed to throughout the lesson as she spoke. Sam followed along quite well and answered all the comprehension questions correctly.

Later, Lisa wrote the prefix and base word for each key word on the board. She had students come up to the board, one by one, to underline the base word and put a square around the prefix. When one child put a square around the base word and underlined the prefix, Lisa quickly corrected him. Sam took two turns at the board and responded correctly both times.

Mrs. Evans stood near Sam for most of the lesson and drew diagrams and wrote key words in Sam's pocket notebook. These would later be reviewed with Sara North. A small box of tissues was on the corner of Sam's desk.

By Lisa's invitation, Sara was also in the room. Lisa wanted her to observe the entire group before they began their team teaching. As Sara was about to leave, Lisa said, "Thanks for coming in. I can tell Sam is participating more, and I'm seeing less disruptive behavior. I hope this continues."

Sara took a deep breath and replied, "So do I. So do I."

Additional Readings

Andrews, J., & Mason, J. (1991). Strategy usage among deaf and hearing readers. *Exceptional Child, 57*, 536–545.

Arnold, K. M., & Hornett, D. (1990). Teaching idioms to children who are deaf. *Teaching Exceptional Children, 22*, 14–17.

Johnson, D. W., & Johnson, R. T. (1985). Mainstreaming hearing impaired children: The effect of communicating on cooperation and interpersonal attraction. *Journal of Psychology, 119*, 31–44.

Luckner, J. L., Rude, H., & Sileo, T. W. (1989). Collaborative Consultation: A method for improving educational services for mainstreamed students who are hearing impaired. *American Annals of the Deaf, 134*, 301–304.

Part C

That Evening

Susan Johnson looked over the assignments for language and realized that the situation wasn't as dim as it first appeared.

We need to explain to Lisa that she will be working in the same language book as her friends, she thought. The words may be difficult for her, but we don't expect her to understand each one. Plus, Mrs. Carey will help her with the words she can't read. Lisa's seatwork and homework would have to be geared to a second grade level, however. A second grade language book could be used for seatwork assignments, which would allow Lisa to participate in the weekly assignment in a modified fashion.

Susan prepared seatwork for Lisa for the next day. She thought about tomorrow's lesson. Mrs. Hill would be reviewing the homework assignment in class. Since Lisa did not have a homework assignment, she would have to think of a way to include her in the activity.

Susan Johnson thought Sarah could copy the correct verb on the board as the students gave their answers. Mrs. Hill could then call on Lisa to give her a verb that described one thing she did the night before. Sarah Hill would copy Lisa's verb on the board, as she did for the other students in her class.

Susan Johnson slept peacefully that night knowing that, given her own materials and adaptations, Lisa could participate in the assigned classroom activities. She knew Sarah would approve of the modifications.

Tuesday

Both teachers met at the end of the day. Susan asked, "How did it go with the language lesson today?"

"Great," Sarah replied. "Even I couldn't believe how smoothly it went. Lisa seemed very proud that she could participate in the lesson. Trisha, who sits next to her, even commented on what a good job she did, and during snack time they played tic-tac-toe together."

Susan said, "I have a great idea for tomorrow's lesson. Lisa is learning about different jobs, and we are now discussing the restaurant business. Lisa can participate in the writing assignment by writing to . . . maybe Trisha . . . about a job she could do in a restaurant."

Susan and Sarah smiled as they reviewed the week's language assignments and the modifications necessary for Lisa to participate. As Susan Johnson was ready to leave, her colleague said, "Oh, by the way, next week we are working on adverbs from Unit 6." Mrs. Johnson left her classroom dazed. "How can I modify adverbs for Lisa and relate that lesson to her individualized goals?"

Additional Readings

Bilken, D. (1985). *Achieving the complete school.* New York: Teachers College Press.

Brown, L., Long, E., Udvari-Solner, A., Davis, L., Van-Deventer, P., Ahlgren, C., Johnson, F., Gruenewald, L., & Jorgensen, J. (1989). The home school: Why students with severe intellectual disabilities must attend the schools of their brothers, sisters, friends, and neighbors. *Journal of the Association for Persons with Severe Handicaps, 14*(1), 1-7.

Brown, L., Long, E., Udvari-Solner, A., Schwartz, P., Van-Deventer, P., Ahlgren, C., Johnson, F., Gruenewald, L., & Jorgensen, J. (1989). Should students with severe intellectual disabilities be based in regular or in special education classrooms in home schools? *Journal of the Association for Persons with Severe Handicaps, 14*(1), 8-12.

Brown, L., Schwarz, P., Udvari-Solner, A., Kampschroer, E., Johnson, F., Jorgensen, J., Gruenewald, L., University of Wisconsin, & Madison Metropolitan School District. (1991). How much time should students with severe intellectual disabilities spend in regular education classrooms and elsewhere? *Journal of the Association for Persons with Severe Handicaps, 16*(1), 39-47.

Davern, L., & Ford, A. (1989). *The Syracuse community-referenced curriculum guide.* Baltimore, MD: Paul H. Brookes.

Thousand, J., Fox, T., Reid, R., Godck, J., Williams, W., & Fox, W. (1986). *The homecoming model: Educating students who present intensive educational challenges within regular education environments.* Burlington, VT: University of Vermont, The Homecoming Project Center for Developmental Disabilities.

Reynolds, M., Wang, M., & Walberg, H. (1987). The necessary restructuring of special and regular education. *Exceptional Children, 53*(5), 391-398.

CASE 13

A Child's Disability—A Teacher's Handicap?

Barbara Heinisch

Part C

The School's Response

A PPT meeting was quickly scheduled. While the details of acquiring software and the arrangements for hiring a rehabilitation engineer were worked out, Hallie was given use of the computer for her classwork. She was working very slowly without the benefit of the adaptive software, but at least she was productively involved while the others were working.

Ann found that she did not need to spend as much time with Hallie, and was much less stressed in the classroom. She still worried about what would happen when the new software arrived. Who would teach her how to help Hallie use it? She knew better than to expect a great deal of help from John Watson. He was enraged when he had discovered that Hallie had been evaluated at an outside facility for computer use, which he had felt to be inappropriate. Ann worried about finding the time to actually learn computer skills. She had used a computer for games before, but she was not familiar with using it as a tool for producing writing. What would happen, she wondered, when she had to place Hallie with another teacher for next year? Most of the other teachers in the school were no more experienced with computer use than she was.

Additional Readings

Behrmann, M. (1988). *Integrating computers into the curriculum.* Boston: Little, Brown.

Geisert, P., & Futrell, M. (1990). *Teachers, computers and curriculum.* Boston: Allyn & Bacon.

Green, P., & Brightman, A. J. (1990). Independence day: Designing computer solutions for individuals with disabilities. *Exceptional Parent, 20*(2), 32.

Guzzo, P., & Guzzo, B. (1991). Scott's IEP includes technology. *Exceptional Parent, 21*(8), T2-T5.

Heinisch, B. (1992). Assistive technology application for students with learning disabilities: obstacles and opportunities. *Disability Studies Quarterly, 12*(4), 21-23.

Heinisch, B. & Hecht, J. (1993). Word Prediction software. *Technology and Media Newsletter, 8*(3), 4-9.

Milone, M. N., Jr. (1992). Special resources for special ed students. *Technology and Learning, 12*(5), 92-93.

Wisniewski, L., & Sedlak, R. (1992). Assistive devices for students with disabilities. *Elementary School Journal, 92*(3), 30-31.

CASE 14

The First Mistake

Robert Piazza and Judith B. Buzzell

Part C

The Following Monday

Ms. Berlein presented a math lesson which she hoped would provide crucial review for all students, but particularly for Emily. She reflected on the day's math lesson to a fellow teacher:

> I wanted to review the division of whole numbers with remainders. I thought it would be best to use manipulatives as a way to ensure that students were understanding the underlying concept rather than just manipulating the figures. By using the place value blocks, they would be able to see the actual process of division and see the blocks left over. I think this kind of experiential learning is especially important for students who have some difficulty with abstractions.
>
> I had learned about cooperative learning in my teacher preparation program and felt it might be an effective strategy to use, especially with Emily. In a group of students with mixed abilities, Emily wouldn't feel constantly pitted against the best students, and this might bolster her confidence. Moreover, all students would be responsible for helping each other to master the task, so she would have guidance from students who were more advanced.
>
> I explained to the class that we would be dividing whole numbers with remainders today. In order for them to better understand the concept of division and the steps in it, they would be using place value blocks. I suggested that they might wish to think of division as "sharing." When I said this, Emily's drawn face visibly relaxed. It seemed to help her when I used a familiar idea to explain a technical term.
>
> I divided the class into six groups of four students each. Emily's group included Emily, one student from the highest math group, one student from the average group, and one student from the lowest achieving group. Although Emily was in the highest group, she had not been performing at their level.
>
> Each member of the group was assigned a role as either facilitator, recorder, encourager, or checker. I assigned Emily the role of checker—she would be responsible for checking to see that the problems were correctly solved. So, after having helped to solve each problem initially with the whole group, she

would then double-check each one. In this role, she actually would go through the process twice. I hoped this would provide added reinforcement of the concept of division for her.

In this particular activity, there was no reporting of each group's findings to the entire class. That didn't seem necessary. However, to build in "individual accountability," at the end of the class, I gave a short quiz that required each student to solve independently three new problems.

To begin the activity, the cooperative learning groups initially spent fifteen minutes exploring with the place value blocks. First, they used the blocks to show a three-digit number. Then they divided that number by 3 or 4. They had to divide the blocks so that each block cluster had the same number. Finally, they recorded the number in each cluster, and the number left over. I reminded them to be careful when they traded the ten block for one blocks. If they didn't count the blocks carefully, they would have an incorrect number of ones, which would affect their answers. After the exploratory period, they had a worksheet of division problems to complete using the place value blocks. For example, 145 ÷ 3 was one of the problems.

I circulated around the room while the groups worked. Emily was actively participating and seemed confident. She animatedly explained her checking of each problem. When I scored the results of the individual quizzes, she had gotten all the problems correct.

Although clearly pleased with the results, Ms. Berlein realized that this lesson was a review. "How," she wondered, "should I introduce decimals to Emily next week?"

Additional Readings

Case, L. P., Harris, K. R., & Graham, S. (1992). Improving the mathematical problem-solving skills of students with learning disabilities: Self-regulated strategy development. *Journal of Special Education, 26*, 1-19.

Davidson, N., & Kroll, D. L. (1991). An overview of research on cooperative learning related to mathematics. *Journal for Research in Mathematics Education, 22*, 362-65.

Goldman, S. (1989). Strategy instruction in mathematics. *Learning Disability Quarterly, 15*, 43-55.

Johnson, D. W., & Johnson, R. T. (1989). Cooperative learning: What special education teachers want to know. *Pointer, 33*, 5-11.

Slavin, R. E. (1989). Comprehensive cooperative learning models for heterogeneous classrooms. *Pointer, 33*, 12-19.

CASE 15

Chen Yang

Judith B. Buzzell

Part C

Early December

Jim continued to be concerned about Chen. In reading, Chen had taken small, incremental steps. The reading teacher was overjoyed a few weeks ago when Chen read aloud for the first time. But it was still unclear how much Chen understood. He was decoding on the second or third grade level, but his comprehension lagged. On the Jostens computer program (which includes comprehension skills), he was at the first grade reading level.

Jim had been encouraging Chen to read more books; the fact that Chen hadn't done so led Jim to suspect that Chen's comprehension was poor. Jim felt that Chen preferred the computer to books because there were obvious picture clues that made it easier for Chen to comprehend. For example, on the screen, there would be the single word *kite* and a picture of a kite. Through the headphones, he could also hear the word *kite*. Jim felt that Chen liked to learn and needed the sense of achievement the computer gave him.

With the help of the ESL teacher, Chen had written some short pieces to contribute to the class's literary magazine. One was about Halloween, and another was about Thanksgiving. Jim lamented that he couldn't spend more time giving Chen the kind of individualized help he needed with his writing.

"It took the ESL teacher one or two months to get him going, and she can only see him for a half hour, three times a week. That's not enough," he commented.

Mathematics continued to be Chen's special strength, and it boosted him socially. The other kids vied to have him in their math group. Chen was very confident of his math skills. "He's a computational whiz," said Jim. "He's way ahead of the other kids in multiplication and division." Jim felt that only language limitations kept him at the third grade level on the Jostens computer program.

Still, Chen had no real connection to the other kids. "I've never seen him make an overture to someone else," remarked Jim. During reading and writing sessions, Chen seemed content to sit at his desk and do nothing for long periods. When this happened, Jim asked Chen if he'd like to use the computer and gave him a choice of either a math or language program.

But even though Chen was frequently alone, *he was* smiling more.

The Second Parent Conference

As Chen's mother described the operation her son needed next year, tears welled in her eyes. Chen had a serious back condition that required surgery. There was a risk that the surgery would cause paralysis. Chen hadn't wanted his mother to tell Jim about this because he was afraid he wouldn't be allowed to go to gym. He wanted to fit in and be part of his class in every way.

Jim was stunned to learn about Chen's desire to belong since that was not his perception of the often solitary student.

An Anniversary Party

During the frenzy of the holiday season, Jim realized that in January it would be a year since Chen had arrived in this country. He was toying with the idea of throwing a party to mark the occasion. At the party, Chen could talk to the class about his life in China, and Ming Lo could translate.

Jim mused that there had been no curriculum activities or discussion related to China. He thought he should have done this earlier. Chen's anniversary seemed like a good time to do it.

The Pupil: Final View

It was about 10:30 on Wednesday morning. Working in groups on their research projects on the human body, students were making diagrams and charts, reading from a variety of resource books, and planning together. Jim was rotating among the groups to help them.

Chen was sitting next to Lamar and Sam, his project partners. They conferred chummily over a book on the human eye, while Chen stared ahead aimlessly. After a few minutes, he got up and found a plastic math game with movable parts and toyed with it. About ten minutes later, Jim came over to this group. He reminded Lamar that they had neglected to list Chen's name as a member of their group on one of the charts they'd made. Lamar looked abashed and wrote it in above the other names, as an afterthought.

Jim asked Lamar and Sam how they intended to include Chen in their presentation. Lamar excitedly described their plan. Then he called Chen over to the blackboard to draw a diagram of the eye.

"Take your time," he coached, as Chen drew an oval outline. "Now make the pupils," Lamar said, demonstrating by making a circle with his finger and holding it to his eye.

Sam was about to take over, but Lamar protested, "Let him do it!" He insistently cheered Chen on. "You know what it is—*pupil, pupil!*"

Chen walked away. He moved to his desk and leafed through a book. Finding a diagram of the eye, he showed it to Lamar, pointing to the word *pupil.*

The Teacher: Final Reflections

"Chen can literally go for days without talking," said Jim. "And I'm *still* not sure how much of his communication problem is caused by lack of knowledge of English, or by shyness, perfectionism, cultural differences—or even by worry about his upcoming surgery."

Reflecting back to the beginning of the year, Jim felt that it was amazing that he had no warning of Chen's language problem. He felt that there should be a system to inform teachers of language problems in advance. Chen's records had not arrived from his former school until a week after school started.

Jim seriously questioned whether Chen should be in his class. He believed Chen needed more individualized teaching. Chen's time with the ESL teacher was too short.

> "I'm not saying that he shouldn't be in the mainstream," Jim hastened to qualify. "It's not that he's any kind of a problem for me, but it's frustrating and painful for me to see a child go without speaking. I don't know what I'm doing for him. I'm trying to fill in that gap by putting him on the computer more."

Additional Readings

Conteras, R. (1988). *Bilingual education.* Bloomington, IN: Phi Delta Kappa.

Fradd, S. H., & Weismantel, M. J. (1989). *Meeting the needs of culturally and linguistically different students: A handbook for educators.* Boston: Little, Brown.

Genishi, C. (1989). Observing the second language learner: An example of teachers' learning. *Language Arts, 66*(5), 509–515.

Leung, E. K. (1988). Cultural and acculturational commonalities and diversities among Asian Americans: Identification and programming consideration. In A. A. Ortiz & B. A. Ramirez (Eds.), *Schools and the culturally diverse exceptional student: Promising practices and future directions* (pp. 86–95). Reston, VA: The Council for Exceptional Children.

Moore, S. A., & Moore, D. W. (1991). Linguistic diversity and reading (Professional resources). *Reading Teacher, 45*(4), 326–327.

Ramsey, P. (1987). *Teaching and learning in a diverse world.* New York: Teachers College Press.

Sleeter, C., & Grant, C. (1987). An analysis of multicultural education in the United States. *Harvard Educational Review, 57*(4), 421–444.

Yao, E. L. (1987). Asian immigrant students: Unique problems that hamper learning. *Bulletin of the National Association of Secondary School Principals, 71*(503), 82–88.

Zuk, D. (1986). The effects of microcomputers on children's attention to reading. *Computers in the Schools, 3,* 39–50.

CASE 17

The Performance

Denise LaPrade Rini

Part C

"How do you think Matt feels about school right now?" Christina asked Mrs. Andrews.

Mrs. Andrews replied thoughtfully, "He's pretty quiet about it, except that he talked about his part in the civics project. He liked that a lot. I think he's feeling a little lost in this school still."

"Do you think he is aware of how his speech is different?" Christina continued.

Mrs. Andrews blushed. "Matt is a lot like I was at his age. You've probably noticed that I stutter. It got very embarrassing for me when I became a teenager. So I just found things to do that wouldn't take much talking. But I don't want Matt to go through what I did. Last year, when the director of pupil personnel told us Matt didn't qualify for services because he was such a good student, I was proud. I didn't know where we could go for help after that."

Christina explained that according to the speech pathologist they would need some specific reasons related to school performance in order to justify services for Matt. Christina reviewed aspects of Matt's schoolwork with Mrs. Andrews. They made a list of the reasons they felt this referral for evaluation and therapy should be pursued: Matt was experiencing difficulty completing oral assignments because of his speech difficulty; apparent self-consciousness concerning his speech was causing him to withdraw from class participation; and his adjustment to class and relationships with classmates were being compromised. They wrote up the referral together and decided to bring it to the principal the next day.

Christina felt that her conference with Mrs. Andrews had been positive and helpful. However, she still had to be concerned about how to help Matt during the period of referral and evaluation. What could she do during that time? What would the outcome of the referral and ensuing PPT meeting be?

Additional Readings

Conture, E. G. (1989). *Stuttering and your child: Questions and answers.* Memphis: Stuttering Foundation of America.

Ham, R. E. (1990). *Therapy of stuttering.* Englewood Cliffs, NJ: Prentice-Hall.

Johnson, W. (1967). An open letter to the mother of a 'stuttering' child. In Johnson, W. and Moeller, A. (Eds.), *Speech handicapped school children.* (pp. 543–544). New York: Harper and Row.

Kidd, K. K. (1984). Stuttering as a genetic disorder. In Curlee, R. & Perkins, W. (Eds.), *Nature and treatment of stuttering: New directions.* (pp. 149–169). San Diego: College-Hill.

Shames, G. H., & Rubin, H. (1986). *Stuttering then and now.* Columbus: Charles E. Merrill.

Shames, G. H., & Wiig, E. H. (1990). *Human communication disorders,* (3rd ed.). New York: Macmillan.

Van Riper, C. (1982). *The nature of stuttering* (2nd ed.). Englewood Cliffs, NJ: Prentice-Hall.

Wall, M. J., & Myers, F. L. (1984). *Clinical management of childhood stuttering.* Baltimore: University Park Press.

CASE 19

The Reluctant Freshman

Robert Piazza and Linda Pica

Part C

Midterm Reports

For the next few weeks, Richard Hernandez had an uneasy feeling about Jodi's progress in history. Mr. Higgins did allow her to tape his lectures, but apparently none of the other modifications were being implemented. Jodi had commented that she really didn't feel comfortable in his class, but in her own words, "The rest of her teachers were great."

It was a rainy October afternoon, and Jodi reported to Mr. Hernandez's resource room for her fifth period lesson. "I got my midterm grades in the mail yesterday," Jodi said.

"How were they?" Hernandez asked.

"Okay, I guess. Here they are."

Hernandez opened up the envelope and studied her grades.

English - B–

Math - C+

History - D

Science - A–

Health - B

P.E. - B+

The resource teacher looked at Jodi and nodded his approval. "Great start, Jodi. We're just going to have to work a bit harder in history. I'll talk to Mr. Higgins as soon as I can and see what the problem is." "Thanks, Mr. H. You're great," replied Jodi.

Mr. Hernandez stared out the window and gritted his teeth. "I'll be right back," he said as he rushed out of the room.

Additional Readings

Cook, L., & Friend, M. (1991). Principles for the practice of collaboration in schools. *Preventing School Failure, 35*, 6–9.

Deshler, D. D., & Schumaker, J. B. (1986). Learning strategies: An instructional alternative for low-achieving adolescents. *Exceptional Children, 52*, 583–590.

Ellis, E. S., Deshler, D. D., Lenz, K., Schumaker, J. B., & Clark, F. L. (1991). An instructional model for teaching learning strategy. *Focus on Exceptional Children, 23*, 1–24.

Schaeffer, A., Zigmond, N., Kerr, M. M., & Farra, H. E., (1990). Helping teenagers develop school survival skills. *Teaching Exceptional Children, 23*, 6–9.

Wiedmeyer, D., & Lehman, J. (1991). The "House Plan" approach to collaborative teaching and consultation. *Teaching Exceptional Children, 23*, 6–10.

CASE 20

The Letter

Judith B. Buzzell

Part C

Sophomore and Junior Year

Jennifer returned to Van Buren High at the beginning of her sophomore year. She took Louise's parenting class in both her sophomore and junior years. Students were permitted to take the class as long as they wished. Louise simply felt that students who took it were acknowledging that they still needed the support that the class provided.

According to Louise, Jennifer was worried and anxious for much of the sophomore year. Her friendships were in a state of flux because her life had changed so dramatically. For example, she'd lost the flexibility to make spontaneous arrangements with friends. She couldn't just decide on the spur of the moment to go to a movie, because she had to arrange in advance for child care. But most teenagers don't make dates a week ahead, so she wasn't able to return to her original friendships.

To Louise, Jennifer's quietness in class was a sign of her anxiety. "When she wasn't talkative, then you knew something was going on. That was her style."

In the parenting class, Louise helped the teen moms to deal with three key issues: the boyfriend, sources of support, and school work. Louise felt that it took most teen moms about seven months to work out the relationship with the child's father, longer than teen relationships generally lasted. Just like other teens, teen moms experienced the romance and idealization of a first love. They fantasized about roses and picket fences, and it was hard for them to accept that the teen fathers were not knights in shining armor.

But then the teen moms began to notice the inequities in the father's and mother's relationship to the child. "We have these babies 24–7 (24 hours a day, 7 days a week), while they can come and go as they please," they often said.

Jennifer recognized that George was immature. "All he cares about is his car. He comes and goes when he wants, not when I need him. And he just wants to spend money on himself, not on the baby," she would complain.

After several months, the teen moms would say, "I can't handle this punk, and I want to be rid of him." But they couldn't, because they still had the baby as a bond.

The second concern was where the teen mom would get emotional support and concrete help in meeting her commitments. One of the unique dimensions of Jennifer's situation was that George's parents were very supportive. "That grandmom was just delighted to take care of that pretty little baby," said Louise. "She was always a backup, someone Jennifer could call in a crisis, especially considering that both of her own parents worked. It's a myth to believe that most grandmothers are waiting in the wings, ready to take care of their daughter's babies. Most grandmothers are young, and they're out working themselves."

The third issue that teen moms contended with was their school work. Jennifer was in the top track, but she always had experienced ups and downs in her level of achievement. Math was particularly difficult for her, and Louise would encourage her and urge her to get extra tutoring.

Typically, there are periods for teen moms when it's hard to concentrate. The beginning is a rocky adjustment. Then, when the baby gets sick, the mother has to juggle child care. Jennifer's good attendance had helped to keep her grades from plummeting.

Eventually, Jennifer started connecting with other teen moms. Louise felt that this was difficult for her in part because, generally, they were not as "future-oriented" as Jennifer was. Louise explained:

> As I see it, the adolescent task is to begin to look to the future. You need to set goals and build a dream. Being a teen parent interrupts all of that. You're pulled back to the present, and making it through the day is a major achievement. You could consider homework as a metaphor for that: students need to do their homework in order to successfully master the present and create a future for themselves. But completing homework is a major effort for most teen moms because of competing demands.
>
> My goal is to help teen parents to rebuild the dream or to build a new one, to get them back on the developmental track. This is an up-and-down process; it doesn't just happen overnight. In fact, many experts feel that teen pregnancy results in the first place when teens don't have a dream; they're more likely to defer getting pregnant if they have a dream. I help students to avoid another pregnancy and to stay in school. Building a dream helps students reach both of those goals.

Louise pointed out that building a dream can be hard for disadvantaged kids. She thought about it in terms of Maslow's hierarchy: if you don't have your basic needs taken care of, how can you work on self-fulfillment? How can you think about going to college, if you don't have a roof over your head? "A lot of kids feel hopeless," she said. Although Jennifer had more advantages than many, there were often days when she felt that it was all too hard to do. But she never gave up.

Senior Year

Although Jennifer saw herself as "coming up" during her junior year—making a lot of friends and becoming well known—Louise felt that it wasn't until her senior year that Jennifer was back on track. By then, she had built her dream and felt independent enough to leave the comfort zone of Louise's class. She faced the healthy concerns and developmental tasks of a typical senior: she applied to college and then worried about getting in and handling the finances of a college education. She anticipated the separation from her close friends.

Louise reflected that Jennifer's relationship with her daughter, Sonia, had also grown. After Sonia's delivery, Jennifer was proud that she returned to the Ernestine Johnson School almost immediately. In fact, the staff at the school were somewhat concerned that it may have been too fast and that perhaps Jennifer was not bonding sufficiently with her new baby. Louise felt that Jennifer was probably just scared about the responsibilities of caring for a baby, as many new parents are. Now, it was clear that Jennifer was definitely attached to her daughter and had matured as a parent.

A confident mother, she understood and met her daughter's needs. She even offered to do extra baby-sitting for her acquaintances' children, although it was rare for teen moms to take on more child care. Furthermore, she had taken a late afternoon job at a day care center where she worked with toddlers and preschoolers. At the end of the day, she came home and devoted her time to Sonia. She continued to complete her homework during her study period at school.

In her senior year, Jennifer also became a "senior buddy," which Louise saw as another sign of success. At Van Buren High, three senior buddies were assigned the major responsibility for teaching a study skills class for one period every day. In her role as teacher and guide, Jennifer had been personally responsible for keeping one student from dropping out of school. Her experiences teaching as a senior buddy and in the day care center had led to her decision to go to college to become a teacher.

The crowning success for Jennifer came when she ran for "Miss Van Buren," a popularity contest, and won. When asked what made her so popular, Jennifer had explained, "I'm nice, caring, and always there for my friends. I'm supportive and very open." She acknowledged that her closest friends were not teen moms. "I just don't hit it off as well with them," she said.

Miss Van Buren traditionally wore red to the pageant, and Jennifer arrived at the dance looking gorgeous in a red satin gown. She proudly marched to be crowned with her daughter, Sonia, by her side, dressed in a pretty red dress as well. Jennifer had received her acceptance to the state university only a few weeks before, and this moment felt like the culmination of all of her achievements.

Unresolved Issues

Louise thought that Jennifer *should* feel proud because "she had gone through hell and made it." The future for many teen mothers does not look as promising. Only about 60 percent of teen mothers who give birth between the ages of fifteen and nineteen complete high school. (And Jennifer had become pregnant even earlier at thirteen.) Furthermore, teen mothers who don't finish high school are significantly more likely to be poor and to stay poor through their twenties. Nationally, one-third of mothers in their mid-twenties who gave birth as teenagers are poor, compared with one-sixth of mothers of the same age who gave birth after age twenty.

Still, the picture was not quite as rosy as Jennifer liked to paint it. Although Jennifer reported that, in her senior year, she was getting all As and Bs, in fact, she was failing math and almost didn't graduate because of it.

Louise saw Jennifer still experiencing emotional swings, too. Jennifer's father had never forgiven her, and there was a distance between them. Louise sensed that there were other issues at home, as well, but she didn't know what they were. Jennifer just alluded to "problems," without offering any details.

As a teacher, Louise felt that she was in over her head and that Jennifer needed other guidance. "I've tried to teach Jennifer the skill of asking for help when you need it and to model it for her, but she still needs to work on this. She waited too long to discuss her problems in math, too," she commented.

She connected Jennifer with the social worker at the school health clinic again, but the relationship was uneasy, and Jennifer never went to see her more than a few times. Louise suspected that Jennifer again was experiencing denial; she was afraid to tell the secret about the turmoil at home, just as she had been afraid to tell about her pregnancy.

Additional Readings

Buchholz, E. S., & Gol, B. (1986). More than playing house: A developmental perspective on the strengths in teenage motherhood. *American Journal of Orthopsychiatry, 56*(3), 347–359.

Carnegie Council on Adolescent Development. (1990). *School and community programs that enhance adolescent health and education.* New York: Carnegie Corporation of New York.

Dryfoos, J. G. (1991). School-based social and health services for at-risk students. *Urban Education, 26*(1), 118–137.

Guetzloe, E. C. (1989). *Youth suicide: What the educator should know.* Reston, VA: Council for Exceptional Children.

Hechinger, F. M. (1992). *Fateful choices: Healthy youth for the 21st century.* Carnegie Council on Adolescent Development. New York: Hill and Wang.

Henshaw, S. K., Kenney, A. M., Somberg, D., & Van Vort, J. (1989). *Teenage pregnancy in the United States: The scope of the problem and state responses.* New York: Alan Guttmacher Institute.

Slavin, R. E., Karweit, N. L., & Madden, N. A. (1989). *Effective programs for students at risk.* Boston: Allyn & Bacon.

CASE 22

Acceptance or Achievement

Linda Powell and Judith B. Buzzell

Part C

The Decision

After several meetings, a committee of teachers came up with a plan. They designed a program that would offer four courses specifically to meet the needs of their most able students. To be chosen for the program, students had to be nominated by three teachers. Half the students would have received grades at the highest levels; the other half would be conscientious, industrious students who were working toward that level.

Two of the courses would draw students from all four grades to allow them to meet, stimulate, and encourage each other in class. Thus, although this would clearly be a higher track, the students would still be mixed. These two courses would not be traditional subjects; for example, one course to be offered was "The Literature of Protest."

The other two courses would be traditional subjects, such as U.S. history, and would draw students only from one grade level (e.g., the sophomore year). These courses would have only eight to ten students each. Since there were only two such classes, this program would not pose any logistical problem. The teachers decided to meet over the summer to plan the program, which would be instituted in the fall.

The Luncheon Chats

Celena took the test for the ISP program; the results would not be available for eight weeks. She continued to eat lunch with the two seniors in Mrs. Robinson's room. Since it was their last semester, Karen and Yolanda shared their excitement about end-of-school activities. Both were receiving special recognition: Yolanda's play was being produced, and Karen had received a leadership award.

One day, the seniors were discussing their summer plans. When Celena announced that she had no plans at all, Karen enthusiastically described her experience in a special summer program open to the city's public school students. It was held at a local university and included morning seminars, in areas such as sociology or psychology, and afternoon activities like volleyball. Over the course of several days, the seniors convinced Celena to apply for the program.

Mrs. Robinson, who had continued to eat lunch in her room to be available to the girls and talk with them, decided to pick up the application for Celena, who wasn't always good at following through with her intentions. She felt Celena needed extra encouragement. She speculated that perhaps Celena didn't perceive herself as bright or had ambivalent feelings about her intelligence because it made her stand out from the other students.

April Grades

When report cards came out, the girls shared them at lunch. Celena's grades had dropped a little. For the first time since the December outburst, Mrs. Robinson heard Celena complain that the work was too easy in some of her classes and that she didn't feel challenged. As Mrs. Robinson left the room, because of her discomfort with hearing kids discuss other teachers, she mused about whether Lyceum was the best school for Celena. Celena was going through an academic slump. Perhaps she hadn't rebounded yet from the experience of feeling taken advantage of by her fellow students.

In fact, in May, Celena arranged for her grades to be sent to Jefferson High School, one of the large comprehensive high schools in the city. She planned to transfer there for the fall. Yolanda had introduced her to a friend who attended Jefferson and would be attending the university summer program along with Celena. The friendship took, and this new friend sparked Celena's interest in Jefferson.

Transitions to Celena's Junior Year

Celena attended the summer program and got a B on her work. She decided to transfer to Jefferson High School in the fall but returned to Lyceum in January. When Mrs. Robinson asked her how her experience was, Celena shrugged, "I'm back." Mrs. Robinson sensed that her student wasn't completely resolved in her decision to leave or to return. She seemed to have mixed feelings about both high schools.

By this time, Lyceum's teachers had developed and instituted the special courses for high-achieving students. Celena took them during the spring and performed very well. In addition, she had received the results from the entrance test for the ISP. The test assessed verbal and abstract reasoning and numerical ability. The system considered students whose scores were among the top 5 percent as gifted, and Celena's scores met that criterion. In fact, although she had taken the test as a sophomore, she had the highest test scores of all twenty-five students in the school, in all four grades, who had been identified and taken the test. She planned to take the ISP seminar in her senior year.

Personal Awareness

In June of her junior year, Celena decided she needed some personal counseling. She felt frustrated by her shyness. She was acutely aware of how uncomfortable she was with her peers. Moreover, there were still problems at home. Leaving her daughters with their grandmother, Celena's mother had gone to Arkansas for a month in the summer to be with her boyfriend, but the relationship had not worked out. Then, in January, she lost her job, which was stressful for the family.

When meeting with her guidance counselor, at his request, about scheduling her courses for the fall, Celena asked about the possibility of counseling. The guidance counselor arranged for her to receive counseling through a community mental health agency.

Epilogue

Despite Celena's concerns, Mrs. Robinson saw evidence that she was beginning to open up socially through her involvement in the school magazine. Celena reviewed the poems and short stories submitted and drew illustrations. "I think she has found her niche through her art. The kids won't let her sit back. They realize what she has to contribute. The art is her form of self-expression and a way to communicate with others."

Indeed, at the end-of-year awards ceremony, Celena won departmental awards at the junior year level in *every* academic area—English, math, science, history, and Spanish. Her artistic ability had been honored as well. After her paintings had been displayed in a citywide student show in the art gallery of the prestigious university downtown, she was awarded a $1,000 scholarship to the university's summer program in painting.

Additional Readings

Colangelo, N. (1985). Counseling needs of culturally diverse gifted students. *Roeper Review, 8*, 33–35.

Fordham, S., & Ogbu J. (1986). Black students' school success: Coping with the burden of "acting white." *Urban Review, 18*(3), 176–206.

Gamoran, A. (1992). Is ability grouping equitable? *Educational Leadership. 50*(20), 11–17.

McPartland, J. M., & Slavin, R. E. (1990). *Policy perspectives: Increasing achievement of at-risk students at each grade level.* Washington, DC: U.S. Government Printing Office.

Neisser, U. (Ed.). (1986). *The school achievement of minority children: New perspectives.* Hillsdale, NJ: Erlbaum.

Oakes, J. (1985). *Keeping track: How schools structure inequality.* New Haven, CT: Yale University Press.

Richert, E. S. (1987). Rampant problems and promising practices in the identification of disadvantaged gifted students. *Gifted Child Quarterly, 31*, 149–154.

Subotnik, R. F. (1989). Teaching gifted students. In J. A. Banks & C. A. Banks (Eds.), *Multicultural education: Issues and perspectives* (pp. 269–285). Boston: Allyn & Bacon.

Welch, O. M., Hodges, C. & Warden, K. (1989). Developing the scholar's ethos in minority high school students: The vital link to academic achievement. *Urban Education, 24*(1), 59–76.

Wolf, J. S. (1990) The gifted and talented. In N. G. Haring & L. McCormick (Eds.), *Exceptional children & youth* (pp. 447–489). Columbus, OH: Merrill.